The Strategic
Bombing of
Germany, 1940–1945

The Strategic Bombing of Germany, 1940–1945

Alan J. Levine

PRAEGER

Westport, Connecticut
London

Library of Congress Cataloging-in-Publication Data

Levine, Alan J.
    The strategic bombing of Germany, 1940–1945 / Alan J. Levine.
        p.   cm.
    Includes bibliographical references and index.
    ISBN 0–275–94319–4 (alk. paper)
    1. World War, 1939–1945—Aerial operations. 2. Germany—History—
Bombardment, 1940–1945.   I. Title.
    D790.L484   1992
    940.54′42—dc20   91–45610

British Library Cataloguing in Publication Data is available.

Library of Congress Catalog Card Number: 91-45610
ISBN: 0–275–94319–4

First published in 1992

Praeger Publishers, 88 Post Road West, Westport, CT 06881
An imprint of Greenwood Publishing Group, Inc.

Printed in the United States of America

The paper used in this book complies with the
Permanent Paper Standard issued by the National
Information Standards Organization (Z39.48–1984).

10 9 8 7 6 5 4 3 2 1

73140

To my uncle, Israel Levine,
and his comrades of the 389th Bomb Group.

Contents

*The Strategic
Bombing of
Germany, 1940–1945*

1

Origins, Prelude, Doctrine

The Allied strategic bombing campaign against Nazi Germany was one of the most destructive, complex, and controversial aspects of World War II. Although it started slowly, the strategic air offensive lasted for nearly the whole war (1940–1945) and strongly affected its course. Only the vital defensive Battle of the Atlantic lasted longer. At first little more than a series of ineffectual pinpricks against a victorious Germany, the Allied air offensive culminated in a torrent of destruction without precedent.

There have been few overall accounts of the campaign as a whole, although it formed a major part of the Allied war effort, and those few have generally been biased, emphasizing either the British or American side of the story and often giving too little attention to what happened in Germany.

The story of the campaign is an intricate one, in which many reverses precede a long-delayed success. The British and American efforts were interwoven, but the two air forces employed very different methods. The story of the strategic bombing campaign also touches on other issues and problems, some of which at first seem far removed from it, ranging from the development of aviation and electronics to the economy of Nazi Germany and the land fighting of 1944–1945. Nor did the story start in 1939. The experience of World War I and a great deal of theorizing—only occasionally backed by experiment—in the period between the wars, had much to do with it.

Strategic bombing is best defined as the use of air power to strike at the very foundation of an enemy's war effort—the production of war material, the economy as a whole, or the morale of the civilian population—rather than as a direct attack on the enemy's army or navy. A strategic air campaign almost always requires the defeat of the enemy's air force, but not as an end in itself. While tactical air power uses aircraft to aid the advance of forces on the ground or on the surface of the ocean, usually in cooperation with those forces, strategic air power usually works in relative independence of armies and navies, although its effects may complement those of a naval blockade—the operation of war most comparable to strategic bombing in its attack on the sources of enemy power.

AIR POWER IN WORLD WAR I

As with many other aspects of the modern world, air warfare came out of the trench deadlock of World War I. Air power did not break the deadlock alone, but it was an increasingly important factor in the fighting.

Specialized bombers were developed. As early as May 1915, the Germans were bombing billets, transportation facilities, and dumps well behind the lines in Russia. And by 1917–1918, planes were being used en masse to support armies, in battles that increasingly resembled those that would take place in World War II. In the fall of 1918, Allied fighters and bombers helped turn the retreats of the Turkish, Bulgarian, and Austrian armies into routs. Aircraft also became important in naval warfare, primarily for reconnaissance but for other purposes as well. While German and British torpedo bombers scored minor successes, aircraft played a more important role in the Allied campaign against German submarines. They actually destroyed only half a dozen U-boats, but proved very effective at spotting them for surface escort ships and forcing them to submerge. Although many generals and admirals still stubbornly ignored or minimized its importance, there was no reason to doubt, when World War I ended, that *tactical* airpower would be a major factor in future wars.[1] Whether that would be true of *strategic* air warfare was far less certain, although strategic bombing had already been tried out on a small scale, first by the Germans, then by the Allies.

Oddly, as airplanes improved, strategic bombing did not develop as an extension of tactical air operations, but in parallel with them. Odder still, for a considerable time the Germans' main "strategic bomber" was the airplane's fragile predecessor, the dirigible airship. Despite the oddities of this practice and its small scale, the course of the not very effective German strategic bombing campaign against Britain foreshadowed that of some later strategic air campaigns.

During 1914 German single-engine planes crossed the English Channel to bomb British coastal targets. But the Germans had something more powerful than the primitive planes used in these first attacks; the rigid airship or Zeppelin. The Zeppelin was bigger and more complex than the blimp ("nonrigid airship") familiar to modern Americans, which is just a powered balloon, a single large gasbag. The Zeppelin had a hull with a duralumin framework, and numerous separate gas cells. It had great lifting capacity; the ultimate war Zeppelin of the L30 class of 1916 hauled nearly five tons of bombs, a load not equalled by planes until the 1940s.

The German people strongly admired Count von Zeppelin and regarded his ships as a war-winning device, and from the start of the war they, and the German admiralty, clamored for attacks on Britain. But the Kaiser reluctantly authorized an offensive against Britain only in January 1915, insisting that only military establishments and targets clearly related to the war effort—for example, docks and oil storage tanks—be attacked. Until May 1915 he forbade attacks on London. But it soon became clear that plans to hit only specific targets of military importance—what would be called "precision bombing" in World War II—could not be carried out. The complicated bombsight used in the Zeppelin was capable of considerable accuracy, but the crewmen had not been properly trained to use it. In any case, the opposition was such that the Zeppelins could attack only at night. Winds caused large errors in navigation. Zeppelin raids (the biggest was launched by 16 airships) only occasionally damaged an important target. During the whole war, 51 airship attacks dropped only 196 tons of bombs on Britain, killing 557 people.

Although the Zeppelins' effectiveness was so limited, the British made considerable efforts to stop the attacks; they could not allow attacks on their capital and biggest city to go unopposed. By the end of 1916, twelve squadrons of planes and 17,341 men were stationed in Britain to defend against Zeppelins. Although full of highly flammable hydrogen, Zeppelins were harder to destroy than might be expected, but in late 1916, British fighters, climbing to the Zeppelins' standard heights of 12,000–13,000 feet and firing newly developed incendiary bullets, finally made the attacks too costly.

However, the Germans continued to hope that attacks on Britain would pay off by lowering British morale and forcing the British to keep important forces at home. They pursued two lines of endeavor to overcome the British defenses, introducing airplanes, and new airships that could fly over the British defenses. New Zeppelins that could fly higher were introduced in March 1917. They had lightened frameworks, smaller control cars, and fewer machine guns and carried a maximum bomb load of just two tons. They attacked between 16,000 and 20,000 feet, above the ceiling of antiaircraft guns and the fighters that had stopped the earlier attacks, carrying oxygen for their crews. These "height-climbers" flew less often than their predecessors and were hampered even more by winds and weather, but were nearly immune to the defenses. Only two were shot down before the war ended.[2]

In March 1917 the Germans began sending twin-engine Gotha bombers against Britain. They flew high for planes of that day, over 14,000 feet, and the crews wore oxygen masks. Carrying auxiliary fuel tanks they could just reach London, but they caused a surprising amount of damage and were a considerable shock to the British. A single attack on June 13 killed 162 people and injured 432 more. The defending planes were old and unable to hurt the bombers, and late-model fighters were hastily rushed home from France. The army's Royal Flying Corps was greatly expanded, while an elaborate organization, the London Air Defence Area, was formed to deal with the attacks.

The new defenses shot down enough bombers to stop daylight attacks; the Germans switched over to night bombing on September 3. When the decision to bomb at night was made, it was clearly understood that it was impossible to hit precise targets at night. The Germans would engage in what would be called "area bombing" in World War II, attacking a whole city or at least a section of it, rather than a specific installation. There was no question of hitting targets that were of military importance, or directly related to the war effort, except by accident. In the same month they introduced even bigger bombers, the Giants (Riesen) with four engines (some later models had five or six) and crews of up to nine men. In size and carrying capacity they were not far short of the Flying Fortresses of World War II. In October the Germans began dropping mostly incendiary bombs. The night attacks on Britain lasted until May 1918; the largest consisted of 43 planes. Growing losses from the increasingly tough defenses then made the Germans switch their efforts to attacks on Paris. The Gotha and Giant raids had killed 836 people and injured 1,982.

The German raids on Britain did not critically damage the British war effort. They caused only minor harm to war-related industries. The effect on British morale was unclear. Some maintained that the bombing was producing signs of panic in London, at least in the slums of the East End, and that by scaring workers and causing absenteeism it slowed war production out of all proportion to the physical damage caused. Other observers felt that the English people endured the raids with their usual stolidity and that, at worst, cabinet members were projecting their own reactions onto the mass of ordinary people. (The idea that air attacks could cause a complete social collapse, it should be noted, predated World War I and had been suggested by H. G. Wells, among others). Minister of Munitions Winston Churchill, although a strong advocate of air power, scoffed at fears that British morale would collapse. He rightly argued that what the experience actually proved was that trying to break the morale of a civilian population through bombing was impractical. (In World War II, Churchill was to take a very different position, as we shall see in Chapter 2.)

Any damage to civilian morale from the air attacks of World War I was temporary and minor, but the attacks made a permanent impression on many British leaders. By contrast, many German officers who had hoped that bombing England would have a terrific impact were disappointed; they were disenchanted with the whole notion of strategic air attack. Others, however, realized that the attacks on Britain had had one very useful effect—they had tied down very considerable British resources. By the end of the war 384 planes, 706 searchlights, 480 antiaircraft guns, many barrage balloons, and a large number of men were pinned down to a defensive role at home. That made the Gotha and Giant raids worthwhile, from the German point of view. For a small expenditure of resources on their part, they had diverted a far greater British effort in 1917–1918. Whether the effort put into Zeppelin attacks had been worthwhile was more doubtful. Building Zeppelins, producing hydrogen, and manning their bases—which required a great many men—was very expensive, and unlike the Gothas and Giants, the Zeppelins were being diverted from a potentially far more useful job. Carrying fuel instead of bombs, they could have patrolled over the Atlantic well west of the British Isles, locating Allied convoys for the U-boats.[3] Some features of the German strategic air campaign were repeated in later strategic air campaigns: the failure of "precision" attacks aimed at specific targets of undoubted military importance was followed by more indiscriminate attacks employing incendiary weapons and by efforts to evade defenses by flying at night or at unprecedentedly high altitudes. The main effectiveness of the attacks had not been in causing fatal damage to the enemy's war effort but in leading him to tie up resources in a defensive effort. And the strategic air effort, or at least its Zeppelin element, had been competitive with the support of naval efforts.

The German attacks helped spur the formation of an independent Royal Air Force, although they did not actually cause it. It had long been widely believed that a single combined independent air force would be more efficient than the army's Royal Flying Corps and the Royal Naval Air Service. The Gothas, however, guaranteed that they would be merged into one force in 1917, rather than after the war. Nevertheless, the creation of an independent air force was, in itself, neither necessary nor sufficient to insure a concentration of strategic air operations. The United States Army's Air Corps, and its successor, the Army Air Force, were decidedly oriented toward strategic bombing, while the independent French and German air forces concentrated on tactical operations. But the circumstances in which the RAF was formed, and the views of its most fervent advocates, insured that it would concentrate on strategic bombing. Gen. Jan Christiaan Smuts, whose reports to the cabinet on air matters inspired the decision to form the RAF, had written that "the day may not be far off when aerial operations with their devastation of enemy lands and destruction of industrial and populous centres on a vast scale may become the principal operations of war, to which the older forms of military and naval operations may become secondary and subordinate."[4]

The RAF created its own counterpart to the Gothas and Giants. The British were not the first on the Allied side to begin strategic bombing; the French, in 1915–1916, had tried it on a small scale, sending planes deep into German territory to attack war plants at Essen and Ludwigshafen. But opposition had made them switch to night bombing in 1916, and they had been disillusioned with the results. When the British formed an Independent Air Force in 1918 to bomb targets well inside Germany, the French were unhappy, fearing that such attacks would merely inspire German retaliation against French cities—a reaction that reappeared in 1939–1940. The British went ahead anyway, and when the armistice came they were getting ready to bomb Berlin, using three of the new four-engine Handley-Page HPV/1500 bombers. (A similar plan to bomb Moscow during the intervention in the Russian Civil War—in 1919—was aborted when British officials lost their nerve.) The Independent Air Force was not very large—it mustered 122 planes—nor very effective. It dropped only 550 tons of bombs, on enemy airfields and railroad targets. But the Germans committed 240 planes to counter it; like the German raids on Britain, the Independent Air Force tied down considerable forces in defense. Sir Hugh Trenchard, who commanded it, remained convinced that its attacks had done much to undermine German resistance.[5] Trenchard, a man of commanding personality, became the chief of the Air Staff during the RAF's formative years and helped to focus it toward strategic operations, at least in theory.

THE RAF BETWEEN THE WORLD WARS

Up to the mid-1930s, the RAF's commitment to strategic bombing remained largely in the realm of theory, and rather confused theory at that. In the 1920s another world war seemed a remote horror, even to most professional military men. The general world view of British officials was embodied in the "ten years rule," which based defense planning on the assumption that no great war need be feared in the next ten years. The rule remained in effect until 1931. The attitudes of the people at large, and their political leaders, were affected by an almost paralyzing fear of another war. In 1924, even Churchill remarked that in another war civilization would perish. This was a common view in the 1920s and 1930s, preserved for posterity in William Cameron Menzies's remarkable movie *Things to Come*. There was no need for nuclear weapons to render war "unthinkable"— that idea was already widespread in the period between the world wars. The general public, as did air power enthusiasts, believed that in another great war cities would be obliterated by an avalanche of high explosives and poison gas. (Fire, the real killer in air attacks during World War II, somehow escaped attention.) People thus achieved the considerable feat of imagining that World War II would actually be worse than it was! Such fears, and a sincere revulsion against war—genuine pacifism was far more common between the world wars than it is today—were a strong influence in favor of appeasement in the 1930s.

In its day-to-day work, however, the RAF did little that was relevant to anything it was liable to do in a major war. It executed a policy of "air control" in the more disorderly corners of the British Empire and its mandates—notably Iraq, Somaliland, and the Northwest Frontier of India—bombing rebellious tribesmen into obedience. Air control proved an effective means of policing the empire and enabled the British to economize on troops. This proved relatively cheap in both British and native lives, but it was an undemanding task that did not prepare the RAF for what it would face in the 1940s.

Preparation for a major air war, such as it was, was dominated by Trenchard's ideas. He insured that the RAF would be overwhelmingly bomber oriented, even though its bombers were unsuited to a major war with an advanced industrial country. The Staff College had wanted to have almost as many fighters as bombers, but at Trenchard's insistence the RAF maintained three bombers to every fighter. He and many other officers were sure that the bombers would get through any defense with or without fighter escort, although his Independent Air Force had needed fighter escort in 1918. Many believed that if they could not operate in the day, night bombing would be just as good. Some even deemed night bombing preferable, arguing that experience in the world war had shown that navigation and bomb aiming at night was little more difficult than during the day. Night bombers, less likely to be intercepted, could haul less defensive armament and more bombs. Unfortunately, this belief in the effectiveness of night attack rested on a misinterpretation of the evidence. Even though night attacks had been carried out in deceptively favorable conditions of good weather and bright moonlight, and at low altitudes, all of which aided navigation over very short ranges, the attacks had not been accurate.

Just what the bombers should try to accomplish in the event of a major war was not clear. During the 1920s Trenchard and others sometimes spoke of attacking an enemy civilian population to break its morale. In 1925 the Air Staff suggested that the morale effect of bombing would outweigh the material damage caused. On the whole, however, this did not represent the considered opinion of the RAF leaders. In 1928 Trenchard emphasized that indiscriminate bombing to terrorize people was improper; bombers should attack production, transportation, and communication facilities, the destruction of which would also have tremendous impact on the morale of enemy civilians. The RAF did not claim to be able to win a war on its own, although its staff may have privately hoped it could do so. It aimed at a policy of "strategic interception," cutting off the supplies of the enemy's armed forces at their sources, enabling the army to attack successfully. But the idea of striking civilian morale, like that of evading enemy defenses at night, lurked under the surface and made it easier for the British to turn to these concepts during World War II. The practicality of the RAF theories, and the crucial problems of navigation and bombing, were not analyzed in the 1920s and 1930s. Trenchard invested much of its small budget in luxurious bases, rather than in aircraft development or in experimental stations for the study of war techniques. The RAF was confident in the destructiveness of its small, high-explosive bombs. It was assumed, on the basis of miscalculations made from World War I experience, that a ton of bombs dropped on city targets would kill or injure 50 people. (In reality each ton killed or hurt 15–20 people.)

When Hitler seized power in 1933 and the prospect of a new world war became real, the RAF had a corps of fine pilots, but was technically behind foreign air forces. The degree of rearmament that began in 1934 was still oriented toward imperial policing.[6] Of its 41 squadrons, 22 had light bombers known to be useless in a European struggle. It was dominated by a conservative, bureaucratic Air Ministry and Air Staff. Britain had lagged behind in the revolution in aircraft construction of the late 1920s and 1930s. A few years had seen a change from wooden biplanes with open cockpits and fixed landing gear to metal monoplanes with enclosed cabins, retractable wheels, an immense increase in engine power, and the ability to fly at high altitudes. Variable-pitch propellers and automatic pilots had been introduced.

The general belief was that, as Stanley Baldwin said in November 1932, "the bomber will always get through" despite any defenses. The only way to prevent a devastating air attack on Britain—a "knockout blow" that could make it impossible to fight on—seemed to be the threat of a similar blow to keep a potential enemy in check. "Parity" with Germany in bombers became the aim, and the RAF gained priority over the other services. (As with the fear that the next war would destroy civilization, the concepts of "strategic deterrence" and "parity" thus preceded World War II and the development of nuclear bombs.

A series of rearmament schemes, all stressing bombers, succeeded each other over the next few years. The Air Staff promoted a transition to improved twin-engine "medium" bombers and in 1936 planned the "heavy bombers" with four engines that would come into service in World War II. The Short Stirling and the Handley-Page Halifax were designed to these specifications. Less successfully, a two-engine "medium heavy," the Avro Manchester, was also ordered. (It was a failure, but was redesigned and became the four-engine Lancaster, the most successful heavy bomber of all.) Wanting a big force as soon as possible, the British built many obsolescent planes, like the horrible Battle light bomber. The all-out priority for bombers, however, was ended by a turn toward air defense.

For a time the development of fighters lagged behind that of bombers. But in the late 1930s the development of radar, and faster and more heavily armed fighters, suggested that the bomber might not get through a properly designed defense system after all. The worries of Prime Minister Neville Chamberlain and others over growing defense costs inspired a review of defense issues by the newly appointed minister for defense coordination, Thomas Inskip—in 1937. Chamberlain wanted to show that the resources to increase the army, as well as the air force and the navy, did not exist, but the review had farther-reaching effects. Inskip had no experience in military affairs and was widely regarded as unfit for his office, but he was astute enough to consult a brilliant civil servant, Maurice Hankey. In December 1937, prompted by Hankey, Inskip concluded that the RAF's proper role was not to launch a knockout blow before the Germans could, but stop an enemy attack. Quick victory could not be expected, but the RAF could and should secure the British Isles as a base for an offensive during a long war. Therefore fighters, not bombers, must be given priority. These ideas were accepted, and the aim of numerical parity with the Germans in bombers was abandoned. Thus the most crucial decision affecting Britain's military buildup before World War II led—fortunately—to a deemphasis on strategic bombing. This did not instantly abolish the fear of a knockout blow by the German air force, the strength of which was then greatly exaggerated. This fear was a factor, although not a central one, in the surrender at Munich.[7]

The decision to stress air defense of Great Britain had been taken in the teeth of the predominant opinion in the RAF. But the defense system built under Lord Dowding (head of Fighter Command from 1936 to 1940) proved almost the only element of the British military that was genuinely ready when war broke out.

The RAF had not been lucky in its senior commanders, nor had the Air Ministry met its responsibility well. Most of the RAF's best planes stemmed at least partly from private initiatives that the ministry at first resisted. The remarkable Mosquito fast bomber and fighter was developed by the De Havilland Company despite Air Ministry opposition; it was only ordered in December 1939, after the war began. The designers of the Spitfire and Hurricane fighters, Reginald Mitchell and Sydney Camm, were dissatisfied with the inadequate specifications laid down by the Air Ministry in 1930, and a new set of specifications was written in 1934 to accommodate the superb designs their companies had already produced. The Air Staff preferred heavy, two-seat fighters with guns mounted in a turret behind the pilot. The few twin-seater Defiant fighters that were built proved disastrous failures in 1940. Only strenuous efforts by Dowding secured priority for single-seat fighters with forward-firing guns. The Air Staff was also content with the inadequate light .303 machine guns that British fighters were stuck with for the first year of the war. British bombers were saddled with these guns for almost the whole war.

In the last years before the war, the RAF's Bomber Command, formed in 1936, began confronting reality. In 1937 the centralized industrial Intelligence Committee of the civil departments of the government began collecting information on the German economy, and serious war planning started. A series of "Western air plans" were formulated, each aimed at attacking a particular element of the enemy's war effort. Some plans were for direct attacks on the German air force and its supporting industries, and against the German fleet, but these were not regarded as very practical because the German forces were too dispersed or too well defended. Some plans were based on the recognition of what turned out to be real soft spots in the German war economy. WA 4 (Western Air Plan 4) aimed to smash the German railroad system, but it was realized even in 1939 that the German rail network was too dense for the available forces to make much of an impression. A more popular plan, WA 5, aimed to wreck the great heavy industrial region of the Ruhr by bombing power plants and coking plants. Yet the Air Ministry doubted that the relatively delicate power plants could be hit, or the coking plants wrecked if they were hit. Bomber Command warned that WA 5 called for more sorties than would probably be possible, and that the plan counted on using light bombers—Blenheims and Battles—that probably could not penetrate into Germany. The Air Ministry noted that a simpler way to paralyze the Ruhr would be to destroy the Möhne and Sorpe dams, which supplied water for its industries. But no existing bomb could smash the dams. WA 6 aimed to destroy the core of Germany's fuel supply—14 synthetic oil plants and as many major oil refineries. The optimists hoped they could be bombed fairly soon, if not at the start of a war, and this became the favorite war plan.

But as the plans were laid, it was becoming clear just how feeble Bomber Command really was. From September 1937 to April 1940, after the expansion of the force had begun, its commander was Sir Edgar Ludlow-Hewitt, a realist who saw how poorly based the RAF's theories were. He warned his superiors that Bomber Command was unready. Navigators, gunners, and even pilots were poorly trained. Nor had research been done on the problems of bombing or gunnery; no facilities for this had ever been built. The few experiments made were discouraging; in 1937 it was found that the average crew could not drop bombs closer than 250 yards from an aiming point. This was worse than expected, but much better than could be hoped for against enemy opposition. (The Americans' Eight Air Force, with far better equipment, would only approach this degree of accuracy after years of experience.) An oddity of the RAF was that it did not have specialized bombardiers; until 1942 the overburdened navigators ("observers") had to aim bombs as well as find the way to the target. Only in 1938 did the RAF admit the need for a 1,000-pound bomb for use against heavy structures like bridges. Some special 1,200-pound bombs were procured to deal with battleships, although they were far too small for that. The RAF's bombs were not only small but weak. Their explosive charge to weight ratio was barely half that of German bombs. The RAF not even have an adequate bombsight.

Ludlow-Hewitt suspected that even the planned heavy bombers could not defend themselves against fighters. In August 1938 he urged developing escort fighters, arguing that experience in Spain and China had shown that they were needed to overcome enemy defenses. If necessary, he argued, the escorts and even many bombers could be based in France. But given the prevalent conviction that it was impossible to build a fighter with the range of a bomber, or at least one that could tackle enemy interceptors, he made little headway. Ideas for increasing the armament of the bombers, perhaps fitting them with 20 mm. cannon, were not welcomed by the Air Ministry. Ludlow-Hewitt also wanted a small fast bomber, roughly like the later Mosquito, to supplement the heavies; it might get through defenses that would stop the bigger planes, albeit with a smaller payload. But the Air Ministry was not interested in this until the war began.

The British failed to come to grips with a paradox. They expected to stop German bombers from attacking them, at least in daylight, yet they expected to penetrate German fighter defenses with acceptable losses, although their equipment was no better than that of the Germans. Some of their strategists already suspected that fighter opposition would force Bomber Command to attack at night, but it had not trained for this. It never flew in bad weather, and when it flew at night, which was not often, the navigators depended on city lights and railroad lines as landmarks. Flying over a blacked-out countryside in wartime would be very different. The few experiments at lighting up targets with flares were not encouraging. The only available flares bright enough to do the job were too heavy for normal use.[8]

When the war began Bomber Command had 33 operational squadrons, 16 of which were classified as "light," with vulnerable Blenheims and Battles. The Blenheim would be of little use against targets in Germany; carrying a load of only half a ton, it was slow and weakly built. The Battle, a clumsy single-engine plane nearly the size of the twin-engine Blenheim, could not take part in a strategic bombing campaign, and was relegated to direct support for the army. Incredibly, the Air Ministry had let manufacturers go on grinding out Battles even though the Hawker Henley, a ground-attack plane and dive-bomber far superior to the German Stuka, could have readily replaced it. (The few Henleys built were used as target tugs!)

The 17 "heavy" squadrons, which were soon reclassified as "medium" and had just over 200 operational planes, were only somewhat better off. Until 1942 Bomber Command's main force was equipped with planes comparable in size and bomb load to those used by the tactical air forces to support Eisenhower's armies in 1944–1945, rather than those of the strategic air armadas that would devastate Germany's industry and cities. These planes, Hampdens, Whitleys, and Wellingtons, were poorly streamlined; the first two types were obsolescent even by prewar British standards. Only the Wellington was an outstanding design; the Air Ministry had been reluctant to buy it. These three types of planes took most of the men serving in Bomber Command in September 1939 to prisoner-of-war camps or graves.

Except for its fighters, the RAF had few good planes during the first two years of the war. Its only truly successful strike aircraft in this period were the Wellington and the Beaufort, a fine torpedo bomber built only in small numbers. The RAF had neglected maritime aircraft and the support of the army. After many years of effort, it had formed a small, poorly equipped strategic bombing force that would turn out to be unable to reach its targets during the day or find them at night, and in fact could not have done much damage even if it had.[9] The reputation of the RAF would be redeemed, and Britain's safety insured, by Fighter Command.

THE ARMY AIR FORCE AND ITS DOCTRINE

The United States Army Air Force entered World War II in 1941 with a doctrine of strategic bombing that was like the RAF's, but more carefully worked out. The United States Army's air element, although very small, was more interested in the technical problems involved in strategic bombing and formulated its ideas more explicitly. The development of a U.S. strategic bombing force was more closely tied to a specific plane, the famous Boeing B-17. Although flawed, the achievements of the American airmen were remarkable given the strong hostility of the dominant element in the United States Army and Navy, which climaxed in the court-martial of Gen. Billy Mitchell. During the 1920s the Army General Staff harassed and snubbed the airmen. Although the chiefs of staff in the 1930s, generals Douglas MacArthur and Malin Craig, were relatively enlightened on the subject of air power, many crusty reactionaries had little use even for air operations in direct support of ground forces. Gen. Hugh Drum, who might well have become chief of staff in 1939 instead of George C. Marshall, held that antiaircraft fire could deal with any attack and that the Army did not need any plane capable of flying more than three days' march ahead of the infantry. Fortunately, General Mitchell himself, his less well known contemporary and rival Gen. Benjamin Foulois, and a group of younger men, of whom the most prominent were Frank Andrews, Henry H. Arnold, Carl Spaatz, Ira Eaker, and George C. Kenney, all generals in World War II, formed an outstanding group of leaders.

The American interest in strategic bombing dated back to World War I. In 1918 a relatively junior officer, Lt. Col. Edgar S. Gorrell, inspired by ideas picked up from the British and from the Italian aircraft designer Giani Caproni, had proposed an air campaign against targets in western Germany. He favored bombing the railroads that connected the iron mines in Lorraine with Germany. Gorrell's ideas had had only a limited impact; the Americans concentrated their air efforts on targets in or just behind the lines. They only carried out one attack on the railroads. But Mitchell, Foulois, and others were impressed by Gorrell. Unlike the British, they did not feel compelled to exaggerate the effect of bombing in World War I, but looked forward to further technical advances.

Mitchell became the chief prophet of air power. His ideas revolved around the central importance of strategic bombing, although they were not limited to it. Some of his other views led to a clash with the Navy. He insisted that bombs and air-dropped torpedoes could sink any surface ship and that airpower alone could defend the United States against invasion. He seemed to prove this in 1921, when seven bombers sank the German battleship *Ostfriesland*. Die-hard battleship men, who dominated the Navy until 1941, argued that *Ostfriesland* and the two U.S. battleships Mitchell's men sank in 1923 had been unmanned anchored hulks. Things would be different against ships able to maneuver and shoot back. That was not a convincing reply; even in 1921 it should have been obvious that the striking power of planes would increase more than the ability of ships to defend themselves or survive being hit. But Mitchell, who at first had conceded the value of aircraft carriers and submarines, foolishly antagonized the whole Navy by asserting that land-based planes would render them unnecessary too. He also assumed (although he was not dogmatic about this) that unspecialized high-level bombers could deal with moving ships, a belief inherited by the Army Air Force. Experience in World War II showed that he was wrong; attacking ships at sea was a specialized business requiring dive-bombing, low-level attack, or torpedoes.

But the focus of Mitchell's thought was offensive. An air force must defeat the opposing air force to win control of the air; then it should strike at production and transportation centers. The bomber was the primary instrument of air power; Mitchell thought that a few bombs would cause tremendous destruction. Like most people between the world wars, he underestimated the ability of people to stand up to bombing and industry's ability to recuperate from attack.

American air doctrine stemmed from Mitchell. Like the British, the Americans had been little influenced by outside ideas after 1918, despite a long-standing myth that British and American airmen were disciples of the Italian Gen. Giulio Douhet. Later the best publicized air theorist of the era between the world wars, Douhet argued that a small bomber force could fight its way through any defense, and by dropping gas bombs, virtually exterminate the population of a target country, killing 4 million civilians in just eight missions! But Douhet had no influence at all on the RAF. His ideas were known to American airmen, but they rejected his notions about air strategy, proper targets, and weapons. American airmen had no faith in bombing civilians or in gas. At most, they welcomed Douhet as a fellow proponent of the omnipotence of war planes. His only real influence may have lain in tactics; he reinforced the dogma of the self-defending bomber.

During the 1920s and 1930s the Air Corps Tactical School elaborated, but also in some ways dangerously simplified, Mitchell's ideas. It assumed that fighters and bombers must first deal with the hostile air force; bombers would then strike industrial and transportation targets and power plants to disrupt the enemy war effort. It early concluded that daylight attacks would be more effective. In 1926 it suggested that one way to defeat an enemy air force might be to attack aircraft assembly plants, while in the long run, strategic bombing might so disrupt the enemy as to destroy his will to resist independent of other military operations. Although it was occasionally questioned, there was a growing assumption that a properly constituted bomber formation could defend itself against interceptors. The assumption seemed necessary, because officers associated with fighter aircraft, as well as the bomber advocates, thought that "pursuit" planes could not have enough range to accompany bombers to distant targets. Even fighter advocates like Captain Claire Chennault, while deriding the self-defending bomber, did not believe in escort. The question of what would happen if the daylight bomber could not defend itself was not really faced; some suggested that in that case night operations would be undertaken. But the self-defending bomber concept and the related premise that fighters could never attain the range of bombers hardened into dogma. This was a near fatal flaw in the work of men otherwise brilliant and farseeing.

The Tactical School settled on a doctrine calling for high-level attacks by the largest possible formations of bombers, aimed at disrupting what was believed to be the delicately balanced, complex fabric of a modern industrial economy. Given the range limitations of bombers in the foreseeable future, this meant that an offensive against any likely enemy must be based overseas. The United States would require allies to supply bases. So, although Army air power advocates often argued that an invasion of the United States could be defeated by land-based aircraft alone, their ideas were nevertheless incompatible with the military premises of isolationism.

During the early 1930s the Tactical School refined its ideas about the proper targets for an air offensive, stressing the enemy's electric power plants, oil industry, and aircraft production. Unlike the RAF, it carefully studied the problems of bombing.[10] And it acquired equipment to implement its theories: the B-17 bomber and the Norden bombsight.

In the early 1930s the Air Corps, far in advance of the RAF, had acquired modern bombers, the B-9 and B-10. Led by General Foulois, it sought a major role in defense against invasion. It wanted both a large experimental four-engine bomber and a smaller "multi-engine" bomber to replace the B-10; the multi-engine bomber should carry 2,000 pounds of bombs over 1,000 miles at a top speed of 200 miles an hour. The Air Corps got its way; in 1934 the Boeing Company received a contract for the experimental plane, the XB-15. This underpowered monster supplied useful data. Boeing also bid to build the new operational bomber.

Model 299, an experimental version of the B-17, was designed and built in just 11 months. It included many innovations that were startling in 1935: electrical operation of flaps, bomb bay doors, and landing gear; "control tabs," which harnessed air flow to help move control surfaces; and soundproofing, insulation, and heating. The new plane also had streamlined "blisters" as gun positions, built to hold .50-caliber Browning machine guns instead of the .30-caliber weapons usual at the time. The B-17's performance considerably exceeded the Air Corps specifications and easily beat out its rivals. It lacked power turrets and tail guns and so, compared to its descendants during World War II, it was very lightly defended. But for 1935 it was a tough and impressive airplane. The nickname coined by a reporter, Flying Fortress, stuck.

In another sense the name jibed neatly with the justification most often given for building the B-17; defense against invading enemy fleets. This was not entirely disingenuous; the Air Corps brass believed, until well into 1942, that high-flying formations of B-17s could deal with enemy warships at sea. They did not entirely hide its main task; in October 1935 Foulois's successor, Gen. Frank Andrews, publicly alluded to long-range strategic bombing of enemy factories, refineries, and power plants.

An accident greatly hindered the B-17's development. In October 1935 an Army pilot crashed and destroyed the only existing prototype, and the Air Corps was forced to order the much feebler twin-engine B-18. With great difficulty, the Air Corps obtained permission to buy just thirteen YB-17s as well. The YB-17s were assigned to the Second Bombardment Group, which, as the first heavy bomber unit, played an important role in developing techniques and tactics. Using the secret Norden bombsight, it achieved remarkable accuracy in tests in California, often hitting within 50 feet of the aiming point from four miles up. Unfortunately, combat conditions in Europe, where the Fortresses would usually be a few thousand feet higher, rarely allowed the results attainable in the clear, dry, and peaceful air over the desert.

There was a long struggle over whether to build more B-17s. The traditionalist elements on the Army General Staff and in the Navy both disliked four-engine heavy bombers. Against much resistance, a few dozen improved B-17s were ordered in spurts, from 1937 to 1940—the last batch just in time to prevent Boeing from leaving the bomber business.

The Army also managed to initiate work on a newer heavy bomber, the Consolidated B-24 Liberator, which was test-flown in 1939. Awkward looking, with a slab-sided fuselage, high wings, and a twin tail, it was faster than the B-17 and could fly farther with a ton more of bombs. It became a teammate rather than a replacement for the B-17, although eventually more B-24s were built than Fortresses. The B-24 never became a legend, as the older plane did; men who flew both types preferred the B-17. Although the final model of the B-17 carried more guns than the B-24, the latter may have been just as well protected in practice. But the B-24 was less stable and harder to fly in formation—an exhausting job even in the B-17—and was more likely to catch fire when hit. Using hydraulic systems for many functions that were carried out electrically on the B-17, the Liberator was more vulnerable to damage and flew less well when it lost an engine. But it was an invaluable workhorse, although the B-17 remained the preferred plane in Europe, the toughest theater, throughout the war.

As World War II began, the Army Air Corps had the nucleus of a well planned strategic bombing force. The obverse of its commitment to some outstanding heavy bomber designs was the backwardness of its fighters; it had developed in precisely the opposite way from the RAF. This was a serious handicap during the first years of the war. Even the new Bell P-39 and the Curtiss P-40 were inferior to European fighters, because these new American fighters were hobbled by inadequate Allison engines with poor high-altitude performance. The Americans had concentrated on air-cooled radial engines, preferred for civil airliners, navy aircraft, and army bombers, and had lagged behind the British and the Germans in work on liquid-cooled engines, for which army fighters were the sole American market. The Army's third new fighter, the Lockheed P-38 Lightning, was an outstanding plane of unusual design. It had twin engines mounted in long booms, the pilot and guns housed in a small nacelle between them. But it was hard to manufacture, and production was delayed because the Army recklessly used the sole prototype to attempt to set a speed record in February 1939. It crashed, setting back the P-38's development by nearly two years.[11] In 1940, as two British historians of the Battle of Britain wrote, "there was nothing President Roosevelt could do to help Fighter Command" because *none* of the fighters being built in the United States were suitable for combat in Europe. As World War II began, the Army Air Corps was a small force, and save for its heavy bombers, had second-rate equipment. It consisted of less than 26,000 men and just 1,500 planes, and was a fraction of the size of the Luftwaffe.[12]

THE ENEMY AND THE TARGET

The British and the Americans were almost alone in developing strategic bombing forces. A major factor in this was probably the fact that, as all but the most optimistic proponents of strategic bombing realized, a successful strategic bombing campaign would take a long time. Britain and the United States were sea powers and did not maintain large standing armies. They had always expected to take considerable time, in any major war, to build up their strength and bring it to bear against the enemy. A continental land power with powerful neighbors, tempted by or exposed to invasion on the ground, and seeking or fearing a quick decision, was almost bound to have less interest in strategic air attack.

Advocates of strategic bombing forces elsewhere were not very successful. The Soviets, who had the largest air force in the world in the 1930s, built some well designed heavy bombers comparable to the B-17, but seem to have envisaged using them to strike the "deep rear" of an opposing army and air force—railheads and bases far behind the front—rather than for true strategic attacks on war production or on basic elements of an enemy's economy. In any case, the proponents of heavy bombers fell afoul of Stalin and were wiped out in the Great Purge.[13]

The Luftwaffe's founders had more interest in strategic bombing but it became a tactical air force, designed to support surface operations. It was headed by Hermann Goering, the most important Nazi next to Hitler himself. Air power had a high place in the Nazi scheme of things. Hitler firmly believed in its importance, although he did not exert the close and continuous influence over the Luftwaffe that he maintained over the army. Instead he trusted in Goering's judgment until it was too late. Goering, a renowned ace in World War I, was a technical ignoramus. Much of the Luftwaffe's development was really due to the efforts of the air ministry's state secretary, Erhard Milch, and its first chief of staff, Gen. Walter Wever. Unlike Milch, Wever favored developing a strategic bombing force. Prototypes of two four-engine heavy bombers, the Dornier 19 and the Junkers 89, were built in advance of comparable British planes. But they were underpowered, and their fuel tanks were too small. Despite all the Weimar Republic's efforts to evade them, the restrictions of the Versailles Treaty had left Germany's aircraft industry in poor shape. Engine development in particular, lagged until the mid-1930s. Lack of suitable power plants finally led to the cancellation of the Dornier 19 and Junkers 89. Wever's death in 1936 did not, by itself, abort the building of heavy bombers, as is sometimes said; efforts to develop them went on. The Germans even built a prototype of the Messerschmitt 264, intended to bomb the United States from bases in the Azores.

But Wever's death did remove some of the impetus for such aircraft. Hitler himself assumed that the Luftwaffe's medium bombers had sufficient striking power for any task that was liable to be encountered in the conquest of Europe and Asia. General Albert Kesselring, Wever's successor, was more interested in the ground support role. Wever's death was fortunate for the Allies, for none of his successors were so capable, and none got along well with Milch. Goering deliberately undercut Milch, whose talents focused on production rather than on the promotion of technical innovations, by building up the influence of General Ernst Udet, another famous airman, who, like Goering, was a dilettante in technical matters and a poor manager. The Luftwaffe's technical development became disorganized, and the Air Ministry became a bureaucratic jungle. Udet had no less than 24 departments reporting to him.

Germany's aircraft industry and fuel supply may have been unequal to the task of building and flying a fleet of four-engine bombers even had suitable engines been developed, but technical blunders ended any chance there had been for a workable heavy bomber. The designers of the Heinkel 177, intended to succeed the Dornier 19 and Junkers 89, tried to overcome the engine problem in a novel way. Lacking engines with the desired horsepower, they decided to reduce the drag that would be produced by four separate engine nacelles by coupling two engines together in the same nacelle to drive a single propeller. But this produced dreadful mechanical problems and many fires. The logical solution, going to four separate engines, was foreclosed by the development of a mania for dive-bombing, promoted by Udet. The Luftwaffe's best medium bomber, the Junkers 88, had unexpectedly proven an effective dive-bomber. Such a capability was now demanded of the Heinkel 177. A conventional four-engine bomber could not be expected to dive-bomb, and the coupled-engine design would be vital if the new bomber were to do so. Many months were wasted before it was admitted that the arrangement was unworkable. By then any chance to build a heavy bomber force was long gone; the Luftwaffe was in a desperate struggle for survival.[14]

Despite its perhaps inevitable failure to develop a strategic bombing force, the Luftwaffe proved a formidable enemy. In the Messerschmitt 109 it had a first-class interceptor, which until 1943 was superior to any Allied plane except the Spitfire. It had sound, although slow and poorly armed, bombers. Its pilots, crews, and technicians were well trained, many with combat experience from the Spanish Civil War. That war had taught valuable lessons about close support for ground troops and the need for radio aids for navigation and bad-weather operations. The Luftwaffe was far ahead of the Allies in "blind-bombing" devices to guide bombers at night. Without the still greater ingenuity of the British in developing methods of jamming these systems, Britain would have suffered even more damage in the Blitz of 1940–1941. In Spain the Germans learned that bombers required fighter escort when they would be opposed by interceptors. They also discovered, or rather rediscovered, the proper tactics and formations for fighters. The Luftwaffe had a large air transport force and a mobile organization. It could shift bases quickly, which proved helpful in the defense of the Reich as well as in the conquest of Europe. Lastly, the Luftwaffe controlled Germany's antiaircraft defenses, which were proportionately stronger than those of any other power. Hitler, and other Nazi leaders, had greater faith in the power of antiaircraft guns than they had in fighters.

However, the Luftwaffe and its supporting industries had serious weaknesses. Some of these were hidden by success in the early part of the war, only to be exposed by the Battle of Britain and later reverses. One amazing lapse (although rarely noted) was Germany's failure to keep up in the development of aviation gasoline. While the United States and Britain had developed 100-octane gasoline, the Germans flew, right through the Battle of Britain, on 87-octane fuel. In 1940–1941 they obtained a 95- to 97-octane gasoline, but they never went beyond this, while new blending agents and additives gave the Allies the equivalent of 140-octane performance. The better performance of Allied piston-engine planes in World War II was often partly due to better fuel.

The aircraft industry was short of skilled workers, and production—partly because of the lack of will to increase it, rather than sheer inability—was low. When the war began, the Luftwaffe was short of reserve planes, fuel stocks, bombs, and flak ammunition; only their victories and the Allied passivity in 1939 enabled the Germans to make good these shortages. The Luftwaffe lacked torpedo bombers, and largely because of Goering's jealousy and hostility, cooperation between the German air and naval forces in the Battle of the Atlantic remained poor. As a result of the disarmament before 1933 and the rapid expansion afterward, the Luftwaffe was also short of mid-level officers. Despite the blind-bombing aids discussed earlier, it was otherwise backward in making use of electronics. When World War II started, the Germans had excellent radar and used shorter wavelengths than the British did. But radar development was promoted by the navy rather than the Luftwaffe. The British made better use of their initially crude radar, and soon took an unbeatable lead by developing the cavity magnetron, which made microwave radar possible.

While the Luftwaffe saw the need for fighter escort, its effort to get adequate escorts misfired. It developed the Messerschmitt 110, a heavy twin-engine, twin-seat fighter ("Zerstorer"), for this. The Me-110 had the range to do the job, but lacked the performance to survive against modern Allied single-engine fighters. (The American P-38 seems to have been the only twin-engine, propeller-driven *day* fighter of World War II that could compete fairly equally with single-engine fighters; as we shall see, even it did not do well at this in the "big league" of air fighting over Northwest Europe.) The Me-110 was exposed as a failure in the Battle of Britain. In an incredible blunder, the Me-109 was not equipped to carry droppable auxiliary fuel tanks until the Battle of Britain was nearly over, although the Heinkel 51, its biplane predecessor, had carried such tanks in Spain. The Battle of Britain showed that the Me-109s lacked the range, and were not numerous enough, to beat the RAF. The Germans failed to draw the correct conclusion about their lack of sufficient single-engine fighters or the vulnerability of the twin-engine fighter; this would impede the defense of Germany.

Nazi politics and erratic decisions on research and development hampered the Luftwaffe's development. Good as the Me-109 was, the Germans could have had an even better fighter, the Heinkel 100, which was faster and more rugged. But the Nazi leaders liked Willy Messerschmitt, and they disliked Ernst Heinkel, who was too frank. (Many Nazis also suspected, wrongly, that Heinkel was part Jewish.) As we shall see, the prejudice against Heinkel would rebound further against the Luftwaffe. Blunders before the war, and a series of cutbacks in research, first on programs that were not expected to have a quick payoff, and later when an early end to the war was expected, retarded the development of conventional planes and jets. The Nazis gave priority to a small number of propeller-driven designs expected to succeed those with which they had started the war, then spread the rest of their efforts on 40 different types of planes. Their new bombers were inadequate or were outright failures. The Me-209 and Me-210, intended to replace the Me-109 and Me-110 respectively, both failed. The Me-210 was hastily redesigned as the Me-410, although the whole idea of a "heavy fighter" should have been suspect.[15]

The Germans' inadequate plane production and reserves of planes, and other shortages at the outbreak of war, stemmed from one of the most astonishing facts of World War II. Nazi Germany had failed to fully mobilize for war, and did not do so until 1942. Contemporary observers were taken in by Goering's boasts that the Nazis preferred "guns to butter." But it was a natural assumption that the most warlike of all states would have completely harnessed its economy for military purposes even before the war. People further believed that

Germany's economy must already be badly strained, and that stocks of raw materials were especially short. This implied, or seemed to imply, that almost any bomb damage would hurt war production. Since, supposedly, the civilian sector of the economy had already been cut to the bone, the Germans were not considered able to shift production from civilian goods to weapons. The belief that German civilians were in a straightened situation was one of the reasons why people in the Western powers believed German morale soft.

All of these ideas were wrong. Neither the economy nor civilian morale was strained or vulnerable. Before 1939 German expenditures on armaments and supporting industries and "infrastructure" were considerable—about one-and-one-half times that of Britain and France combined—but this was far from a total mobilization of the sort the Allied countries undertook when the war began, and that Germany neglected. From 1940 to 1942, British production of planes, tanks, trucks, and other war items was actually higher than that of the Germans, despite the latter's bigger economy and control of a conquered Europe. German living standards remained high, higher than those of the British, until 1944. There was a "cushion," and a thick one, of unused capacity that could be used to repair bomb damage and increase production.

The Nazis' failure to fully mobilize was not recognized until after the war. It has often been suggested that they coherently planned a "blitzkrieg economy," to support short, victorious campaigns, since they foresaw a series of short offensives, tackling one enemy at a time, rather than a long, multi-front war against a coalition, which was what they got. There are indications, too, that during the 1930s they did not expect a really big campaign until 1942 or 1943. Hitler thought that he did not have to mobilize his economy fully to support a war or wars of the type he banked on, and he was reluctant to reduce living standards, lest it hurt his popularity. Although the Nazis pretended that Germany had been defeated because it was "stabbed in the back" by treason, Hitler, at least, knew better, and he feared subjecting the German home front to hardships like those of World War I.

In fact, although these ideas about Hitler's war plans were roughly accurate, it is doubtful that Germany's economic preparations were closely geared to those plans, or that they reflected a coherent program for a "blitzkrieg economy." The Nazis' emphasis on what was called "rearmament in width rather than depth"—that is, a quick payoff in the actual production of weapons, rather than expansion of the base of the economy by expanding the production of basic industrial materials—did fit in with the "blitzkrieg" notion. Partly this was the result of underestimates of British and French arms production, which made greater efforts seemingly unnecessary. But Hitler had no great interest in, or comprehension of, economics, and he did not impose an overall plan.

Instead, the war economy, at least up to 1942, was the object of bitter feuds between elements of the Nazi party, agencies of the armed forces, and the ministry of economics. The result was that while in some sectors of the economy planning was based on the expectation of a short war or wars, planning in other sectors assumed the need for self-sufficiency for a long time and the danger of major air attacks. The Nazis were fairly successful in making Germany self-sufficient in food production. Elaborate industries to produce synthetic oil, rubber, fibers, and nitrogen were built. Yet reserves of raw materials seem to have been set up erratically. Stockpiles of oil, rubber, and materials for alloys were small, and in 1939–1941 the Nazis were lucky to be able to increase them by trade with the USSR and by conquest. The synthetics plants were concentrated, and vulnerable to air attack, although they would have been hard to disperse even if the Nazis had wanted to do so. But certain industries directly related to weapons production were carefully dispersed and protected. Aluminum, aircraft, and ammunition production was vastly expanded in the 1930s. The government encouraged their dispersal to areas of the country far from the Western frontiers. Particular care was taken with the aircraft plants. New ones were built in open country, outside cities, and well spread out in a number of buildings, all very strongly constructed. Most of the aircraft production processes were duplicated. And if the factories were damaged, the Germans were in a good position to repair them. Germany's machine-tool industry was lavishly equipped, and so was its transportation system. The only weak spot, perhaps, was a strained electrical power system. Otherwise, there were few weak points in the German war economy, and they were not obvious.[16]

The Failure of Bomber Command, 1939–1941

Since at least some of Bomber Command's limitations were generally understood, the British government welcomed President Franklin D. Roosevelt's request on September 1, 1939, that the belligerents refrain from an unrestricted air war that would endanger civilians. This was interpreted as excluding almost any attacks on industrial targets located in or near cities. The Nazis also professed to welcome Roosevelt's appeal. The French favored "restraint" even if the Germans launched a major offensive in the West, lest their poorly defended industry suffer devastation by the Luftwaffe, but the British disagreed.

The British limited their air effort against Germany to attacks on the German navy and to dropping propaganda leaflets on German cities. The Allies would have been well advised to invade the Rhineland while the German forces were tied down in Poland, but the opportunity slipped by without even being noticed at the time—it was beyond the mental horizon of the slow-thinking Allied leaders. Their grand strategy was to build up their forces gradually and launch a major land offensive only in the later stages of a war, after blockade and bombing had weakened Germany. Whatever the defects of the general strategy, the British decision to hold back in the air was reasonable. The British continued to follow this policy after indiscriminate German bombing in Poland released them from the pledge of mutual restraint. Ludlow-Hewitt expected a long war; he planned a gradual expansion of Bomber Command and held back men from front-line squadrons to increase the strength of training units.[1]

That the decision to hold off on bombing was prudent was soon shown when even limited attacks on the German fleet ended disastrously. On September 4, the day after Britain declared war, fourteen Wellingtons and fifteen Blenheims set out to attack the German fleet near Wilhelmshaven. The formations became disorganized in clouds; ten planes turned back, and the rest made ragged attacks. While the Wellingtons bombed from high up, the Blenheims, going in low, damaged a cruiser slightly (one Blenheim crashed into it) and hit a pocket battleship with three or four 250-pound bombs. But these bombs, too light to really harm an armored ship, did not even explode. Five Blenheims and two Wellingtons were lost to German fighters and flak. The RAF wrongly ascribed all the losses to flak.

Inability to find the German fleet delayed a decisive test until December, when only the better armed, more rugged Wellingtons were used. On December 3, twenty-four Wellingtons attacked German warships near Heligoland, without success. German fighters approached the tight British formation cautiously, firing only from long range. The Wellingtons all got home, suffering only some damage to flak. On December 14, twelve Wellingtons patrolling off the German coast ran into fighters. This time the German pilots meant business; five Wellingtons went down and another crashed on landing. The planes that returned claimed to have shot down one German fighter. The RAF again wrongly attributed most or all of its losses to flak. On December 18, twenty-four Wellingtons went out. Two turned back; the Germans detected the rest on radar well out to sea, but took time to assemble their fighters. In earlier encounters the Germans had noted that the Wellingtons' rear turrets were dangerous but that their traverse was limited; there was nothing to oppose a side or beam attack. The Germans intercepted too late to cause much trouble before the British started bomb runs on a battleship and a cruiser. But the British, following orders not to bomb if there was any danger of hitting the shore, did not drop their bombs! Then the German fighters closed in. Only ten Wellingtons returned home; two German fighters went down.

There was no doubt, this time, that fighters had caused the terrible losses. If this episode was typical, daylight attacks on inland German targets without escort would be suicidal. There was a spate of rationalizing by some senior officers. Some blamed the disaster on a failure to keep formation under fire. Others argued that modest alterations to the bombers would make all the difference. They needed self-sealing fuel tanks (armor to protect the wing tanks was already being fitted) and guns to cover the side approach. Others blamed the plan of attack, complaining that a course involving a landfall far north of the target and a flight along the enemy coast had been unwise. Ludlow-Hewitt conceded the truth of the last criticism and suggested that the extent of the defeat had been because the Germans had committed "crack units," which in fact they had not done. He took steps to secure self-sealing tanks and "beam" guns. Slowly, however, the truth sank in, assisted by another disaster, when German fighters downed two of three Wellingtons over the North Sea on January 2.

NIGHT OPERATIONS

The RAF was faced with one of the fateful decisions of the war. It must give up strategic bombing altogether, use long-range escort, or resort to night operations, which would, apparently, reduce the danger of interception. The first choice seemed unthinkable, while the second seemed to be foreclosed by fundamental engineering factors. Any fighter carrying enough fuel to accompany bombers to a distant target, it was believed, would be too heavy and unmaneuverable to deal with enemy interceptors. (In fact, Giro Horikoshi, the designer of the Japanese Zero fighter, had already disproved this notion— unknown to the British.)

Night operations seemed the only choice. Leaflet dropping at night by Whitley bombers of Bomber Command's 4 Group seemed encouraging. They met no effective opposition during the bitter winter of 1939–1940, despite all sorts of operational difficulties. Without heaters or proper clothing, the crews were miserably cold. Oxygen supplies were limited. Planes iced up, and engines cut out or caught fire. Still, there were few losses. Bomber Command hastened to provide de-icers and heaters, but the problem of finding and hitting the target remained. Prewar tests of Bomber Command's navigation at night had not been encouraging, but little had been done about it. Early in the war, navigational equipment consisted only of maps, sextants, and radio direction finders. The latter required considerable skill, and the radio was often jammed. The navigators were not well trained and the planes were not stable; taking star sight (when weather allowed) was not easy. Seeing a target, if someone got there, depended heavily on moonlight. In October 1939, Air Commodore Arthur Coningham, 4 Groups's commander, estimated that on clear nights with more than a quarter moon, individual buildings could be distinguished at heights up to 3,000 or 4,000 feet. Small towns could be seen from 4,000 to 6,000 feet, and small rivers were visible up to 6,000 to 8,000 feet. Only coastal points, major rivers, and canals could be seen from over 12,000 feet. On moonless nights only a coastline or something self-illuminating, like a blast furnace, was visible. Unfortunately, below 10,000 feet, bombers flying in a defended area were highly vulnerable to flak, and crewmen were apt to be blinded by searchlights, so even Coningham's estimate should have shown that the force could not be relied on to hit specific targets at night. (The fact that they *could* be seen below 4,000 feet might have suggested that a few planes, coming in low, could find and mark a target for a main force flying far higher. But it was years before this possibility was seen and acted on.) Nevertheless, Coningham and others believed that targets like synthetic oil plants or factories could be found and hit by making a timed run from some readily identifiable point.

Experiments with this technique in January 1940 were not encouraging, but it was decided that conditions had been unusually unfavorable. In December Ludlow-Hewitt had started another investigation into target finding at night by planes flying over Germany. Their crews were able to spot large railroad yards (which were dimly lit) and factory cooling towers, as well as the Rhine, in moonlight. These flights, however, were made below, often far below, 10,000 feet, and despite Coningham's report, the results were recklessly assumed to be valid for much greater heights. Ludlow-Hewitt decided that training and experience would greatly improve navigation and target finding. In February 1940 he began converting most of his command into a night force. Despite the poor results of the tests in January, crews were trained to make timed runs from recognized landmarks to the target area, where flares would be dropped to help identify the target. But the available flares were not too effective and were dangerous to handle; in practice flares were little used until 1942.

Bomber Command assumed that the enemy's night defenses might improve, but not enough to raise British losses dangerously. Even when techniques and equipment improved, night bombing, even more than other military operations, would be severely constrained, not just by weather but by the phases of the moon and the season. The best results were attained by moonlight; during the early years of the war the grim expression "bomber's moon" replaced "full moon" for a time. (Later, when conditions changed, bombers would avoid moonlit nights.) During the short summer nights, the RAF limited its attacks to western Germany; it could not reach Berlin or targets further east and return under cover of darkness.

Geography was tremendously important to night operations. It was always easier to find targets on a coast or estuary, or along a wide, winding river, than inland. Also, the closer a target was to England, the easier it was to find it. Certain places—the Ruhr, with its maze of similar-looking cities under a perpetual layer of smog; Stuttgart, scattered among deep valleys; and Berlin, spread out over a huge area—were particularly hard to attack. Unfortunately, the geographical layout of the critical features of the German economy was not favorable to the Allies. The cities of the North Sea coast, the easiest to find, were important in a general way, but they did not contain either an overwhelming percentage of German war production or (with one exception, which the Allies overlooked) the production of any critical item.

Beginning as a force used to flying by day in tight formation and facing simple problems of navigation, Bomber Command became a force committed to operating in darkness in an individualistic way. Until 1942 its crews took off at widely varying times and made their own lonely way to the target. There was usually little concentration of effort in time or even space. Overestimating the destructiveness of its small bombs, the RAF would strike several different cities on the same night, or would attack several different targets within the same city. In one attack on Berlin in September 1940 it assigned the bombers 18 different targets!

German air attacks on the British fleet at Scapa Flow made the British less fussy about dropping bombs on Germany. On the night of March 19, 1940, fifty Whitleys and Hampdens with experienced crews set out for a German seaplane base on Sylt Island, off the German coast. All but one plane got home; forty-one reported bombing the target and claimed many hits and resulting fires. But reconnaissance pictures made on April 6 showed no visible damage.

The first analysis suggested that things were as bad as they seemed, and that the average bomber crew could never find a precise target even on the coast, except in the very best visibility. Then, half the crews might bomb the target. But the sort of rationalization that had earlier operated to preserve the concept of the self-defending bomber formation now operated to uphold the effectiveness of night bombing. It was pointed out that the enemy might have repaired or camouflaged the damage before the pictures were made, and that the photos were of poor quality. Bomber Command remained subject to delusions of accuracy until the summer of 1941; in fact, during 1940 an increasingly optimistic reading of operational reports led to the amazing conclusion that some precise targets could be hit even without moonlight.[2] For many months it was firmly believed that precision bombing at night was possible.

THE OFFENSIVE AGAINST GERMANY BEGINS

The switch to night bombing was made shortly before the Nazis invaded Denmark and Norway. Bomber Command's sole role in that campaign was to mount ineffective attacks on the airfields the Germans had seized.

When the Germans invaded Belgium and the Netherlands, restrictions on Bomber Command's operations were lifted. The Blenheims of Bomber Command's 2 Group, operating in daylight, were hurled into the land battle and suffered from German fighters and flak. On the night of May 15–16, the rest of Bomber Command opened the strategic air offensive proper. Executing Western Air Plan 4C, (WA 4C), 99 night bombers set out to attack marshalling yards and synthetic oil plants in the Ruhr. These attacks did little damage.

Bomber Command could not have influenced the Battle of France even had its operations been effective. But after the battle was over, bombers were the only offensive weapon the Allies, what was left of them, had. Britain was alone; Bomber Command was the only, if pitifully ineffective, means with which it could strike Germany. On August 8 Churchill wrote that should Hitler "be repulsed here or not try invasion, he will recoil eastward, and we have nothing to stop him. But there is one thing that would bring him back and bring him down, and that is an absolutely devastating, exterminating attack by very heavy bombers from this country on the Nazi homeland. We must be able to overwhelm them by this means, without which I do not see a way through." In September he put it more pithily. "The Navy can lose us the war, but only the Air Force can win it."

By early June it was clear that the war's next phase would see a desperate struggle for air supremacy. Air Marshal Sir Charles Portal, who had replaced Ludlow-Hewitt in April, was ordered to attack aircraft plants when oil plants could not be found. Several times reshuffling its priorities, the RAF went after aircraft plants and airfields, German ports, and shipping. More units were assigned to mining enemy-controlled waters; this proved an effective and cheap means of sinking enemy ships, superior to direct attacks with bombs and torpedoes.

During August, Bomber Command concentrated on "counter-air" operations against the Luftwaffe's bases and factories, while 2 Group, now flying mostly at night, bombed the ports across the English Channel from which an invasion of Britain was to be mounted. A special operation was launched to stop the assembly of the invasion fleet by wrecking the aqueduct that carried the Dortmund-Ems Canal over the Ems River. Barges and small craft used the canal to reach the invasion ports. On the night of August 12–13, eleven Hampdens with picked crews attacked the canal. While some tried to draw enemy fire, the remainder struck at low level. Despite the diversion there was a storm of flak. Two planes were shot down, but the canal was blocked for ten days. Flight-Lieutenant Roderick Learoyd, who dropped the critical bomb, received the Victoria Cross. In September the other groups joined 2 Group against the channel ports, which proved easy targets; unless the weather was utterly impossible, the ports could be hit even on moonless nights. Bomber Command destroyed over 200 barges, almost a tenth of the invasion fleet.

This bombing alone did not prevent an invasion, although it had done a good job of hindering invasion preparations. The fundamental reason the Germans failed to invade Britain was the Fighter Command prevented them from gaining air superiority. Bomber Command's actions had little direct effect on the fight for air superiority, but indirectly they may have encouraged the Nazis to make a mistake that greatly helped Fighter Command. Despite considerable advice to the contrary, Hitler had ruled that the British capital should not yet be attacked on a large scale, and the Luftwaffe was concentrating its efforts on beating down the RAF. However, since there were more bombers than could be escorted during the day, the Germans employed some at night. And on the night of August 24–25, German bombers seeking oil-tank farms and aircraft plants mistakenly hit residential areas of London.

The British were furious. At the Air Ministry's suggestion, Churchill ordered Bomber Command to Berlin. The British had refrained from attacking the German capital until then; it contained few targets of high priority under recent directives, and on the shortest nights it had been out of reach. On the night of August 25–26 Bomber Command sent 81 bombers to strike industrial objectives in Berlin. Clouds interfered with the bombing, which as usual was inaccurate. More attacks followed, killing a few civilians.

On August 30 Hitler decided to retaliate on London. In this he was following the advice of many Luftwaffe generals, who had long believed that an attack on London would force a decisive air battle under conditions that would favor the Luftwaffe. This was a miscalculation. The attacks on London, which began on September 7, lifted the pressure from Fighter Command's airfields in southeast England, and the RAF did well in the fighting over London. The decision to make London a target, however hard for the Londoners, gave Fighter Command a welcome respite. It is doubtful that this decided the Battle of Britain, as was once widely believed. But the attacks on Berlin, along with Bomber Command's attacks on the invasion fleet, certainly were to Britain's advantages.

THE BLITZ AND THE ELECTRONIC WAR

By the end of September the Germans had "indefinitely postponed" the invasion of Britain. Except for some minor operations, heavy losses had brought daylight bombing to an end.[3] The Germans switched to night bombing, trying to demoralize the British people by bombing their cities. The history of the "Blitz" of 1940–1941 is not, strictly speaking, part of our story, but it influenced or paralleled British efforts against Germany.

British defenses against night attack were weak, and Britain was an easier target for German bombers than Germany was for Bomber Command. The Germans were based close to their objectives; British cities are near the coast and were easily found. Spotting specific targets like factories, however, was difficult for the Germans as well. But, far in advance of the British, they had developed electronic devices to guide their bombers. The first round of the electronic war began as the British tried to jam these systems.

They quickly jammed Knickebein, the simplest blind-bombing device, which could be used by any bomber. The Germans then had to turn to more complex devices requiring special equipment and training. These were used by a special pathfinder unit that preceded the main bomber force, dropping incendiary bombs to mark the target. The marking tactics were less effective, and the British learned to jam these systems too.

The Germans continued to bomb Britain heavily, especially London, which would have been hard to miss even without a guidance system. But erratic target selection by the Luftwaffe, the inefficiency of the pathfinder technique, and the inexperience of many bomber crews prevented the Germans from making good use even of intervals when British jamming was not so effective. Accordingly, the Germans readily accepted "area bombing" for the purpose of terrorizing British civilians. The idea of blasting the residential areas of London to cause the resistance to collapse seems to have lurked in Goering's mind, at least, from the start of the Battle of Britain. Area attacks did not disturb the Luftwaffe's senior officers, even if they regarded them as inferior to striking military installations and war plants.

Contrary to a widespread myth, the Blitz did hurt British morale, but it was far from breaking. The particularly devastating attack on Coventry in November 1940 caused a brief decline in aircraft production but did not permanently hurt the RAF; no vital industry or basic part of the economy suffered decisive damage.[4]

Despite the relatively small effect of German night bombing, during 1941 and 1942 the RAF would copy many features of the German onslaught, including area bombing, the use of electronic guidance systems and pathfinder units to mark the target, and the use of incendiaries and very heavy explosive bombs.

ILLUSIONS, 1940–1941

It should have been obvious that Bomber Command faced a more formidable task than the one at which the Luftwaffe had failed, but the British remained confident that they could do tremendous damage to Germany. With the Nazi attacks on civilian areas, scruples about destroying German residential areas and civilians had eroded. Earlier, British bombers had sometimes returned without bombing if the crews were not sure they had found their assigned target. But on September 9 they were ordered to bomb if at all possible. German civilians were not yet deliberately chosen targets, but letting them suffer "unintended" destruction was now more acceptable. Some wished to go further; in September Portal suggested deliberate retaliatory raids against 20 German cities. But the Air Ministry and the Air Staff disliked deliberate retaliation—apart from the special case of Berlin—and Portal did not pursue it after becoming chief of the Air Staff in October 1940. He already doubted that Bomber Command was really hitting its assigned targets, but Sir Richard Peirse, his successor at Bomber Command, was more rigid and overconfident.

At the height of the anti-invasion struggle, the Air Staff had reminded Bomber Command that attacking the Nazis' oil supply remained the "basis of our longer-term offensive strategy." Bad weather, however, had rendered moot the directives in October that made oil the primary target.

There was little real evidence with which to evaluate early attacks on oil targets. The poor quality of reconnaissance photos, and convoluted arguments based on prewar calculations, were used by optimists to justify big hopes. In mid-December the War Cabinet's special committee on oil matters, chaired by Geoffrey Lloyd, the Secretary of Petroleum, concluded that the 539 tons of bombs that had been dropped on synthetic oil plants—just 6.7 percent of Bomber Command's total effort in the same period—had already cut synthetic oil output by 15 percent. It was further calculated that only 400 aimed 500-pound bombs, carried by 100 bombers, were needed to knock out an oil plant for four months. If only half of the bombers sent out attacked their primary targets, 200 sorties would suffice to smash each plant. Just 3,400 sorties over four months would be needed to knock out all 17 synthetic plants. Given nine clear, moonlit nights a month, this seemed within Bomber Command's present capabilities—and it was about to get its first true heavy bomber, the Stirling.

By some standards this was a modest evaluation. There were group commanders who thought their men, or at least their best crews, could hit oil plants even without moonlight.

The British chiefs of staff were enthusiastic about an all-out attack on oil plants, believing that this would be a decisive blow. The War Cabinet—Churchill in particular—increasingly favored hitting German civilians. Churchill frankly doubted that the oil plan would work. Skeptical of any hard-and-fast calculations about how to win the war, he also thought that it was too bad that oil plants were mostly well away from densely inhabited areas. Shrewd doubts about whether the RAF could do what it promised were thus mixed with less worthy, although natural, motives of revenge. Nevertheless, on January 15 Bomber Command was ordered to make the destruction of the synthetic oil plants its sole primary aim.

Even as these plans to deprive the Nazis of oil were laid, however it was becoming apparent just how little basis there was for confidence in the RAF's ability to hit the oil plants. On December 16 an "area attack" on the center of Mannheim was carried out, on Churchill's order, as a reprisal for the German attack on Coventry. It was frankly aimed at German civilians. Copying German practice, it was led by eight Wellingtons flown by the most experienced crews, dropping incendiaries to mark aiming points for the following planes. There was a full moon. Of 134 planes sent out, 102 reported hitting the target area; 7 went down or crashed in England. But high-quality photos taken by the new reconnaissance model of the Spitfire showed that the bombing had been scattered and inaccurate. A reconnaissance of two oil plants at Gelsenkirchen, in the Ruhr, showed that despite two attacks in which 296 planes had dropped 260 tons of high explosives plus some incendiaries, there was little evidence of damage or even of craters nearby. Inquiries showed that incompetent debriefing had exaggerated the achievements of the air crews. Many were not confident that they had found their targets, and the more experienced men were the least optimistic. Most wanted the target marked by specially picked crews starting fires.

The Battle of the Atlantic

Nevertheless, the house of cards of precision bombing remained standing for a time. The weather in January and February 1941 was so bad that just two attacks were made on oil targets,[5] and by March the threat to Britain's supply lines in the Battle of the Atlantic was so great that the oil offensive could not be pursued. On March 9 Bomber Command received a new directive giving the Battle of the Atlantic priority. For the next four months it concentrated on attacking naval bases, U-boat construction yards, factories making components for U-boats and for the Focke-Wulf 200 Kondor bomber, and the bases of the FW-200 units. (The FW-200s were converted airliners that flew far west of Britain and inflicted heavy losses on shipping.) Most of these objectives were on the French or German coasts and were far easier to find than oil plants.

An attack on the Focke-Wulf plant at Bremen on March 12 finally proved Bomber Command incapable of precision bombing. Of 54 Wellingtons dispatched, 33, carrying 132 HE (high explosive) bombs and 840 incendiaries, reported attacking the target. Photographs showed that despite a full moon and perfect conditions, just 12 bombs had hit the plant, a large and easily located target. It was concluded that the average aiming error, in the best conditions, would be 600 yards; normally it would be closer to 1,000 yards. This analysis, which was still too optimistic, ruled out hitting oil plants at all. Only area bombing would be possible on dark nights—three-quarters of each month. This seemingly left the German transportation system the only critical target, other than German morale, that could be harmed.

Until July 1941 the RAF persisted with the campaign against German sea power, although it was clear that attacks on naval targets in Germany itself often amounted to area attacks on whole German cities. Much of Bomber Command's efforts were directed against German warships in French ports, which were at least easier to find. From March 1941 to February 1942 the battle cruisers *Scharn-horst* and *Gneisenau* were holed up in Brest. Hidden by smoke screens and heavily defended by flak, they were not rewarding targets. Usually sitting in dry docks, they could not be sunk. Although, as Portal and Peirse warned from the start, these ships could not be destroyed. At great cost, Bomber Command helped keep them out of action at a critical time.

The attacks on the big ships, and the belief that the British planned to invade Norway, led Hitler to bring them to the North Sea by the famous "channel dash" of February 1942. During this both ships were damaged, and this would lead indirectly to the loss of *Gneisenau*. The attacks on the ships had paid off; for one thing, repairing them had tied down many men who would otherwise have been employed in repairing U-boats. The effort expended against the bat-tle cruisers, however, might have been better directed against the U-boat bases at Brest, la Pallice, Lorient, St. Nazaire, and Bordeaux. Huge bunkers to pro-tect the submarine pens were still under construction behind watertight caissons, and the Germans considered the pens very vulnerable. The bunkers at Lorient and la Pallice would be finished only by the end of 1941, the rest in mid-1942. But whether Bomber Command could have bombed even these relatively near-by coastal targets accurately was perhaps doubtful.[6]

The Butt Report

On July 9 Bomber Command was released from its overriding commitment to the Battle of the Atlantic, although, as we have seen, it continued to devote many bombs to naval targets. Its new directive emphasized attacks on German morale, alleging that the "morale of the civil population" and the "inland transportation system" were weak points. The former belief, at a time when Ger-many controlled the European mainland and was marching deep into the USSR, and when most Germans at home had hardly been touched by the war, was a remarkable piece of wishful thinking.

Large railroad marshaling yards seemed to be the sole precise targets Bomber Command could hit, at least in moonlight. To smash the whole transport system was too big a task; the immediate aim was to isolate the Ruhr by bombing the nine major railroad centers linking it to the rest of Germany. British railroad experts thought that attacks on a feasible scale would wreck these targets. If possible, the Ems-Weser canals would be attacked and the Rhine mined. To cripple road transport, the main synthetic rubber plants at Hüls and Schkopau would be attacked. On dark nights the RAF would simply blast large industrial cities to demoralize people, hoping that some of the bombs would damage railroad facilities.

Lord Cherwell, Churchill's clever if erratic scientific adviser, had initiated a more thorough inquiry into the accuracy of bombing that showed that this plan too was based on false premises. Even meaningful area bombing was not yet possible. In August 1941, D. M. Butt, a member of the War Cabinet secretariat, analyzed over 600 photos taken by cameras aboard the bombers during June and July, in conjunction with operational reports. The results shocked even pessimists, revealing that Bomber Command's navigation, and not just its bomb aiming, was hopelessly off. Only a third of the crews who claimed to have attacked their targets had even gotten within five miles of them! Success varied greatly with the weather, the amount of moonlight, and the position of the target. As many as two-fifths of the bombers had come within five miles of their targets in attacks on the French ports, but only a quarter did so in attacks on Germany. In attacks on the Ruhr, the proportion fell to a tenth. There were doubts about how well the photographs had been taken; Peirse and others tried to argue that Butt's report was not conclusive. Some claimed that the weather had been unusually bad or that commanders had given the cameras to their worst crews. But the evidence was too clear, or the night bombers were not bombing accurately, because they were usually not even near their targets.

Area Offensive

Bomber Command might have been dissolved if not for (1) hopes that its navigation could be improved, (2) an already strong current of opinion in favor of area bombing, and (3) the fact that it was the only way to strike Germany in the foreseeable future. Churchill expected the Soviets to survive the Nazi attack, and he was even more certain that the United States would enter the war. But he and other British leaders were unwilling to concentrate the whole British war effort on an invasion of Western Europe without some preliminary weakening of the Germans.

During September 1941 the British frankly accepted area bombing. A new radio device, "Gee," under development since 1940, had been successfully tested in May 1941. Its production had been delayed by difficulties with one of its tubes, but it was certain to improve navigation over western Germany; it would let Bomber Command at least find entire cities. (Many hoped that it would permit precision bombing of specific industrial plants, but they were to be disappointed.) Then at least an effective area bombing campaign would be possible.

Studies of Britain's experience in the Blitz suggested that massive area attacks on cities would impair production for a time by injuring the workers' morale and wrecking city services. These calculations were a bit optimistic; the British did not take into account the fact that German bombs were more powerful than British bombs of the same size (the Germans used more powerful explosives and higher ratios of explosive to casing) and that German buildings were more stoutly built than British ones. The Air Staff decided to use a higher proportion of incendiary bombs, rightly arguing that in area attacks they were more destructive, weight for weight, than HE bombs. (Later experience would suggest that this was also true for precision attacks, even against industrial plants built to be fire resistant.)

Although the British used bigger and bigger "high-capacity" HE bombs, ultimately in sizes up to 12,000 pounds, their purpose was mainly to "soften up" cities for fire attacks. These "blockbusters" would rip up roofs, blow open doors and windows, break water mains, and drive air raid wardens and firemen to cover, opening the way for fires. The British would experiment with a wide variety of incendiary weapons, some quite unusual. Like the Germans, they tried oil- or liquid-filled bombs, but these were not too successful. The type the Germans hated most was a thirty-pound weapon containing white phosphorus, designed to smash through to the lower floors of buildings, because the phosphorus inflicted horrible burns on anyone it hit. But the main weapon of destruction was a four-pound bomb similar to one used by the Germans against England. Dropped in clusters, it consisted of a two-pound stick of magnesium with a two-pound iron head to insure that it would slam through a roof. The British were slow to obtain a good ballistic container for it, but along with the blockbuster, this humble-looking weapon would turn the cities of Central Europe into ruins.

Peirse resisted recommendations for marker bombs and a special fire-raising force to lead the bombers, but the Air Staff put forward a full-blown program for area attacks. Skeptical of the Air Staff's calculations and promises, Churchill stressed that while as many bombers as possible would be built, he envisaged an eventual invasion of Europe if the Americans entered the war. Bombing alone could not be counted on. "Even if all the towns of Germany were rendered largely uninhabitable it does not follow that the military control would be weakened or even that war industry could not be carried on." But he conceded that "it may well be that German morale will crack and that our bombing will play a very important part in bringing the result about."[7]

GERMAN DEFENSES

Bomber Command suffered increasing loses. After the fall of France the Luftwaffe allotted a small force—at first only 35 Me-110s—to the very capable Gen. Josef Kammhuber for defense against night attacks. Radar was the key to successful night defense. The Germans had two different radar sets. Freya, an early warning radar using a 2.5 meter wavelength, could spot planes as far off as 75 miles but could not give their height. A tracking and fire-control radar, Wurzburg, operating on 53 centimeters, had a range of 20 miles. It could determine the height of a plane and steer searchlights, flak guns, and fighters onto it. A Freya network covered the German coast when the war started; Wurzburgs became available later.

In 1940, the Germans initially used a system called *Hellenachtjagd*, or illuminated night fighting. Warned of incoming British bombers by Freya, searchlights around the cities tried to light up the bombers for the flak and fighters. This did not work well. Kammhuber redeployed the searchlights in a belt across western Germany, forming a system of "boxes," which the British dubbed the Kammhuber Line. Each box contained a single Freya and searchlights and was patrolled by a fighter. As Wurzburgs became available, they were used to track the bombers. Radar data was passed to the searchlights, which lit up the bombers for the fighters. The Germans had some successes with this system, but the British countered it by diving through the illuminated areas or flying around them. The Germans then transferred the lights to a backup belt behind the boxes; eventually they returned them to the cities to aid the antiaircraft guns there. In the summer of 1941 the Germans introduced Giant Wurzburgs, with a range of 40 miles, and introduced the *Himmelbett* (four-poster bed) system. Each box was allotted one Freya and two Giant Wurzburgs. The Freya detected the oncoming planes and gave bearings to the Wurzburgs; one Wurzburg tracked the bomber, while the other tracked the intercepting fighter. Data from the radars was plotted by Luftwaffe women on a Seeburg Table, a frosted glass screen, in a sector control room, and a controller coached the German fighters onto the bombers. Ultimately a maximum of three fighters could be brought to bear in each box.

This system proved effective, and it was supplemented by a deadly force of night intruders. Late in 1940 a group of long-range night fighters with modified Dornier 17 and Junkers 88 bombers was formed. They followed British bombers back to their bases and attacked them as they landed. Sometimes the Germans, listening to British radio traffic, were able to steer the intruders onto planes that were taking off. These tactics were very successful, but Hitler ordered them abandoned on October 12, 1941, because the German air crews' claims of success could not be checked and because he wished to encourage German civilians by shooting down the enemy over Germany itself. The unit that had perfected intruder operations was transferred to the Mediterranean. The ban was not totally effective; excuses were occasionally manufactured to let crews fly to Britain. But Hitler's order was an important relief for the British.

Nevertheless, British losses mounted. On the night of November 7–8, 1941, thirty-seven planes, nearly a tenth of the force sent out, were lost. An inquiry exploded Peirse's alibis for the disaster. Churchill then enforced a "conservation" policy, which should have begun right after the Butt report. Only small forces would be sent out; distant targets and bad weather would be avoided.[8]

During 1941 Bomber Command's strength had risen to over 500 operational planes, including some four-engine Stirlings and Halifaxes. It now had better bombs, including 4,000-pounders. It had done the enemy some minor damage, and forced him to divert some efforts to defense. But it had not delivered its bombs to crucial targets. It had not performed the task for which it had been formed. More than two years after the start of World War II, its efforts had been a failure.

The Reform of Bomber Command, 1942

During 1941 the RAF had been forced to acknowledge that Bomber Command was not succeeding at precision bombing at night. Since it usually could not single out a particular factory or installation in the darkness, it had backed, at first unwillingly, into area bombing.

At least for a time, it had to be content to attack the centers of German cities, which, with pending improvements of technique, it could hit. Unfortunately, although there were exceptions, the big industrial plants, especially those most important to the enemy war effort, were usually on the edges of cities or even outside them. In the heavily built-up centers of cities, any bomb was likely to cause damage, but these areas were usually residential and commercial, with some small industrial plants. Their destruction would have only a slow, indirect impact.

A policy of deliberate area attacks meant accepting the idea that large numbers of German civilians would be killed. It had always been clear that even the most careful and accurate precision bombing campaign must kill civilians simply because civilians worked in war plants. Not even the tightest bombing pattern could entirely avoid hitting homes or workplaces right next to a target. And even the most skillful force would occasionally make gross mistakes in aiming or dropping bombs. Even if perfectly aimed and released at the right moment, some bombs would go astray because their fins were warped or because their tails had snapped off on the way down. The idea of conducting a war with "surgical strikes" (to use an anachronistic and silly expression) that would entirely spare civilians was a fantasy. That was generally understood during World War II, if not later. But while most people felt that such incidental and unwanted deaths were morally acceptable, there were qualms about deliberately attacking civilians. These reservations were eroded, however, by the Nazis' indiscriminate bombing and their atrocities, and by the desperate situation of the Allies. There was to be far more unhappiness about the area bombing after the war than was felt during it. In later years there would be more doubts about whether it had really contributed much to the victory. After the war the reflection that it was the Nazis who started the indiscriminate attacks on cities, along with committing far worse crimes, did not seem to provide the same reassurance that it had in 1941–1945.

It is worth noting that the British civilian leaders were more enthusiastic about the shift to area bombing than most senior officers of the RAF. This was not a policy pushed by ruthless militarists, overriding delicate civilian scruples. And some important officers, notably the deputy chief of the Air Staff, Air Vice Marshal Sir Norman Bottomley, and the deputy director of bomber operations at the Air Ministry, Group Captain Sidney O. Bufton, hoped to go over to precision bombing as soon as that was possible. But the forced resort to area bombing brought forward a military leadership that would cling to this originally unwanted expedient long after alternatives to it were available.

By February 1942, the Gee and the new tactics were nearly ready. The success of the Soviet winter offensive suggested that it was desirable to hit the Germans as hard as possible. On February 14 Bomber Command received a new directive, written by Bottomley, that ended the conservation policy and formally registered the shift to a policy of area attack, albeit with significant reservations. This directive governed Bomber Command's operations until early 1943, and the policy was not greatly modified until much later. It is a document that rewards close study.

The primary objective was now to attack "the morale of the enemy's civil population and in particular, of the industrial workers." The directive emphasized incendiary attacks on seven big industrial cities in the Ruhr and Rhineland and on the German coast within Gee range (350 to 400 miles from Britain.) Some cities beyond Gee range would be bombed when conditions were particularly favorable. In case Gee made precision attack possible, some precision targets within its range were listed for attack, including the synthetic rubber plant at Hüls and several oil plants and power plants. The other major synthetic rubber plant, at Schkopau, and factories making critical parts for planes were listed too, although they lay beyond Gee range and it was hard to see how they could be hit. A few factories in France would be struck when the weather was particularly favorable there but impossible over Germany. Such targets were few, since they had to be very big, and easy to hit without hurting friendly civilians.

It should be noted that, except for some attacks on the U-boat ports in France, the British government never approved area bombing of the German-occupied countries, including, oddly, Austria. The selection of specific factories in occupied Europe as targets, and some of Bomber Command's actual operations, constituted a left-handed admission that, although Gee had proved disappointing, it was *sometimes* considered possible to carry out precision attacks even with the equipment available in 1942—a fact often ignored.

The February directive was thus not entirely clear. As far as the near future was concerned, Bomber Command was unmistakably committed to area attacks in Germany. But the directive left the way open to, and implicitly favored, precision attack if Gee was equal to the task. Moreover, it left open the option of choosing a policy of "selective" rather than "general" area attack. Bottomley and the Ministry of Economic Warfare favored this idea. Instead of seeking the general dislocation of the enemy's morale and economy, area attacks could be aimed at wrecking a particular industry. Even though it was usually impossible to single out individual factories, production of a particular item might be disrupted by blasting the cities in which it was made. The inclusion of Schweinfurt, the center of German ball bearing production, among the target cities listed in the February directive was at least a gesture in this direction.

Portal felt it necessary to stress area bombing. On February 15 he sent a note to Bottomley remarking that "I suppose it is clear that the aiming points are to be the built-up areas, *not* for instance the dockyards or aircraft factories where these are mentioned in Appendix A. This must be made quite clear if it is not already understood." (Emphasis in the original.) But in practice this point was not taken literally, and in the next few months, many attacks on Germany were of a mixed sort. While most of the force was ordered to bomb the center of a city, part would be assigned a particular factory as an aiming point. On May 5 the February directive was amended; while stressing the aim of attacking morale, it suggested area attacks on cities associated with aircraft production, to be accompanied by precision attacks on the aircraft factories themselves if possible. But Air Marshal Sir Arthur Harris, who led Bomber Command from February 22, 1942, to the end of the war, showed little interest in this.[1]

Harris had ably commanded 5 Group early in the war; later he had served as the deputy chief of the Air Staff and as head of the RAF's delegation in Washington. Even his most ardent defenders admit that Harris made appalling mistakes, especially in the last year of the war, but even his worst critics have agreed that he was a real leader and a vast improvement on Peirse, a man of little initiative or drive. Harris was a man of brutal determination, and his personality impressed everyone. For much of the war he overawed Portal and virtually dictated policy, against his superior's better judgment. His air crews respected him even while they dubbed him "Butcher" Harris. (Whether this referred to his acceptance of heavy losses or to what he was doing to the Germans is unclear.) He was not an innovator. While commanding 5 Group he had been particularly stubborn in insisting that his bombers could defend themselves during the day, and later that they were hitting their targets at night.

Although not so quickly as has often been supposed, Harris became fanatically convinced that area bombing was *the* way to win the war. He became a bitter critic of what he acidly called "panacea" bombing, attacking a specific target system to deny the Germans a critical item, like oil or ball bearings. He claimed there were no "bottlenecks" or vital spots in the Germans' war effort, but that they could not get around his destroying whole cities. Unlike other advocates of area bombing, he had no great faith in smashing morale, although he occasionally stressed this for tactical purposes. Rather, he envisioned the slow crumbling of the enemy's whole economy. In justifying Bomber Command's operations for Churchill in June 1942, he stressed the damage area bombing had done and would do to industry, not what it would do to German morale.[2]

In some of these views Harris was alone. The Ministry of Economic Warfare and many in the Air Ministry never doubted that there were bottlenecks in the enemy economy, even if they were not immediately vulnerable. Indeed, the notion, implicit in Harris's view, that no part of the enemy structure was more important or more vulnerable than any other should have been self-evidently absurd. It is safe to say that Harris himself must have regarded the German attack on the Short aircraft factory in 1940, which had denied the RAF nearly 200 Stirlings, as far more damaging than any number of bombs dropped on houses in London.

The Ministry of Economic Warfare, in particular, continued seeking bottlenecks in the enemy war effort. That an attack on oil would be a decisive blow was still generally accepted; Secretary of State for Air Sir Archibald Sinclair and Maurice Hankey, who headed the government's committee on oil matters, tried to revive attacks on it in 1942. But Portal pointed out that, apart from Gee's inadequacy, only a small part of oil production lay within its range, while an attack on Germany's main natural oil source at Ploesti, in Romania, was not practical either. Accuracy and range problems apart, oil was just too big a target system; there were too many targets for the available bomber force.

The hunt went on for smaller target systems, where a critical item was made in only a few plants. During 1941 the Ministry of Economic Warfare had realized that the enemy was dependent on ball bearings, production of which was overwhelmingly concentrated at Schweinfurt. Synthetic rubber production was also vital, and a concentrated target. Even Harris showed interest in attacking Schweinfurt. But by August 1942 the Air Staff concluded that an attack on it would need a force of 500 bombers, more than Bomber Command's normal strength at this time, and a system of special ground markers that must be laid by British agents on the spot. Later, Harris talked of a low-level attack in moonlight but did nothing about it. Although some British officials remained interested in Schweinfurt, it slipped into the province of the Americans.

The Ministry of Economic Warfare continued to study bottlenecks. By late November 1942 it had settled on a list of five target systems: ball bearings, synthetic rubber, alkalis, fuel injection pumps and electrical equipment for planes, and optical and laboratory glass and instruments. All were concentrated in just ten cities, eight in Germany and one each in France and Italy. Not all these systems were good choices, and while some of them would be struck, it would mostly be by American precision attacks. By January 1943 the ministry had compiled a guide to the economic importance of German cities, the "Bomber's Baedeker." The guide heavily influenced the selection of target cities for the general area offensive.[3] Although Harris rejected selective attacks on particular industries, he did wish to hit economically important cities; those of little industrial importance, such as Dresden, were given low priority for attack and were hit only late in the war.

Curiously, only in early 1942 was there a major debate in Britain about whether to pursue strategic bombing. Although the prospects for bombing had been weaker right after the Butt report the previous August, serious questions were only raised in the winter of 1941–1942. Until then many people had not expected the Soviets to survive; that made an eventual invasion of Western Europe a much better prospect. More important was the shock of defeats in the Middle East and Southeast Asia and the U-boat threat in the Atlantic. Some politicians favored a radical change in priority. But they remained isolated, and Churchill's control of affairs was unshaken.

The real clash over policy took place inside the government; the Royal Navy took the initiative. At first it did not attack the strategic air offensive directly; it just demanded the immediate transfer of six and a half squadrons to Coastal Command and two more to Ceylon for reconnaissance. The Navy's basic perspective was summed up on February 18 by its brilliant scientific adviser, P. M. S. Blackett, who wrote that

the present policy of bombing Germany was wrong; that we must put our maximum effort first into destroying the enemy's sea communications and preserving our own; that we can only do so by operating aircraft over the sea on a very much larger scale than we have done hitherto, and that we shall be forced to use much longer range aircraft. The only advantage that I can see in bombing Germany is that it does force the enemy to lock up a good deal of his effort on home defense . . . the heavy scale of bombing will only be justified in the concluding stages of the war when (or if) we are fortunate enough to have defeated the enemy at sea and have command of it.[4]

The First Sea Lord agreed. At first the Air Ministry weakly responded that Coastal Command was being expanded anyway, while planes taken from Bomber Command would not be of much use since they were not equipped for work at sea. More forthrightly, Sinclair grumbled that it was wrong to disperse to defensive tasks, resources that could carry on an offensive.

Lord Cherwell generated a stronger justification for area bombing on March 30—one that has since often been wrongly supposed to be the basis of that policy. Claiming to have a simple way to estimate what could be done by bombing Germany, he reported that the German attacks on Britain showed that a ton of bombs dropped on a built-up area smashed 20–40 dwellings, making 100–200 people homeless. "Investigation seems to show that having one's house demolished is most damaging to morale. People seem to mind it more than having their friends or even their relatives killed." The British could count on getting 14 operational flights from every bomber built; each bomber should drop about 40 tons of bombs in its lifetime, making 4,000–8,000 people homeless. Even half the total load of the 10,000 heavy bombers expected to be built by mid-1943 could render homeless most of the people of the 58 German cities that had over 100,000 inhabitants. That should break German morale. All this, he pointed out, ignored damage to factories, as well as anything the Americans might do. Cherwell did not submit any calculations of how many Germans would be killed or hurt while being "dehoused." It was probably assumed that the number would not be great, since people in shelters should survive much better than their houses would. It did not work out that way in practice, however.

Churchill, Sinclair, and Portal liked Cherwell's minute, but Sir Henry Tizard, an able scientific adviser to the government, tried to expose flaws in it. Noting that bomber production programs were never fulfilled, he suggested that Bomber Command would drop only half the tonnage Cherwell expected, with less accuracy. The damage would not be decisive. Tizard did not fundamentally oppose bombing, but felt that defensive measures at sea must take precedence. Cherwell replied that he had not meant his calculations to be taken literally; even if Tizard's figures were right, the bombing would still have a "catastrophic effect." But Churchill was content with Cherwell's arguments. He did not expect bombing to win the war by itself; it was only supposed to soften up the Germans. In practice he was willing to delay the growth of Bomber Command by transferring some units to Coastal Command and some to the Middle East. During 1942 Bomber Command lost six squadrons to Coastal Command alone, while another was "loaned" to it.[5]

Elements of Tizard's and Blackett's critiques were sound enough. They were right to insist that vital sea routes must be secured and that planes allotted to that duty would accomplish more in 1942 than they would by bombing Germany. Blackett was wrong only in thinking that defending the sea lanes would require more forces than was actually the case. As it turned out, only a few long-range planes were needed to turn the tide in the Battle of the Atlantic. A more basic problem was that the British were increasingly committed to the vague hope of breaking enemy morale, without a clear idea of what would happen even if that were accomplished. Should the Germans turn out to be too stubborn, or the German defenses be improved radically, they would be in big trouble. The British were losing sight of the desirability of attacking the material basis of the enemy's war effort—the very thing Bomber Command had originally been built to do.

ELECTRONIC GUIDANCE

An important factor in confidence in Bomber Command's future lay in the new equipment it expected. Most important were a series of electronic aids to navigation and bombing: Gee, Oboe, and H2S. (The latter two did not come into service until the winter of 1942–1943, but it is convenient to describe them all at this point.) It cannot be too strongly emphasized that Bomber Command's effectiveness would depend on these three devices.

Gee consisted of three ground stations in Britain and a receiver in the plane using it. A "master" station (A) controlled two widely separated "slave" stations (B and C); the three broadcast synchronized identical pulses similar to those used in radar. A navigator using Gee measured the differences in time of arrival of the pulses from the three stations as they were displayed on a small cathode-ray tube. His plane's position could then be located on a special color-coded Gee chart. The resulting fix varied in accuracy from under half a mile (sometime far less, in skilled hands) to about five miles, depending on the navigator's ability and the range from Britain. Gee's range also varied; in practice it could not be counted on east of the Ruhr. It could be used by any number of planes and, unlike the German devices used in 1940–1941, gave the enemy no clue as to the intended target.

Gee has been proposed by R. J. Dippy of the Telecommunications Research Establishment (T.R.E.) as early as 1938, but its development was not pushed because its range was thought to be short. Concerted work began only in June 1940, when the Air Staff began worrying about the accuracy of navigation. It was successfully demonstrated late in 1940, but problems in producing a vital tube, and the Ministry of Aircraft Production's mishandling of the problem of installing it in planes, delayed its introduction.

In August 1941 preproduction Gee sets were used by Wellingtons in trials over Germany. Only three missions were flown, but one of the planes was lost. The British feared the system had been compromised; the Germans might have salvaged the equipment or maps, or learned something from prisoners. Because of this, Reginald V. Jones, head of scientific intelligence for the Air Staff, set up an ingenious scheme to trick the enemy into thinking that the British were using another device, the J-Beam, so that the Germans would assume that they had mistaken "J" for the similar-sounding letter "G." Misinformation about "J" was fed to German spies operating in Britain under British control. A whole J-Beam system was devised; it was a copy of the German Knickebein system, which could be used with standard RAF gear. During the winter of 1941–1942 J-Beams were actually broadcast; in fact, they were of some use to RAF navigators until the Germans jammed them. The Gee receiver was given a new type of number to lead the Germans to think that it was a simple radio transceiver, while the Gee signals were subtly altered.

Gee came into service on March 8, 1942. It radically improved Bomber Command's navigation and ability to concentrate attacks, and saved many planes returning home to their bases. The Germans recovered a damaged Gee set on March 29 and began jamming Gee on August 4. A simple circuit modification gave some relief from jamming for a time, but the Germans soon rendered Gee useless over most of occupied Europe to most navigators. (Skilled men could distinguish the jamming signal from the genuine article as long as the signal strength of the latter was high.)

A new Mark II Gee set, with wider frequency coverage, was introduced in February 1943. It allowed the Gee stations and navigators to make predetermined changes of frequency while the bombers were en route to a target. That only gave temporary relief, but Gee remained a tremendous help in the first and last stages of a flight, saving many planes throughout the war. The Americans adopted Gee and used a similar device, called Loran, which used a longer wavelength and had a much longer range. Gee also guided ships and landing craft in the great amphibious operations of the war. The Germans finally paid it the ultimate compliment—they used captured Gee equipment and maps to guide their air attacks on Britain in 1944.[6]

Unlike Gee, Oboe, devised by A. H. Reeves and F. E. Jones of the T.R.E., proved to be a true blind-bombing device. It guided a plane right to the target itself. Two ground stations, Cat and Mouse, broadcasting on the same frequency, controlled a single plane. The Cat station's beam kept the plane on course, and the Mouse indicated the point at which the bombs should be dropped. A pulse repeater in the plane amplified and retransmitted signals from the ground stations, enabling them to determine the plane's range. An Oboe-carrying plane normally navigated by other means to within ten miles of the target, then settled on the beam from the Cat. The pilot heard a continuous note in his earphones if he was on course, dots and dashes if he was off course. The Mouse warned the plane when it was near the target, then transmitted a bomb-release signal. Oboe was very accurate—it could be used to drop bombs with an average error of 400 yards—but had severe limitations. At first, one pair of Cat and Mouse stations could control just one plane at a time, although later a system of multichannel control would enable them to control more. And Oboe was a purely line-of-sight device, with a maximum range of 270 miles for a plane flying at 28,000 feet. It was of little use for targets east of the Ruhr until ground stations were moved to France after D-Day. A repeater system was developed, using planes to relay signals from ground stations in Britain to the Oboe planes, but the RAF hardly used it. A plane using Oboe also had to fly a very straight course. The British therefore used it mainly as a target-market device, putting it on Mosquitos, which could fly higher and faster than the heavies; they would drop markers for the main force.

In December 1941 a crude form of Oboe had been used by two Stirling squadrons to bomb the German ships at Brest, but it had proved unreliable. In April 1942 a better system was successfully tested, but its introduction into service, originally planned for July, was delayed until December. It turned out that Oboe was more accurate than the available maps; to calibrate map grids for it, the British had to undertake a special operation. Oboe Mosquitos bombed a German night-fighter sector headquarters in Belgium and the results were reported by Belgian agents, enabling the British to make the necessary corrections. Oboe made a gigantic difference in the accuracy of British bombing, and might have made an even bigger one had it been better exploited. The Mosquitos were rarely shot down, and the Germans did not recover any Oboe equipment until 1944. They began trying to jam the original 1.5 meter Oboe in August 1943, but had little success until November. By then the British were introducing a version of Oboe using centimeter wavelengths. Only near the end of the war did the Germans have some success in jamming this Mark III Oboe.[7]

H2S was the first major electronic aid sought by Bomber Command, but its development was prolonged and difficult. It had been noted, early in the development of radar, that different surface features returned different sorts of echo; this inspired the idea of an airborne radar map-reading device. H2S was a downward-looking radar that scanned the area under a plane. The resulting picture was displayed on a cathode-ray tube called a Plan Position Indicator—a type of radar display far easier to use than earlier devices. Unlike Gee and Oboe, H2S was self-contained; it did not depend on ground stations. It could be used on any number of planes. Reading the picture, however, was a tricky business; using H2S took great skill. Coasts, lakes, and rivers always stood out well, and towns and cities could be picked out from the surrounding countryside. Sometimes small areas or even railroad lines could be identified, but it was often hard to tell which town or what part of a city was on the screen. Hamburg, located on an estuary, gave a clear picture, but Berlin, inland and spread out, gave a very bad one. H2S was thus more of a navigational than a bomb-aiming device, though it served as the latter beyond Oboe range.

Ludlow-Hewitt had wanted such a device as early as 1938, but there seems to have been no drive behind it until the Butt report. Developing H2S posed a difficult dilemma for the whole Allied cause. Generating the really high powered 10-centimeter radar waves necessary for a useful radar map required the use of the highly secret cavity magnetron tube, developed in 1940 by J. H. Randall and Harry Boot. The magnetron gave the Allies a lead in microwave radar the Germans never overcame. But using it in H2S would expose it to capture and duplication by the enemy, perhaps undermining the similar 10-centimeter airborne radar used against the U-boats. Many people, including the Air Staff for a time, opposed using the magnetron in H2S and wished to employ the older klystron tube although it had much lower power. Only proof of the klystron's inadequacy and prolonged argument persuaded the Air Staff to allow use of the magnetron. Sir Robert Watson-Watt, the inventor of radar, persuasively argued that it would take the enemy a year to eighteen months to duplicate it.

In June 1942 the project suffered a terrible setback when half the development team was killed in an air crash while testing H2S. It was finally introduced, in small numbers, only in January 1943. Later a three-centimeter version was introduced. The Germans recovered an H2S set, without a cathode-ray tube, from a shot-down plane as early as February 1943, but it took them some time to realize what it was. By the fall of 1943 they had developed a compact warning device, Naxos, for installation in U-boats and planes to detect the ten-centimeter radars. Night fighters using it could track British bombers from 50 kilometers; Korfu, a similar ground-based device, could track bombers at a range of 125 miles and even pick up transmissions from H2S sets being tested in Britain. Since the British were effectively jamming German radar by then, this was a great help to the Germans. After they captured a Naxos set in mid-1944, the British imposed a partial H2S silence on their planes; the sets were only turned on for short periods when absolutely necessary. Despite the Germans' ability to turn it against the Allies, H2S was extremely valuable. The British developed a three-centimeter version of it, which the Americans copied as H2X, better known to air crews as Mickey.[8]

NEW WEAPONS AND TACTICS

In 1942 Bomber Command's destructive power vastly increased. More Stirlings and Halifaxes became available; Whitleys, Hampdens, and the failed Manchester were withdrawn from operations. The Mosquito and the Lancaster, the backbone of the command for the rest of the war, entered service. The Mosquito was first used by 2 Group for small, unescorted daylight strikes on precision targets deep in Germany as well as in the occupied countries; later an Oboe-equipped night bomber, a night fighter, a fighter bomber, and other versions of the Mosquito were introduced. The group also received new American light and medium bombers, which were used over France and the Low Countries for escorted day attacks. But these operations had little effect on, or relation to, the night offensive.

The Avro Lancaster was more important; it was the RAF's best heavy bomber of the war. It could carry an enormous bomb load. Normal loads were five tons or more (twice that of the American heavy bombers), and special Lancasters later carried a 22,000-pound bomb. It flew higher and was more rugged than the disappointing Stirling and was safer and easier to fly than the Halifax. Harris would have liked to convert Halifax production lines to the Lancaster but never got his way. He also tried to persuade the Americans to build it, but failed.

In March 1942 the British settled on a new standard organization for the crews of their heavy bombers, now largely men who had joined since the war began—many from Canada, Australia, and New Zealand. They stopped carrying copilots and added a specialized bombardier and another full-time gunner. Relieving the overburdened navigator of the job of handling the bombsight was long overdue, but even some senior officers were unhappy about the lack of a copilot. One man had to handle the controls for a whole six- to eight-hour trip. Although perhaps somewhat less difficult than flying a B-17—unlike the Americans, British pilots did not have the strain of keeping formation—a night trip to Germany and back was physically exhausting. Unlike American pilots, many British pilots were only sergeants; nevertheless, they commanded the plane and a crew of six other men: navigator, bombardier, flight engineer, radio operator, and two full-time gunners. RAF four-engine bombers were lightly armed by American standards; there were only three gun positions, all power-operated turrets. The top and tail turrets were manned by full-time gunners; the one in the nose was manned by the bombardier when necessary—the Germans rarely attacked night bombers from ahead. Later the Canadian 6 Group wisely added a belly turret and an additional full-time gunner to its bombers.

The British turrets were excellent—it was only in late 1943 that a comparable turret would be added to the much more threatened nose of the B-17—but they were pitifully underarmed, with .303-caliber machine guns. Plans to rearm them with American .50s were aborted by Pearl Harbor and only resumed late in the war.

The arming of the turrets may not have mattered much, for the German night fighters depended on surprise, trying to remain unseen until they opened fire.

The bombers depended mainly on seeing the enemy first and then taking violent evasive action. Gunners were mainly important as lookouts. The carefully rehearsed "corkscrew" maneuver, rather than their guns, saved many British bombers. The crew of a shot-down plane stood little chance of survival; only a fifth managed to bail out. Until late in 1944 the prospects for bomber crewmen were grim. Losses averaged about 5 percent; 7 percent was about as much as Bomber Command, as an organization, could stand for a long period. Only a fraction of the bomber crews completed a full "tour" of 30 operations. The survivors then went to train new crews (in itself hazardous) for some months, then returned for a second tour of 30. (Occasionally, men serving in a squadron that had suffered exceptional losses were let off before 30 trips.) In May 1943 the second tour was mercifully limited to 20 operations. Crews serving in Mosquitos and in Pathfinder units had longer tours, but with various compensations. The crews usually flew seven or eight times a month, less in the winter. But the strain was worse than such figures imply, for many operations were readied and then cancelled at the last minute because of bad weather. Such last-minute reprieves were generally not appreciated.

During 1942 weapons and tactics changed considerably. Bomber Command shifted over to largely incendiary bombloads; during the summer 8,000-pound blockbusters were introduced, along with special marker bombs for use by the new Pathfinder target-finding force, which will be discussed later. Bomber Command finally obtained an effective bombsight, the Mark 14 stabilized vector sight.

The introduction of Gee meant a change in tactics. Until 1944 Bomber Command emphasized overwhelming concentration in time and space against a single target city, an idea long favored by Harris. Instead of flying singly to the target, planes concentrated in a single "bomber stream," to get as many bombers through the German defenses and over the target in as short a time as possible. This overloaded the Kammhuber Line, for each box was designed to engage one bomber at a time. At the target, the new Shaker technique was introduced. At first only a few bombers had Gee equipment; they were manned by picked crews and marked the aiming points for the rest of the force. Some lit up the target area with flares; then others dropped incendiary bombs to start fires. The rest of the force, with mixed, but largely incendiary, loads, aimed at the fires.[9]

On March 3 elements of the new tactics were tried out in a precision attack on a French target, the Renault works at Billancourt, in the Paris suburbs, which made 14,000 trucks a year for the Germans. Gee was not yet available, and the target was not considered suitable for incendiary bombs, but flares were used to identify it, and the attack was far more concentrated than earlier ones. All planes were to bomb within one hour. The Renault plant was easy to find; it was a densely packed area right on the bank of the Seine, opposite an island. The moon was nearly full and weather was perfect; given the lack of defenses, the British planes could fly far lower than usual. The bomber stream worked even better than expected, concentrating the attack even more than planned.

Many eager crews went in even lower than they had been ordered. Of 235 bombers dispatched—the most to a single target so far in the war—223 attacked, dropping 470 tons of bombs. Only one plane was lost. Production at the Renault works stopped entirely for a month and did not recover fully for several more, costing the Germans 2,272 trucks. They scaled back plans for increasing production. Unfortunately, 367 French civilians were killed, and the plant recovered more quickly than the British expected; this was a frequent vice of Allied assessments of industrial damage. After the war the United States Strategic Bombing Survey calculated that the attack would have had to be repeated at intervals of two to three months to keep the plant knocked out. (It was only attacked again by the Eighth Air Force in April 1943.) Nevertheless, the Renault attack was the first solid success by Bomber Command against a land target. But, as the British official history noted, such a combination of perfect weather and weak defenses seldom occurred over important targets in Germany.

The attack was not typical of Bomber Command's capabilities.[10] Gee, and the full-blown Shaker technique, were introduced in an attack on Essen March 8–9. But this, and seven subsequent attacks on Essen, failed. Despite flares and bright moonlight, the Nazis were defended by their own air pollution. Only one bomb in twenty fell within five miles of Essen! The Ruhr remained an impenetrable fortress for another year. Over other targets the new technique worked better; an attack on Cologne March 13–14 proved quite successful and destroyed an important rubber plant.

On March 28 Harris, perhaps to provide a spectacular if not too important success, attacked the Baltic coastal city of Lübeck. Although beyond Gee range, it was easy to find, lightly defended, and an ideal target for fire bombing. Its center was of medieval wooden construction. Part of the force, however, was assigned a precision target—a machine-tool plant. There was a full moon and fine weather. Of 234 planes sent out, 191 attacked, dropping over 400 tons of bombs. Many planes went as low as 2,000 feet, and in spite of the weak defenses, losses were heavy. The old town was destroyed, with 190 acres of buildings burned out, along with some moderately important factories, and 312 people were killed. A series of four similar attacks was launched against another Baltic port, Rostock, starting on April 23. Again, destructive area attacks were combined with precision attacks, on the Heinkel aircraft plant in the suburbs; the Heinkel plant was only hit on the third attack. The Lübeck and Rostock attacks upset the Nazi leaders for the first time in the war, although production in the two cities recovered quickly.

The limitations of the techniques in use became clear. A series of attempted precision attacks by small forces on more French factories failed more often than not, while a mixed attack on Stuttgart, in which part of the force tried to attack the Bosch plant, a vital source of generators, injection pumps, and magnetos for planes, hurt neither the city nor the factory.[11]

Harris now decided to show what Bomber Command could do, not with the force at hand, but with what he might have in some years. At a time when his force normally numbered 416 planes, he decided to assemble a special force of 1,000 planes and send it against a single city, at the risk of deranging the future growth of the command. He mustered every available plane from Bomber Command's operational units, its conversion units (on which crews transitioned to new types of planes), and training groups. (He gained a promise of 250 planes from Coastal Command, but the Admiralty blocked its participation.) On the night of May 30–31, 1,046 bombers set out for Cologne. It was purely an area attack. Cologne, Germany's fourth-largest city, was easy to find and there was a full moon; the attackers dispensed with flares, as 868 planes bombed the city. The British lost 41 bombers, along with 3 night intruders sent by Fighter Command in an attempt to disrupt enemy night fighter operations, and 12 more bombers were damaged beyond repair. The attack was very effective, destroying 600 acres of built-up area and 36 factories and killing 500 people; 13,000 homes were destroyed or damaged.

Harris kept the "thousand force" together for a few more blows. On June 1 he sent it against Essen; only 31 planes were lost, but the attack failed, just as others against the Ruhr. On June 25–26 an attack by 960 planes was launched on Bremen. This was partly a precision attack; 5 Group was ordered to bomb the Focke-Wulf plant, while 102 bombers on loan from Coastal Command, which the Admiralty had finally allowed to participate, attacked a shipyard. The British lost 49 planes and did not consider the attack a success, although the Focke-Wulf plant was severely damaged.[12]

Bomber Command returned to normal operations. Harris had scored points with his superiors and the public and had revived faith in bombing, but he was in something of an impasse. The available techniques did not usually produce very successful area bombing; even within Gee range only cities on the coast or on a large, winding river made good targets, and only in good weather. Precision results could rarely be attained, and only against light defenses. Losses had begun to rise again as the Germans added depth to the Kammhuber Line and more night fighters appeared. Some of Harris's group commanders favored frankly recognizing their limitations. Oxland of 1 Group, in particular, strongly urged conserving strength and mounting a few heavy attacks on fine nights against easy targets. He believed that more targets like the Renault plant—that is, ill defended and easily located precision targets valuable to the enemy—could be found. (Indeed, a return to the Renault plant itself would have been a good idea.)

Harris rejected this as a policy of weakness. He tried some unusual tactics, even sending forces of four-engine bombers in daylight against shipyards on the German coast and on one occasion deep into France, to strike the Schneider armaments plant at Le Creusot. They used heavy clouds to hide from interception, planning to bomb at dusk and return in darkness. But clouds thick enough to offer protection usually prevented accurate bombing, while delays caused the bombers to reach their targets after sundown. For a time in late 1942 Harris even pondered returning to regular daylight operations, depending on the bomber's ability to defend themselves. Although he had advised the Americans to drop their own plans for daylight attacks, their initial successes impressed him. But he soon dropped the idea; if anything, he was becoming increasingly fixated on "pure" area bombing at night. He launched only one or two more "mixed" attacks of the sort made on Rostock and Bremen. But for every successful area attack, there were two or three failures.[13]

THE PATHFINDER FORCE

Since March 1942 the Air Ministry had wanted to form a special target-finding force within Bomber Command. Harris and his group commanders opposed this. Finally the Air Staff ordered Harris to form a separate force with regular squadrons drawn from the other groups. He appointed an outstanding officer, Group Captain Donald Bennett, to command the new Pathfinder Force (later it became 8 Group), and gave him his full support. The pathfinders began operations in August. They flew tours of 45 missions instead of 30, but were given a step up in rank and pay as long as they were on operations. Target-marker bombs were introduced; they were filled with benzol, rubber, and phosphorus to provide distinctively colored fires. The 250-pound "red blob fire" was first used in late August; in September the huge 2,800-pound "pink pansy" was introduced. These early markers were not very good, but the results justified the formation of the Pathfinder Force. The concentration of bombing increased greatly, although overall accuracy improved only slightly. The main force could see and aim at the markers fairly well, but the markers could not be placed accurately enough. Oboe and H2S would be needed to do that regularly.[14]

During 1942 Bomber Command was finally hurting the enemy. Some damage was inflicted on German production, although not enough to prevent its actually rising during the year. More important, German efforts were diverted into defense and into ineffective retaliatory measures. The German fighter and flak defenses grew considerably. Reinforcing the small bomber and fighter-bomber force on their western front, they diverted it from mine laying and attacks on ships to costly revenge attacks against Britain, at a time when every plane was needed in Russia and the Mediterranean. The most foolish diversion of effort, however, was yet to come. On December 22 Hitler would give the V-2 rocket the highest possible priority and authorized its mass production, at great cost in scarce resources.[15]

The Climax of Area Bombing and the Defeat of Bomber Command, January 1943–March 1944

Bomber Command continued blasting German cities until the spring of 1944. Harris was sure, and others hoped, that he could smash Germany before the invasion of France. He was largely allowed to ignore inter-Allied directives dealing with the strategic bombing campaign; he stuck to a policy of general area attack and only occasionally, and evidently reluctantly, tried precision attacks. Until February 1944 he evaded attempts to cooperate with the Americans by selective attacks on cities connected with the production of planes and ball bearings, although these were strongly favored by Bottomley and Air Commodore Bufton. Bomber Command had smashed much of Germany's cities to rubble, and damaged the enemy war effort. But it had not even come close to wrecking the German economy or morale. Instead, the attempt to evade German defenses under cover of darkness ended in failure. The very development of electronic devices that enabled the bombers to find their targets let the Germans find the bombers and inflict prohibitive losses.

NEW TACTICS AND DEVICES

During the winter of 1942–1943 Bomber Command perfected the equipment and tactics that allowed regular, effective area bombing. During 1942 its numerical strength had not risen greatly; in January 1943 it numbered only 515 operational planes, only about a hundred more than a year earlier. But it was now largely a force of four-engine bombers. It now had 178 Lancasters and 58 Mosquitos.

During the winter it stopped operating on moonlit nights; moonlight was too helpful to the growing enemy night fighter force. Henceforth only a few precision missions against very important targets took place when the moon was close to full. To confuse and overwhelm the German defenses, the bomber stream was even more compressed, and the bombers flew at varying heights.

The bombers' effectiveness depended on the long-delayed introduction of Oboe and H2S, and marking techniques enabling the pathfinders to direct the main force. On December 31, 1942, Oboe-equipped Mosquitos went on their first mission to Germany, marking for a small attack on Düsseldorf. H2S was introduced in late January, and a new, more effective 250-pound marker bomb was introduced in an attack on Berlin on January 16–17, the first since 1941. When a barometric fuse set it off in the air, the bomb showered 60 colored candles, which burst into flames before hitting the ground. Another device, the sky marker, was introduced on the December 31 Düsseldorf mission. Sky markers were parachute flares, dropped by Oboe- or H2S-equipped Pathfinder planes over the aiming point when the ground could not be seen. The main force then aimed at the sky markers. They drifted and were only briefly visible, and were basically inferior to marker bombs, but they let the RAF attack even through unbroken cloud cover. These devices made possible three basic techniques: (1) Parramatta, blind dropping of marker bombs on electronic guidance; (2) Wanganui, sky marking; and (3) Newhaven, a mixed technique in which flares were dropped on electronic guidance to light up the target and then the Pathfinders tried to aim the marker bombs at it visually. When Oboe, rather than H2S, was used, these methods were referred to as Musical Parramatta, Musical Wanganui, and Musical Newhaven.[1]

The British also took the offensive with electronic countermeasures. During 1942 they had learned a great deal about the enemy's radar systems. On February 27 a spectacular raid by paratroops on Bruneval, on the French coast, had captured a Wurzburg radar and brought part of it back to England. (Later in the year, a largely intact Wurzburg was captured at El Alamein.) And in August 1942, during the raid on Dieppe, a radar technician was able to look over a Freya station. In December the British introduced Mandrel, a jammer to deal with Freya, and Shivers, a device to jam the Wurzburg. Another device, Tinsel, jammed communications with the night fighters. These devices were only moderately successful, however.

The Germans had begun equipping their night fighters with an airborne intercept radar, Lichtenstein, in February 1942, operating on a wavelength of 62 centimeters and with a range of two miles. The British detected its broadcasts but were uncertain what they were. On December 3, 1942, a specially equipped "ferret" Wellington was sent to find out whether the Germans had an airborne radar and to determine its characteristics. Accompanying the main force to Frankfurt, it deliberately invited attack by night fighters. Everyone aboard was wounded and the plane had to ditch off the British coast, but the mission succeeded; it gave a complete picture of the enemy radar. The British then fitted a search receiver, Boozer, to their bombers to pick up both Wurzburg and Lichtenstein. They also installed Monica, a tail-warning radar, on their planes. Unfortunately, Boozer and Monica had too short a range to do much good. Monica interfered with Oboe and, as we shall see, had an even worse drawback.[2]

To its disgust, Bomber Command was ordered to smash the ports in France where the U-boats were based—the only area attacks ever authorized on targets outside Germany. It was vaguely hoped that these attacks would interfere with submarine operations by damaging maintenance facilities and power supplies outside the invulnerable submarine pens. On April 6, after St. Nazaire and Lorient had been leveled without any effect on the pens and with the loss of 38 planes, Harris was released from his commitment to attack La Pallice and Brest. Although these attacks on the French ports had generally been launched when the weather over Germany was impossible, this campaign did delay the start of the Battle of the Ruhr. It is hard to believe that some more effective way of striking at the enemy could not have been found.

HAPPY VALLEY

The British had long been fascinated by the great Ruhr industrial region. It was a classic center of coal, steel, and heavy machinery production. The Ruhr was heavily defended by flak and hidden by perpetual smog; the men of Bomber Command sarcastically referred to it as Happy Valley. The British were almost obsessed by the great Krupps works (Gustahlfabrik Friedrich Krupp), which covered 1,088 acres in Essen, a fabulous center of the German armaments industry. In fact, the British somewhat exaggerated the importance of the Krupp plants, and of the Ruhr. Except for the synthetic oil plants located on the outskirts of some of its cities, the Ruhr did not produce much that was immediately vital to military operations. It furnished only about a quarter of Germany's war material; it produced only a tenth of Germany's tanks and had only one aircraft engine plant. Nor was the type of machinery in the Ruhr plants susceptible to bomb damage.[3]

The Battle of the Ruhr was the first of the major "battles" Bomber Command fought in 1943-1944. In each battle—more properly, campaign—it concentrated its attacks on a certain area: the Ruhr, Hamburg, or Berlin. But it interspersed its efforts against the main objectives with attacks on cities elsewhere in Germany. And it carried out several interesting and important operations against precision targets.

The Battle of the Ruhr, which included heavy attacks on nearby Rhineland cities such as Düsseldorf, Aachen, and Cologne as well as on the Ruhr itself, began on March 5, 1943 with an unprecedentedly effective attack on Essen. Unusually, for this period of the war, the aiming point was an industrial plant, the great Friedrich Krupp works. (Since the works formed the center of Essen, the British could hardly have aimed at anything else.) The attack was a fine example of area attack using the Parramatta technique. The first Oboe Mosquito arrived over Essen at 8:58 P.M., two minutes early, and dropped its red target indicator bombs. Others followed at intervals of several minutes. Behind them, 22 heavy bombers of the Pathfinder Force dropped green marker bombs, at intervals of a minute or two, aimed at the red markers. To help with navigation they dropped yellow markers on the way to the target. Three waves of the main force followed, with orders to aim at the red markers if they could see them, and the green markers if they could not. Of the 442 bombers dispatched, 61 (including 3 of the 8 precious Oboe Mosquitos) aborted the mission or could not attack the primary target, while 14 bombers went down. Of those that attacked Essen, 153 bombed within three miles of the aiming point. The Krupps works and the city, hit by 1,000 tons of bombs, were heavily damaged; 160 acres of built-up area was completely destroyed, and three-quarters of the buildings in another 450 acres were destroyed or damaged. These were remarkable results against the toughest target in Germany.[4]

It soon became apparent, however, that such results could not be expected beyond Oboe range. On March 8–9, Bomber Command sent 335 planes against Nuremberg, planning to use H2S and the Newhaven technique. But visibility was bad, and some Pathfinders had to drop their marker bombs on H2S. Some H2S sets failed. Both the markers and the bombing were scattered. While considerable damage was done to the suburbs and some factories, this was a lucky accident.

The Ruhr and Rhineland cities suffered greatly; on March 12 Essen was blasted even more heavily than a week earlier. But even within Oboe range, weather, mistakes, and bad luck sometimes nullified even the best efforts. Duisburg, the target of more sorties than any other city during the battle, survived four big attacks well but was terribly damaged by a fifth and final blow. The loss of life in the Ruhr and Rhineland, was far greater than from any earlier air attacks of the European war. Two attacks on Barmen-Wuppertal in late May and June killed 5,200 people. The first attack on that city, on May 29, showed how accurate Parramatta could be in good conditions; 475 of the 611 bombers attacking dropped within three miles of the aiming point, devastating a city just two miles across.

Beyond Oboe range Bomber Command did not achieve accuracy of this sort, although it sometimes even attempted precision targets. Two attacks on the Skoda works, a target somewhat like the Friedrich Krupp plant, located on the edge of the small Czech city of Pilsen, failed badly. The Pathfinders could not find it. But the center of Stettin, which was industrial in character, was devastated on April 20.

It is noticeable, however, that Harris dispatched fewer planes on these missions than he usually did on attacks on orthodox, that is, nonindustrial, area targets. His disbelief in the prospects of success, at least against distant targets, was not unreasonable in this period. But whether his pessimism was justified about targets covered by Oboe is a different question. Essen was the only place within Oboe range where the British aimed at a particular factory. The British official historians admitted that other very large factories might have been hit in the same way, but they insisted that aiming errors were still great, so attempting precision attacks on specific industrial targets would have meant that most of the bombs would fall on suburban areas or even open fields. "Nothing like the devastation which was produced by the area offensive would have occurred and it is highly improbable that the destruction of factories and other 'military objectives' in and around the Ruhr would have been any greater than, or perhaps, even as great as, in fact it was."[5] This argument is unconvincing, for damage to housing and commercial areas had no impact comparable to damage to factories. But it is true that in the spring of 1943 Bomber Command was an "effective bludgeon," not a rapier. The very big industrial plants that might have been good targets for Oboe-guided attacks were rare. In general, area bombing was still unavoidable.

By the end of the Battle of the Ruhr, on July 14, Bomber Command had badly damaged the Ruhr and some other areas and had caused indirect disruption. The important Rheinmetal-Borsig plant in Düsseldorf had been safely evacuated, but its machinery, sent away for dispersal, was never used again in the war. The Ruhr-Rhineland area as a whole probably lost the equivalent of about one-and-one-half months' production in this period. The British wishfully supposed that they had permanently crippled these areas, reduced overall German war production, and delivered a terrific blow to German morale. The lesser blow they had in fact dealt had been costly. They had launched 43 major attacks, comprising 18,506 sorties, with 872 bombers destroyed and 2,126 damaged—some of which had to be scrapped. On several attacks the British had sent over 700 bombers. The overall loss rate had been 4.7 percent—near the maximum Bomber Command could sustain for a long time.[6]

THE ATTACK ON THE RUHR DAMS

While the Battle of the Ruhr raged, a small force carried out one of the most spectacular operations of the World War I, the famous attack on the Ruhr dams. Had it succeeded completely, it would have left much of the Ruhr's industry useless. As it was, it inflicted damage equal to that of many conventional attacks and helped to develop new methods, which ultimately made precision bombing at night a regular possibility.

The British had long known that a system of dams supplied water vital to the Ruhr industries. When the Western air plans were drawn up in 1937, it had been noted that destroying the most important dams, the Möhne and the Sorpe, would be a cheaper way to wreck the Ruhr than a massive attack on the industrial installations themselves. Hankey also suggested that destroying the nearby Eder Dam, while it would not affect the water supply of the Ruhr, might hinder traffic on inland waterways. Bomber Command was initially unenthusiastic, for destroying such massive structures would not be easy. The task was complicated by the fact that the two critical dams were of different types. The Möhne was an arched gravity-type masonry dam, while the Sorpe was an earth dam with a watertight reinforced concrete core. The weapons and tactics suited for one dam might not work against the other. Attention settled early on the Möhne, as the easier target. Attacking the water side of the dam with conventional bombs, torpedoes, or mines was considered as late as 1940, but these were probably not powerful enough to break the dam even in the unlikely event they hit it. After the war started, the Germans laid protective nets against ordinary torpedo attack.

More exotic devices were considered. Serious work began on a radio-controlled drone plane, but the fall of France made the target too distant from friendly bases and the project was dropped. Rocket-assisted bombs, glider weapons, and a "hydroplane skimmer torpedo" were all studied; an attempt was made to build the last weapon in 1940–1941. None of these devices proved satisfactory. Combined Operations and the Special Operations Executive independently proposed destroying the Möhne by sabotage operations; paratroops, or commandos landed by flying boats, would plant charges to break it. In early 1943 this idea was a serious rival to a proposal for an air attack using yet a new special weapon.

Barnes Wallis, the brilliant engineer who had designed the Wellington bomber, had long been interested in attacking all the enemy's sources of energy, not only dams, as an alternative to direct attacks on industry. (He was later wrongly credited with the whole idea of attacking the dams.) In 1940 he designed a huge 22,400-pound "penetrating" bomb that was to bury itself in the ground before exploding. This "earthquake" bomb would wreck the foundations of any structure. It would also break dams like the Möhne (the importance of which he was well aware) if exploded in the reservoirs within 150 feet of the dam face. He designed a huge six-engine Victory bomber, to drop the bomb from 40,000 feet. Wallis attracted some support, but in May 1941 the Air Staff rejected the Victory bomber and the big bomb; the plane was unlikely to be finished during the war. Later on, a 12,000-pound version of the earthquake bomb, called the Tallboy, would be produced. It turned out that a modified Lancaster could haul a full-scale 22,000-pound weapon. Called the Grand Slam, it would be introduced in 1945.

Wallis turned to the narrower problem of attacking dams. His solution was to explode a relatively small charge directly against a dam's water side. He proposed a round bomb, really a depth charge or mine, that would be dropped at low altitude after a backspin had been imparted to it. Skipping over the surface of the water, it would clear or smash through protective booms and hit the dam. Then it would sink, sliding down the dam side, and explode when it reached the right depth. Wallis was sure it could destroy both the Möhne and the Sorpe. He was backed by Tizard, and the Admiralty was interested in his work; a smaller version of the weapon might sink enemy capital ships, especially the well-protected *Tirpitz*.

Tests showed that Wallis's method would work, but Harris regarded it as ridiculous. He was sure that either the spinning device would wreck the Lancaster or the mine would be torn off. Even if delivered he did not think it would work, and anyway, he maintained, the dams were just another "panacea" target. But Portal overrode him. Two versions of the spinning mine were to be built: Upkeep for the dams and the smaller Highball for ships (the latter to be delivered by

Mosquitos). Upkeep, in its final version, was a cylinder rather than a ball, 5 feet long and 50 inches in diameter. It weighed 9,250 pounds, 6,600 of which were Torpex explosive. A belt run by an electric motor would spin it backward at 500 rotations per minute, and it was set to go off 30 feet below the surface of the water.

Work on Upkeep was still going on when Bomber Command formed 617 Squadron under Guy Gibson, an exceptionally able and experienced pilot. Delivering Upkeep was a tricky business. The attack had to take place in moonlight at a low level; to insure surprise the approach had to be at low altitude as well. To destroy the Möhne and other dams of the same type, Upkeep had to be dropped while flying at exactly 220 miles an hour, from a height of exactly 60 feet, 450 yards from the target. Unlike Bomber Command's normal attacks, this one had to be directed by a single commander on the spot. New VHF transceivers were installed in the bombers for quick and reliable communications. The Lancaster's bomb bay doors and top turrets were taken off and a spinning mechanism was installed. No altimeter was precise enough for the job; finally the problem of keeping an exact height was solved by setting two spotlights on the underside of the planes. Their beams would intersect only when the bombers flew at 60 feet.

It was originally hoped to use Highball against the *Tirpitz* and Upkeep on the dams at the same time, because countermeasures against this type of weapon would be simple once the enemy saw it in action. But Highball's tests did not go well, and its chances of success against the *Tirpitz* were not rated as particularly high. The Air Staff did not want to miss the moonlight period in May, when the water in the reservoirs would be highest, and it was decided that using Upkeep might not necessarily compromise Highball. On May 14 the chiefs of staff approved an attack at the first possible date.

The Air Staff had originally supposed that destroying the Möhne alone would cause a catastrophe in the Ruhr and that the Eder was nearly as important. But the Ministry of Economic Warfare explained that the destruction of both the Möhne and the Sorpe "would be worth more than twice the destruction of one" and that the Eder's destruction would not have a major impact. Sir Norman Bottomley urged attacking the Möhne and the Sorpe simultaneously; the Eder would be hit only if there were unexpended mines.[7] Bomber Command's operations order for what was called Operation Chastise stressed the Sorpe's importance, but somewhere down the line someone became confused, or decided that there was a greater chance of success against the Eder and that this overshadowed the Sorpe's importance. The final plan thus gave the Sorpe third priority, after Möhne and Eder. Three less important dams would be attacked if the first three were smashed. The attacking force was divided into three waves. The first wave of nine planes, led by Gibson himself, was to destroy the Möhne, then the Eder. If any planes still had Upkeeps, they would then go to the Sorpe. A second wave of five planes would fly right to the Sorpe. It had been decided that different methods were needed there. The Upkeeps would not be spun, and the bombers would fly along the length of the dam, as low as possible, dropping the mines in the water just short of the centerpoint, although some people, such as Barnes Wallis, believed that some simple experiments would have suggested a better method of attack. A third wave of six planes—in the actual event, only five planes were available—was to follow Gibson's route. The third wave would be recalled if all three main targets were destroyed; if no message was received, it would attack the Möhne and then the Eder.

On the night of May 16–17, 617 Squadron set out on its incredibly dangerous mission, threading its way through gaps in the heaviest defenses in Europe. The first wave had one plane shot down en route to the Möhne. The dam itself proved lightly defended; there were only six 20-millimeter guns instead of the dozen 20-millimeter or 37-millimeter guns that had been expected.

Gibson attacked first. His mine exploded short of the dam. The second plane went in; its mine bounced right over the dam, and the explosion brought down the plane. Incredibly, two of the crewmen survived. The third plane was damaged on the way in; its mine blew short of the dam. The fourth plane attacked in company with the third, while Gibson tried to draw the enemy's fire. Its Upkeep hit, but seemingly had no effect. But then, as the fifth plane made its run, the dam burst; the fifth mine also hit. Two planes went home; Gibson took the other five, with three remaining Upkeeps, to the Eder. The dam was undefended. All three Upkeeps had to be dropped; the last smashed the dam. The first wave then went home, losing two more planes en route.

The second wave, assigned to the Sorpe, proved unlucky. Flak downed two planes, and another was damaged and returned home. A fourth hit the water near the Dutch coast. The Upkeep was ripped off, but the plane, improbably, reached home. The fifth plane, after great difficulties, hit the Sorpe, causing a small break at the top of the dam.

The reserve force had even worse luck. While it was en route to Germany, someone at 5 Group reconsidered and ordered four of the planes to the Sorpe and a fifth to strike the Ennepe, one of the minor dams. The plane ordered to the Ennepe apparently attacked the Bever dam instead, but failed to destroy it. Two of the planes ordered to the Sorpe were shot down, and a third got lost and went home. The fourth reported hitting the Sorpe without effect.

A huge gap had been blown in the Möhne, unleashing a great flood. More than a thousand people, most, unfortunately, foreign slave laborers, were killed. Eleven factories were destroyed and 114 damaged; 25 bridges were swept away, and much farmland was rendered useless. The Eder attack unleashed a lesser but still destructive flood.

The Sorpe had not been severely damaged, but a shocked Albert Speer, flying to the stricken area, thought that had the mine hit a bit lower the dam would have been destroyed. He was puzzled that the British had bothered to go after the Eder instead of making sure of the Sorpe.

Had both the Möhne and the Sorpe been broken, the consequences would have been at least as great as the optimists on the British side had supposed.

As it was, only the recent installation of an emergency pumping system bringing water from the Rhine prevented a serious crisis in the Ruhr; had the attack been made a year earlier, it would also have been more effective. The Germans made frantic efforts to repair the Möhne and Eder in time to catch the fall rains. They brought 7,000 workers to the Ruhr to restore water and power supplies; another 20,000 were taken from work on coastal defenses in the West to repair the dams and other damage. The gap in the Möhne was closed on September 23, just in time to catch the rain. Partial repairs on the Eder were finished at about the same time, although its reservoir had to be kept at a lower level until complete repairs were made after the war.

Speer was surprised, and Wallis was disgusted, that the Germans were allowed to finish the repairs on the Möhne. Both thought that even a few bombs would have wrecked the reconstruction effort. However, it is true that the Möhne, and many other dams, were now heavily defended by flak guns, rocket launchers, balloons, searchlights, wire aprons, and even mines to blow up low-flying planes. Nets and wooden deflectors were laid to block a second attack with Upkeeps. (The German precautions rendered Upkeep unusable over Germany, but Wallis thought it might still have been used against Italian targets.)

Perhaps over 10,000 troops were permanently tied down in defense of the Ruhr area dams. The enormous effort the enemy had to expend in the repair and defense of dams would alone have made the Ruhr dams attacks worthwhile, despite the heavy losses that had been suffered by the small force—losses that were but a fraction of those suffered in orthodox attacks that had caused the enemy far less trouble. But errors in planning the attack, the ill luck of the planes assigned to the Sorpe, and the failure to follow up the success against the Möhne prevented the operation from dealing the truly crippling blow that it might have.

Low-level attack by heavy bombers was not likely to become a standard tactic, but the dams attacks saw the first use of what became known as a "master bomber," a leader who stayed in the target area and directed the attack. It had forced improvement of air-to-air communications and encouraged more attention to precision bombing. Some inspiration, or a desire to placate Bottomley and Bufton, caused Harris to keep 617 Squadron in being to perform small-scale precision attacks. Techniques that it developed were ultimately applied by the rest of Bomber Command.[8]

FRIEDRICHSHAFEN

A month after the Ruhr dams attack, when moonlight again made major air attacks on Germany too dangerous, Bomber Command carried out some more operations that pointed toward the development of greater precision in bombing. On the night of June 19–20, 290 planes attacked the Schneider works. The weather was good and the defenses weak, and the attack was made from relatively low altitudes. The pathfinders dropped flares but did not mark the target; instead, the main force tried to aim visually—and missed. The attack failed.

The following night the RAF departed from its usual methods more creative-ly. At the urging of Jones, it attacked the huge Zeppelin works, at Friedrichshafen on Lake Constance, which made Wurzburg radars. Unknown to the British, V-2 missiles were also to be built there. Friedrichshafen, although a small city, had an amazing concentration of plants important to the German war effort.

A force of just 60 Lancasters—4 were pathfinders and the rest from 5 Group—flew to Friedrichshafen, from which they were to fly on to North Africa. A master bomber supervised the attack, in which several new techniques were used. The pathfinders were to mark the target visually, under the light of flares dropped by H2S guidance and under the direction of the master bomber, and then they were to use offset marking. A marker right on an aiming point would often be obscured by flames, smoke, and dust during an attack, so 5 Group had developed the idea of putting the markers on an easily seen point *away* from the target; the main force would then add a precalculated "overshoot" to their bombsights to compensate for the difference so their bombs would hit the aiming point. In effect this was a modified version of Newhaven. Part of the force, however, would not be using the markers at all. Instead, it would make a timed run from a clearly visible landmark outside the target area. This was a pet idea of 5 Group's able commander, Ralph Cochrane, a man who many later thought would have made a good replacement for Harris.

The Friedrichshafen attack went well despite mishaps. The original master bomber lost an engine, so his deputy took over; heavy flak forced the British to bomb from a higher altitude than planned. An unexpected wind change caused the marker bombs to be slightly misplaced, so the bombing by most of the force was only moderately accurate. The time-and-distance runs, however, went very well. The Zeppelin works was wrecked, and the Germans gave up plans to build V-2s there. Neighboring plants making diesel and aircraft engines were damaged as well. No planes were lost. On the return trip from North Africa, the force attacked an Italian Naval base, but the master bomber technique failed because of radio interference.

Jones later wrote, "Had we realized the improvement in our bombing technique we might have abandoned area bombing earlier, or at least put more effort into precision attacks at night." Friedrichshafen had established a precedent. "Here we used the Master Bomber technique, and when it was combined with Oboe pathfind-ing, precision attack became distinctly feasible. Even without Oboe at Friedrich-shafen, the random bombing error was no more than 400 yards."[9]

But Harris showed little interest in exploring these possibilities. The Master Bomber technique was used only on a few more attacks in 1943, then set aside until 1944. A month after Friedrichshafen, on July 15–16, an attack on a Peugeot factory at Montbéliard in France, by 165 Halifaxes using the standard Newhaven technique, misfired despite being conducted at low level and in good visibility.[10] Attempts at precision bombing were still having erratic results, if only because of poor tactics. Harris showed little interest in refining those tactics, as Bomber Command readied the most horrible of all area attacks.

THE BATTLE OF HAMBURG

At least since May, Harris had planned to follow the Battle of the Ruhr with a series of attacks on Hamburg, Germany's second biggest city and Europe's largest port. Its industries were a major factor in German war production and included aircraft plants, a variety of machinery plants, and shipyards. The latter produced more than a third of all the U-boats built in Germany during the war. Hamburg also had the largest concentration of crude-oil refineries in the Reich (28 percent of German production). Moreover, three large refineries there made vital lubricants. The enemy oil industry as a whole was not yet a ripe target. The Americans did not yet have enough bombers to deal with the many targets involved, nor the fighter escorts to reach deep into Germany, while the British could not yet normally bomb accurately enough at night. But an attack on the three big lubricating oil refineries at Hamburg, the Strategic Bombing Survey later concluded, might have had "catastrophic results" for the German war effort.

Hamburg, its suburbs, and its satellite city Harburg, sprawl in a north-south corridor straddling the river Elbe. The bulk of Hamburg, including its oldest sections and most of the residential and commercial areas, lies north of the Elbe. The modern port area, and most of the industry, are largely located in a narrow east-west strip, on islands south of the main course of the Elbe and on its south bank. South of the industrial area lie more residential areas and Harburg, which has an industrial section of its own. The greater Hamburg area is thus unusual, in that much of its industry is located in the approximate center of the built-up area, albeit spread out and cut up by waterways. But it was not that part of the city that Harris intended to bomb, although he set out his aim as Hamburg's "total destruction," in a series of attacks that would drop at least 10,000 tons of bombs. Surprisingly, in view of what happened, Hamburg was not considered a good fire target, having few really old or flammable buildings. It was arranged for the Americans to attack precision targets—aircraft plants and U-boat construction yards—during the same period as the RAF attacks were scheduled.[11]

Despite heavy losses in the Ruhr battle, Bomber Command's strength had risen to nearly 900 operational planes and a thousand ready crews. And it had some new tricks up its sleeve to deal with the German defenses, the most important of which was Window, or "chaff."

It had been known for years that masses of metal foil strips cut to the proper size—preferably half the wavelength of the radar to be interfered with—would swamp the enemy's receivers with false echoes. Window could have been introduced as early as the spring of 1942, but an initial decision to use it had been reversed when some warned that the Germans in turn would use it to render Britain's defenses ineffectual. (In fact, the Germans were well aware of the effectiveness of Window, which they called Duppel, but withheld it for the same reason!) Harris was uninterested in pushing its use. During April 1943 the decision was reconsidered, but it was found that the strips being produced were of the wrong size. The introduction of Window was delayed again until after the Allies landed in Sicily, when after a final argument its use was authorized for the Battle of Hamburg. Bundles of 2,200 paper strips with aluminum foil on one side, each strip 26.5 centimeters long, designed to interfere with Wurzburg and Lichtenstein, were delivered to each bomber. Until automatic launchers were available a man would have to hurl them out, one bundle a minute, for one hour before and one hour after bombing the target. Bomber Command also had another new countermeasure, Cigar, a jammer designed to interfere with enemy VHF transmissions to night fighters. In June a more active measure against the enemy's defenses had been introduced: Serrate night fighter support. These Beaufighters carried both their own radar and a device called Serrate, which could home in on the Lichtenstein radar. But the Beaufighters were too slow to deal with the German fighters, and their operations were not very successful.[12]

On the night of July 24-25, Bomber Command dispatched 752 bombers to Hamburg. The aiming point for the attack was in a residential area north of the Elbe, between the river and the Alster lakes. Marking was somewhat more complicated than usual. The first pathfinders were to drop both flares and yellow marker bombs under H2S guidance; later pathfinders would try to visually aim red markers in the light of the flares. The "backers-up" who were to maintain the marking were to aim green markers at the reds, or if they could not see them, at the yellows. The main force was to aim at the reds or the greens.

The flight to the target proved easy; Hamburg was almost within Gee's unjammed range and gave a very clear picture on H2S screens. The approach route was calculated to bring the British planes in from the north, where attack was not expected. Window blinded the enemy. Nevertheless, despite clear weather, the markers were scattered. Some fell in the dock area south of the Elbe, attracting enough bombs to do some unplanned damage to shipyards. Of the 728 bombers that reported attacking the city, 306 bombed within three miles of the aiming point. The bombing killed 1,500 people and caused severe damage; the fires were so bad that they seriously interfered with an American attack the next day. RAF losses were low. Only 12 planes went down; another had to be scrapped after returning home.

There was so much smoke over Hamburg on July 25 that Harris shifted that night's attack to the prepared alternative of Essen; the RAF again heavily damaged the Krupps works. The Americans returned to Hamburg on July 26; smoke again hid their primary target, a U-boat yard, but this time it was a smoke screen deliberately laid by the Germans. The American attacks caused a good deal of damage to industry, although much of this was not to the planned targets, at the cost of heavy American losses.[13]

Bomber Command rested on the night of July 26-27. On the night of July 27-28 it sent 787 planes to Hamburg. The aiming point was to be the same as in the first attack, but pure "blind" marking was used. This time the British carried a much larger proportion of incendiary bombs; this was decided on in order to lighten the loads of the Halifaxes and Stirlings.

The Germans were already responding to Window. They had two new night-fighting tactics, the highly non-kosher Tame Sow and Wild Sow. In Tame Sow they let night fighters fly around freely, leaving the boxes. A controller gave them a running commentary on the location not of individual British bombers but of the entire bomber stream. Wild Sow used slightly modified single-engine day fighters, usually flown by ex-bomber pilots. Without radar, they flew over a city under attack, using the illumination provided by flares, searchlights, and the fires below to find the bombers. Some Wild Sows had operated earlier over Cologne and in the first Hamburg attack. But these measures did not save Hamburg; on this night the defenses proved only slightly more effective, destroying 17 British planes.

Two minutes before the planned opening of the attack, yellow marker bombs crashed into the Billwarder area, a lower- and lower-middle-class district. This was two miles from the aiming point, but the markers were well concentrated. So was the bombing. Of 722 bombers claiming to have struck Hamburg, dropping 2,326 tons of bombs, 325 bombed within three miles of the aiming point.

It was soon clear to the middle and rearguard of the bomber force that something unusual was going on. Men smelled smoke in their oxygen masks and found their planes covered with soot. They looked down and saw not many fires, *but a single fire that covered four-and-a-half square miles.*

A tremendous concentration of bombs in a densely built residential area in unusual weather had produced the world's first firestorm. (A contributing factor was the absence of most of the fire fighting equipment, which was still fighting fires from earlier attacks.) There had been a long spell of hot and very dry weather around Hamburg. A pocket of warm, unstable air went up to 10,000 feet above the city, with cold air above and all around it. As the fires raged and combined, the air above them heated and rose. The cooler, oxygen-rich air all around was sucked in and acted as a bellows. Winds of tremendous force developed.

For years Germans had been carefully indoctrinated to stay in air raid shelters while an attack lasted. Those who took refuge in the multistory public surface shelters, built of reinforced concrete, with gas-tight doors and set apart from nearby buildings, generally got out alive. But they had to step through fat that had run from the melted bodies of those who had come too late. And there were few such shelters in the firestorm area. Most people went down to modified apartment basements, or in a few cases to specially built underground shelters below businesses. These were well built (better than those available to British civilians) and normally safer against large HE bombs than surface shelters. Now, however, they were death traps. Unless the inhabitants realized in time that they had to get out, and were very lucky, they were doomed. Most, mercifully, did not burn to death; they were poisoned by carbon monoxide or smothered by smoke. As the heat rose their corpses melted, or in some shelters they burned so completely that only a thin layer of ash remained on the floor. Those who realized that they had to leave the shelters before they were overcome by smoke, and before the exits were buried by collapsing buildings, sometimes died more horribly than those who stayed. Some were killed by falling debris as they struggled against the hurricane-force winds. Some were burned alive when flames spurted from buildings or even when sparks set their extremely dry clothing on fire. Some were picked up by the winds and sucked into the flames. Some were caught when asphalt on the streets melted. The lucky ones, who got out of the heart of the firestorm area, found safety in canals or in parks and open spaces. The firestorm ended only when everything that could burn was gone. At least 40,000 people were killed, and even this may be an underestimate. Air attacks killed larger numbers of people later in the war, but this may have been the heaviest toll exacted by an air attack deliberately aimed at an almost purely residential area.[14] Fortunately, firestorms were not a common result, even of the heaviest attacks. Bombing was horrible, but not typical.

After this horror the last two attacks on Hamburg were something of an anticlimax. On July 29–30 strong winds scattered the bombing; it did much new damage, but many of the bombs fell into the glowing ruins of the firestorm area. The final attack, on August 2–3, ran into bad weather and was a failure. In all the British lost 100 planes in the attacks on Hamburg, including those lost in related actions or scrapped after return; 552 men were killed and 65 captured. The destruction of the city had required 3,091 sorties and the dropping of 8,344 tons of bombs.[15]

The Germans were near panic. Speer warned Hitler that attacks of this sort on six more major cities would halt arms production. Hitler was more confident, assuring Speer that he would straighten it all out. In fact, the RAF could not repeat the success at Hamburg, which had stemmed from several unusual circumstances: a long period of good flying weather, odd weather conditions in the target area, atypical paralysis of the defenses, and easy location of the target on H2S. (In spite of this, the marking at Hamburg had not been very accurate.)

The disaster was local and temporary, but deep. Although herculean efforts were made to rush help to the shattered city, Gauleiter Karl Kaufmann urged people to flee (not that urging was really needed), and 1.2 million did so. The city was left without water, gas, power, or public transportation for some time. The port was at a standstill for lack of labor more than anything else, besides which some railroad facilities, 122 cranes, and nearly 500 warehouses had been destroyed or damaged. Although the main industries had not suffered great direct damage—the RAF had not aimed at them, and smoke had rendered the American attacks inaccurate—the destruction of many small workshops and the general disruption probably cost the city 1.8 months of full war production. Production returned to 80 percent of the preattack level in five months, but never did recover fully. The attacks cost Germany 20 to 27 U-boats and delayed introduction of the new Type 21 and Type 23 high-speed U-boats. Nevertheless, the destruction of Hamburg was not one of the more glorious episodes of the Allied war effort. It is hard not to feel that the 8,000 tons of bombs dropped on the city would not have caused more damage to the Nazis if aimed at the industrial areas south of the Elbe.[16]

Peenemünde

After the last attack on Hamburg, Bomber Command attacked targets in Italy to prepare for the coming invasion there and to pressure its new government into surrendering to the Allies. The RAF did not resume major attacks on Germany until August 17. Then it launched an unusual and important blow against the German missile development center at Peenemünde on the Baltic. There the German Army was developing the V-2 ballistic missile for use against Britain, while the Luftwaffe tested the V-1 pulse-jet powered cruise missile and the Messerschmitt 163 rocket fighter.

The British had received reports about German rocket development as far back as 1939; reconnaissance planes had photographed Peenemünde in 1942. But its importance was not realized until more reports encouraged a careful investigation in May and June 1943. Aerial photos convinced the responsible officials that something must be done. Had the British known how inaccurate the V-2 was and that its warhead held just a ton of explosive, they might have worried less. Even some Germans realized that the V-2 was not worth the vast expenditures on it, and that it would be wise to give the Wasserfall antiaircraft missile priority. But during 1943 and 1944 the Allies feared German secret weapons and invested considerable efforts to stop them.

On June 29 the War Cabinet ordered an all-out attack on Peenemünde, but the attack could not be carried out until August, when longer nights allowed trips to distant targets. Harris knew that his usual methods would not be suitable. Accuracy had to be high. He had to smash three small, widely separated targets: the main experimental station, the housing estate where the scientists and engineers lived, and the factory that was to mass-produce the V-2s. He even pondered a daylight attack, using clouds to hide a force reaching the target at sunset. But that had not worked well in 1942, and he discarded the idea. Instead, he decided to strike in moonlight at relatively low altitude, using the tactics employed at Friedrichshafen. A master bomber would guide the attack, while 5 Group would carry out time-and-distance runs in case the markers could not be seen or were obviously misplaced. A new type of marker bomb, the "red spot fire," would be used. It ignited at a height of 3,000 feet and burned on the ground for ten minutes with a very distinctive color.

An elaborate bluff was prepared to put the enemy off guard. Small diversionary attacks by Mosquitos had been a feature of Bomber Command operations for months. Harris had Mosquitos fly past Peenemünde for several nights before the attack there. They struck Berlin from the north, accustoming the Germans to expect attacks on the capital and to ignore apparent threats to Peenemünde.

The attack on Peenemünde used much the same route, while Mosquitos mounted another diversion to Berlin.

On the night of August 17–18 Harris dispatched 596 bombers to Peenemünde—a relatively small force by this part of the war. Some planes had returned from Italy the previous night, too late to get ready for Peenemünde, and the number of available crews was reduced by leaves, which were usually concentrated in moonlight periods. To preserve security, Harris had not reduced leaves.

Some pathfinders, using H2S, were to drop the new red spot fires on Ruden Island to establish a final checkpoint for the run into the target. They would then drop markers and flares over the targets. Finally, six planes would aim yellow markers visually at the aiming points.

Gulled, the Germans concentrated their planes over Berlin; only belatedly did junior officers send the fighters north. The attackers reached Peenemünde without trouble, but the initial marking was poor. The red spot fires fell on Peenemünde itself, and some markers, overshooting by two miles, hit the slave labor camp at Trassenheide, attracting many bombs. The visual markers did better, and the master bomber steered most of the main force to them. Most of 5 Group dropped on the markers. Those who trusted their time-and-distance runs, however, did better. In the last stages of the attack, smoke hid the targets and the master bomber lost control, and German fighters arrived. The British lost 40 bombers (one more crash-landed at home) and 290 men. As many as 200 planes might have been lost had the diversion not tied up most of the Germans over Berlin. (Three of the eight Mosquitos sent there were lost.) The attackers wrecked the housing but were less successful at the experimental station and the factory. Over 700 people were killed; unfortunately, as in the Ruhr dams attack, most were slave laborers. The effects of the bombing were only moderate, because the V-2's development was too far along, but the facilities at Peenemünde had to be dispersed. The V-2 was delayed by about two months. An attack a few months earlier would have found Peenemünde far less ready and would have had more impact.[17]

Friedrichshafen and Peenemünde might have pointed Bomber Command toward precision bombing. Jones's evaluation, quoted earlier in this chapter, may have been a bit overoptimistic, for neither attack was a good model for "normal" operations. Both were carried out in moonlight from relatively low altitude, against easily located targets. Nor, in the case of Peenemünde, was the bombing particularly accurate. But the equipment, and nearly all the techniques, that made precision attacks possible in 1944—Oboe, H2S, good VHF communications, red spot fire markers, the master bomber technique, offset marking, and time-and-distance runs—were already available by late August 1943. Harris, however, showed little interest in the possibilities they offered. He let 617 Squadron continue to practice precision techniques, and even made a few experimental precision attacks with the main force, but on the whole, these were fewer than before. He resisted calls to bomb Schweinfurt and concentrated more than ever on area attacks.

Right after Peenemünde Harris had seemed ready to try new techniques. On the night of August 22–23 he sent 462 bombers to Leverkusen, aiming not at the center of the town but at a chemical plant. No master bomber was used. But the Oboe gear partly failed, and clouds hid the markers. Although this misfire was due to bad luck and unfavorable circumstances, Harris did not repeat the experiment. The fact that he had sent only three-quarters of his Lancasters and Halifaxes, and used the night to rest the Stirling units, suggests that he had undertaken it without much conviction.

Harris apparently wanted to start a campaign against Berlin to force Germany's surrender. Given all-out concentration, he thought it possible to beat Germany in 1943. On August 23–24 he struck Berlin with 719 planes. The attack failed; 62 bombers were lost. Two more attacks on Berlin, on August 31–September 1 and September 3–4, also went wrong. The British estimated that for all three nights, just 27 planes dropped their loads within three miles of the aiming point, while losses averaged an unbearable 7.2 percent. Berlin was heavily defended, and so big and spread out, with so few distinct landmarks, that its picture on an H2S screen was incomprehensible. And for the last 100 miles of the long trip to Berlin, it was hard to dupe the enemy into thinking that the bombers were going elsewhere. So Harris decided to wait, evidently hoping a few months would make Bomber Command readier to deal with Berlin. By November he would have three-centimeter H2S and some new electronic countermeasures and other devices to support the bombers. In the meantime he concentrated on the "road to Berlin," striking targets in central and southern Germany. The attacks mostly depended on H2S and did not cause destruction comparable to that inflicted earlier. One attack, on Kassel, set off a firestorm, killing 5,200 people. British losses remained fairly low; in the period of July 24–November 18 they lost 695 planes, not counting planes that crashed in England or were scrapped after return, a loss rate of 4.1 percent.[18]

THE DEFENSES

The bombers faced a growing threat from German fighters, although they coped with the Wild Sows, a tactic the Germans abandoned when too many poorly trained pilots crashed trying to land at night. The regular night fighters, using Tame Sow tactics, were the real threat. The Germans largely neutralized Window by steering the fighters to the bomber stream farther from the target areas. Some skilled radar operators could tell the difference between Window and the bombers on the edges of the bomber stream; finally, the Germans modified the Wurzburg radar to use the Doppler effect to distinguish the slow-moving Window from the bombers. In October they introduced SN-2, a 3.7-meter airborne radar immune to Window, with a longer range than Lichtenstein. Ground and airborne detectors for H2S appeared, along with Flensburg, which could home in on the RAF tail-warning radars. The Germans began replacing the old Me-110s with the better Junkers 88s and later a few

Heinkel 219s, designed specifically for night fighting. Their fighters were becoming better armed. In August 1943 they introduced Schrage Musik (jazz music), a cannon mounted to shoot upwards. This let a German fighter slip unseen below a bomber, giving an easy shot at its engines and fuel tanks.[19]

For a time the British contained the fighter threat with their own new devices and tactics. There were more and more diversionary operations by Mosquitos and deceptive routing, with feints and sudden changes in direction. This and the further compression of the bomber stream, reducing the time over the target to 26 minutes, had helped to defeat the Wild Sows. But the latter trick was no help in dealing with the standard night fighters. In November 1943 Harris formed the 100 Group to orchestrate electronic countermeasures and other bomber support efforts. And in October the British introduced Airborne Cigar, wherein some Lancasters carried an extra man who listened for the German controllers and then tuned a jammer to the appropriate frequency. Tinsel jammers tried to drown out the running commentary. Another gimmick, Corona, broadcast false instructions to the fighter pilots. But the enemy beat Tinsel by increasing the power of his transmissions, and after the initial surprise, countered Corona and Cigar too. In December the British belatedly replaced the Serrate Beaufighters with faster Serrate Mosquitos. But Serrate was ineffective against the new SN-2, and the Mosquitos were older models with obsolete radar. The British also introduced new bombing aids. G-H, first used in October 1943, had been proposed much earlier, but its development had been postponed in favor of Gee and Oboe. G-H combined Gee with a sort of Oboe in reverse; a transmitter in the plane measured the range of ground stations in Britain. It had no more range than Oboe, but up to 100 planes could use it at once. The British also introduced a repeater system to extend Oboe's range, using planes as airborne relays. This promising system would have let the British mark Berlin accurately and probably carry out precision attacks deep in eastern Germany. But Harris was not interested; it was never used after October 1943![20]

Unfortunately, by the opening of the Battle of Berlin in November, the RAF had largely exhausted its bag of tricks.

THE BATTLE OF BERLIN

On November 3 Harris explained his plans to Churchill. He claimed to have virtually destroyed 19 German cities as far as their contribution to the war effort was concerned, and seriously damaged 19 more. He concluded that "we can wreck Berlin from end to end if the USAAF will come in on it. It will cost between 400–500 aircraft. It will cost Germany the war."[21] He was sure he could defeat Germany before the invasion of France. On December 7 he justified his optimism in great detail. His policy remained pure area bombing; success was measured in terms of destruction of built-up area. He believed that the destruction of 40–50 percent of the principal towns would cause a surrender, and expected to achieve this by April 1944.

Not everyone agreed. On December 23 Bottomley bluntly told Harris that his reasoning was not convincing. He doubted that more than 11 percent of Germany's people could be "dehoused," and anyhow they could be rehoused in Austria and some other occupied countries. (In fact, the Germans did not bother to do this except in Austria.) The Germans would not surrender even if the predicted degree of destruction were attained. He worried about the growth of the German fighter force and insisted that it was necessary to bomb smaller cities containing vital industries, such as ball bearing and fighter plants.[22]

The Battle of Berlin began on the night of November 18–19. The weather was bad; sky markers had to be used. The attack failed. Three attacks in late November, beginning on the night of November 22–23, went better. An attack on November 26–27 was particularly effective. It damaged the Alkett tank plant, perhaps the most important factory in Berlin, and other war plants. Losses were relatively low, but that was due largely to gross blunders by the Germans and weather of a sort that hindered the night fighters even more than the bombers. The next attack on Berlin, on December 3–4, did little damage, and 40 of the 458 attacking bombers went down. The new H2S sets were not much help, and the planes carrying them suffered a high rate of aborted flights. Bomber Command had more success against Leipzig the next night; then the moon halted attacks until December 16. From then on, losses were usually higher and successful attacks few.

There was no reason to expect destruction in Berlin on the scale seen in Hamburg or the Ruhr. Berlin consisted of relatively low and well built modern structures; its wide streets and many open areas acted as firebreaks. British morale was low, thanks to the high losses and miserable cold. Some planes were overloaded, and many crews jettisoned their blockbusters en route to gain height and speed. What were scornfully called "fringe merchants," who bombed as soon as they saw markers rather than aiming at them, became fairly common. More and more elaborate feints and evasive routing had to be used, forcing reduction of bombloads in favor of fuel. The Germans became harder to fool and their tactics more effective. There was an unusually long stand-down during and after the moonlight period in February. Losses were prevented from rising even more only by turning away from Berlin to other targets, especially in southern Germany, but the worst losses of all were yet to be suffered, over Leipzig and Nuremberg.

After mid-February 1944 Harris launched only one further attack on Berlin. On January 14 he was directed to attack towns that housed key installations making ball bearings and fighters, with Schweinfurt given the top priority. He resisted the directive to attack Schweinfurt and insolently delayed doing so, finally striking it on February 24–25—too late to do any good. (See Chapter 6.) He was only now joining in a true combined offensive with the Americans, over half a year after one had been nominally agreed on. On March 4 he was ordered to attack Friedrichshafen to hurt the production of tank gearboxes and engines and radar, and to make "every effort" to do so during the March moonlight period, itself a sign of the importance attached to this target. But he did not attack it until April 27–28.

In the meantime, it became clear that attacks deep in Germany were no longer possible. An attack on Leipzig on February 19–20 marked the real end of the Battle of Berlin. Harris sent 832 bombers there; winds scattered the bomber stream and gave the Germans plenty of time to steer fighters into it. The British lost 78 planes—9.6 percent of the force. Harris withdrew the older models of the Halifax from attacks on Germany and concentrated on southern German targets. In late March he decided on one more attack on Berlin. Of the 811 planes sent, the British lost 72—9.1 percent—despite careful planning and the cleverest diversionary operations yet.[23]

A final disaster took place when Bomber Command attacked Nuremberg on March 30–31. Even the official history termed this a "curious operation," marked by "unusually bad luck and uncharacteristically bad and unimaginative planning." The moon was nearly half full, normally too bright for an attack, and Nuremberg was deep in Germany. But it was a lush target, not hit recently, and was associated with the aircraft industry. (The aiming point, as usual, was well away from the actual industrial area.) Harris apparently calculated that planned American operations nearby might disrupt the enemy fighter force, and gambled on the weather. Most recent attacks had been farther north; one on Nuremberg would be unexpected. He planned a quick flight while the moon was up, aided by tail winds and covered by high cloud; the return flight would occur after the moon had set. No diversions were planned. The approach was designed to threaten several possible targets, but it involved a long, straight flight near the Ruhr defenses and right past radio beacons the Germans used to rally their night fighters. Some commanders disliked the route. Harris persisted, although late weather forecasts indicated that clouds could not be expected en route but *would* be found over the target. The crews were surprised to be sent out on a moonlit night and horrified at the "long leg" of the course. But 795 heavy bombers took off.

Strong winds dispersed the bombers, slowing them and forcing some off course. There were no high clouds, and the bombers left condensation trails, making them even easier to find. Over 200 night fighters attacked. Some desperate pilots deliberately left the bomber stream; others jettisoned bombs to gain height. Weather forced an emergency resort to sky markers, and the attack failed. In all, 545 British airmen were killed. Bomber Command lost 95 planes; a dozen more were junked. Although the extent of the disaster was clearly due to attacking on a night unsuitable for operations and bad planning, this was not a freakish episode.[24]

The Battle of Berlin had ended in defeat. From November 18, 1943, to March 31, 1944, the British had launched 35 major attacks (16 on Berlin), with an overall missing rate of 5.2 percent; 1,047 bombers had been lost, not counting the ones scrapped after return. Bomber Command was in no danger of destruction; its strength had actually risen, from 864 operational planes with crews in November to 974 in March. But it could not go on facing the sort of losses it regularly suffered deep in Germany. (Losses on attacks on western Germany were still bearable.)

It is arguable that Bomber Command had reached a dead end that had been inevitable, or nearly so, from the moment it switched over to night operations in 1940. The very developments that made it possible for a bomber to reach targets at night effectively exposed it, to an even greater extent, to a night fighter. If Bomber Command and other forces did not cripple Germany before the Nazis made their defenses effective—and Harris's obsession with general area attack sank any chance of that—then the British air offensive had to eventually hit the brick wall it encountered in 1944. Its diversion to preparing for D-Day, which will be more fully described later, prevented general recognition of the defeat. D-Day saved Bomber Command's morale and Harris's face. Eventually the change in the situation created by the liberation of France and by American attacks on German fuel production allowed Bomber Command to return to distant targets. It is possible, however, that new tactics, electronic countermeasures, and greater support from Mosquito night fighters with late-model radar, which appeared in the summer of 1944, might have changed the situation even had there been no invasion or attacks on fuel production. As we shall see, these things played a major role in reversing Bomber Command's fortunes.

The Americans Join In during 1939–1943: The Emergence of the Eighth Air Force

Beginning in 1939, as the British held off the Germans, the United States prepared for eventual participation in the war. The United States Army's small air element began the spectacular growth that would turn it into the mighty Army Air Force, of 2.4 million men and 80,000 planes, the greatest air force in the world. By the fall of 1941 this force, which had been training 300 pilots a year in 1939, was preparing to train 50,000 a year. It is interesting to note that the Army Air Force was the least professional and most civilian-minded of all the American—and probably all Allied—armed services. This, and the high quality of the tiny group of leaders who directed its expansion, was one of the keys to its success. Its commander, General Arnold, was a soldier with a remarkably flexible mind. He was firmly backed by General Marshall, who treated the Air Corps as a quasi-independent service long before it had such status under the law. Arnold became acting deputy chief of staff of the Army in November 1940 and head of the newly created Army Air Force on June 20, 1941.

THE BRITISH AND THE B-17

Strategic bombing, and the four-engine heavy bomber, retained pride of place as the Army Air Force grew. That growth was necessarily delayed by aid to Britain. In May 1941 the British took over 20 B-17Cs, after the planes were refitted with self-sealing tanks, as "Fortress I's." The U.S. Navy would not release the Norden bombsight to the British, who received the harder-to-use Sperry. The Americans advised using the planes only to train a nucleus of crews for later-model Fortresses, but the British, although skeptical of the planes' ability to survive, sent them into combat. They were given to 2 Group, the stepchild of Bomber Command, for unescorted, very-high-altitude attacks deep in enemy territory, in daylight. The RAF again ignored American advice to use the B-17s in as big a formation as possible between 22,000 and 28,000 feet. Instead, they were sent out in tiny numbers at over 30,000 feet. The results were miserable; the British Fortresses flew just 48 combat sorties. It is unlikely that any harm was inflicted on the enemy; the most notable feature of the bombing was that on one mission to Bremen, on September 2, 1941, a "neutral" American civilian technician served as a bombardier! Operations were hampered by icing, oxygen and intercom failures, poor maintenance, and badly designed high-altitude equipment. The Americans rightly grumbled about British blunders, but the Allies learned a lot about high-altitude operations, and some weaknesses in the B-17 were disclosed in time for changes to the new B-17E.[1]

THE FORTRESS REDESIGNED

Ordered in June 1940 and first flown in September 1941, the B-17E was really a new plane, the first model of the armadas the AAF was to send over Germany, in which hundreds of thousands of Americans would fight. It had armor, self-sealing tanks, tail guns, power turrets with twin .50-caliber guns behind the cockpit and in the belly, and better fields of fire for the older gun positions. Installing tail guns required a completely redesigned tail, and the new tail made the plane more stable. The B-17E was a feat of engineering. Although it had the same engines as the B-17D, it was just as fast, despite greater weight and the drag of the gun turrets. It had two serious faults. The original belly turret, a remote-controlled device, never worked right and was later replaced by a manned "ball" turret when the Japanese showed its weakness. And the B-17E was poorly protected against head-on attacks. It had just a single hand-held .30-caliber gun in the nose, while all other gun positions held .50s. When B-17Es encountered the Japanese in early 1942, the crews hastily replaced the .30 with a .50, and often a pair of .50s. In Britain, crews would mount four and even five .50s in the nose, and that would still not be enough.

The B-17F, which began coming off the assembly lines in April 1942, looked much like the E. Its first versions had even less firepower in the nose and were hastily modified in the field. Later B-17Fs had built-in mounts for "cheek" guns on both sides of the Plexiglas nose, as well as at least two guns firing right through the nose, and improved engines. The B-17F series had additional fuel tanks in the wings—"Tokyo tanks"—which unfortunately proved very vulnerable, and new self-sealing oil tanks, as well as broader, "paddle-blade" propellers. One fault of the B-17 was inherent in its basic layout. For lack of space, not lifting ability, no Fortress could take anything larger than a 2,000-pound bomb in its bomb bay. The B-17F had external racks enabling it to carry a 4,000-pound bomb under each wing, but bombs in the racks caused so much drag, and other problems, that they were rarely used. Fortresses normally hauled purely internal loads of 4,000 to 6,000 pounds. The United States Eighth Air Force began operations from Britain with a mixture of B-17Es and Fs and a few B-24Ds. The B-24s were initially less well armed, lacking protection underneath and in front, but a retractable belly turret, lowered only in action, was later added, along with a powered nose turret. Ultimately more B-24s were built than B-17s; the Ford Company built a huge plant the size of a city at Willow Run, Michigan, which after much bungling and delay, turned out 500 B-24s a month. The B-24 replaced the B-17 in the Pacific, where it was also used by the Navy, but the B-17 remained the preferred bomber in Europe.

The B-17s were manned by crews of ten men—considerably larger than those carried by British bombers. The bombardier and navigator worked in the nose and manned the guns there when needed. The pilot and copilot sat above and behind them; aft of them, the flight engineer doubled as the top turret gunner. Behind him was the bomb bay. A catwalk gave access to the colder and draftier rear of the plane. Behind the bomb bay was the radio man. He also manned a .50-caliber gun firing upward toward the rear through a hatch, with a limited field of fire; it supplemented the protection given by the top turret against diving attacks. Behind the radio compartment, four full-time gunners manned the two waist guns, the ball turret, and twin machine guns in the tail. The last two positions were the most uncomfortable; the tail gunner worked on his knees, while the ball turret gunner had to squat for hours in an awkward position inside his turret. (The B-24 layout was roughly similar, save that the radio operator was in front of the bomb bay and its later models had a full-time gunner in the nose.) However uncomfortable they were, B-17 crewmen could depend on their planes. Fortresses got home after being practically torn in two, or as half-burnt-out hulks, or with as many as 3000 holes from bullets and shells.[2]

AIR WAR PLANS

On July 9, 1941, President Roosevelt asked the War and Navy departments to prepare an estimate of the overall production requirements needed to defeat the United States' potential enemies. This required some sort of overall war plan, to determine what the requirements were. The Army Air Force hastened to develop its own plan, lest the War Department prepare an "air annex" to a ground-force-oriented scheme, mentioning only tactical air operations. The Air War Plans Division had been studying the industrial vulnerabilities of Germany and Japan for some time, aided by an RAF intelligence digest on German industrial targets. It completed AWPD-1, "Munitions Requirements of the Army Air Forces to Defeat Our Potential Enemies," in August. It was submitted to the joint board, the predecessor of the Joint Chiefs of Staff, on September 11—the same day that FDR's "shoot-on-sight" order began de facto war with Nazi Germany.

Like previous plans for war with both Japan and the European Axis, AWPD-1 envisaged a primarily defensive stance against Japan while an offensive was undertaken in Europe. It assumed that the United States would enter the war by April 1942. Major operations would not start until July 1943. They would culminate in an all-out attack from April to September 1944. The ultimate offensive force would consist of 98 groups of bombers (6,834 planes.) Medium and heavy bombers would be based in Britain, while very heavy groups, equipped with B-29s and B-32s, currently under development, would be split between Britain and the Suez area. Very-long-range bombers, equipped with the newly designed B-36, would be based in Newfoundland, Greenland, or sub-Saharan Africa. This was based on a wild underestimate of how long it would take to develop the B-36 (it only became fully operational in 1951) and a somewhat optimistic idea of how long it would take to produce the B-29 and B-32.

The bombers would seek to knock out Germany's electric power and transportation systems and petroleum industry; they would also attack aircraft and light-metals plants to aid the air offensive. AWPD-1 assumed that the bombers could defend themselves, although escort was desirable. But it envisaged a heavily armed bomber-type plane in the role of escort, rather than a fighter; this concept led to the development of the YB-40, a modified B-17.

Despite this, and its mistaken assumptions about aircraft development and overoptimism about bombing accuracy, AWPD-1 was a remarkably farsighted scheme. Its ideas about the proper target systems proved basically sound, and better founded than some notions fashionable later in the war. General Marshall and Secretary of War Henry L. Stimson were rightly impressed. After its acceptance, there was no doubt that a strategic air offensive would be a major part of the war.[3]

After Pearl Harbor, Churchill and Roosevelt and their military chiefs met in Washington. They created the Combined Chiefs of Staff, to settle issues of strategy and policy. Churchill learned that the Americans still aimed to defeat Germany first and that they shared his desire to send heavy bombers to Britain to attack Germany. The Combined Chiefs already knew that AWPD-1 could not be carried out without grave delays; they estimated that only 16 bomber and 5 fighter groups could go to England in 1942. The mission of these groups was left vague, but it was accepted that they would initially concentrate on "counter-air" operations against enemy air strength, and not on attacking Germany itself.[4]

THE EIGHTH AIR FORCE

In January 1942 the Eighth Air Force, commanded by Gen. Carl Spaatz, was activated in Georgia. Its ultimate strength was to reach 60 combat groups by April 1943, including 17 heavy bomber groups and 12 fighter groups. But most of its units were still training; in fact, most were inadequately trained even when sent overseas. Nor were its fighter units adequately equipped, except for the few with P-38s. Some groups with P-39s and P-40s were reequipped with "reverse lend-lease" Spitfires.

Spaatz sent General Eaker, who would take over VIIIth Bomber Command, and several staff officers to Britain to prepare for the Eighth's arrival. Despite differences of opinion over tactics and strategy, the Eighth's advance echelon established a close relationship with the RAF that was vital to its success. Eaker became a good friend of Harris and arranged for American bases (the Eighth's most comfortable bases were prewar RAF stations), British training for air intelligence officers and photographic interpreters, and a complete integration of communications. Until well into 1943, all of the Eighth Air Force's radar, and most of its radios, were British built, and it relied on the British Ministry of Aircraft Production for essential maintenance.

In June 1942 the ground element of the Eighth's combat units crossed the Atlantic aboard the *Queen Elizabeth*. Had a lucky U-boat been in the right position there would have been terrible loss of life, and the air offensive against Germany might have been set back a year. The movement of planes was delayed for some weeks as Washington anxiously awaited the outcome of the Battle of Midway; one B-17 group and a fighter group flew to the West Coast in case things went badly. In late June the heavy bombers and the P-38s began leaving Maine for England via Labrador, Greenland, Iceland, and Scotland. Meanwhile, light bombers that had reached Britain by sea carried out the Eighth's first attacks on the Germans, accompanying British units.[5]

American heavy bombers had not even begun operations when it became certain that the air offensive against Germany would be seriously hampered by a massive transfer of forces to Operation Torch, the invasion of northwest Africa, which was decided on July 25. The Eighth Air Force would lose all four of its fighter groups and two of its best prepared B-17 groups, as well as its medium and light bombers, to Gen. James Doolittle's newly formed Twelfth Air Force. Spaatz himself became primarily concerned with preparations for Torch and finally became head of the Northwest African Air Forces under Gen. Dwight D. Eisenhower, the Torch commander. Eaker replaced Spaatz as the Eighth's commander in December 1942. In addition to these movements of complete combat units there were important transfers of men (nearly 30,000) and equipment from other units to make sure the Twelfth was ready.

The Eighth Air Force now had just five B-17 groups and two B-24 groups, one incomplete. It had only one fighter group, the "new" 4th Group, composed of the Eagle Squadrons, made up of American volunteers who had joined the RAF and were transferred to the Army Air Force, along with their Spitfires. The Eagle Squadrons, although formed earlier, had not compiled the spectacular record of the better known Flying Tigers, but they gave the Eighth a core of exceptional pilots. Americans would have even more reason than the British to be grateful for the Eagle Squadrons.

The drain to North Africa did not end in 1942. In early January 1943 the newly arrived 78th Fighter Group lost all its P-38s and almost all its pilots to the North African campaign, while four heavy bomber groups originally intended for Britain went to Africa and other theaters. The Eighth was left without any P-38s, the sole American fighter then capable of long-range escort work. Its B-24s were too few to be useful; they could not fly a big enough formation to stand a reasonable chance of defending themselves. Torch accentuated the Eighth's dependency on the RAF. Many American units arrived without their equipment and supplies; the British provided ammunition, bombs, vehicles, tools, spare parts, and flying clothing, as well as electronic gear. Lubricating oils brought from the United States proved unsatisfactory and had to be replaced by British products. Much of what effectiveness the Eighth Air Force had in 1943 depended on the help given by the British.[6]

That help was all the more generous considering that most of the British had little faith in the American plans. (The Americans had no high opinion of the effectiveness of the British area attacks, but were in no position to make an issue of the matter.) Churchill and Portal were particularly critical of the idea of the self-defending bomber. Portal predicted that the Americans would be unable to defend themselves or bomb accurately under heavy attack. At best, he believed they would be reduced to infrequent and costly area attacks on the Ruhr, and perhaps Hamburg. For an effective force, even by 1944, they would have to switch to night attacks soon.

Churchill was even more vehement. He told FDR's special assistant, Harry Hopkins, that the Americans should turn to night bombing and build Lancasters. Sinclair and Harris urged restraint upon Churchill, lest too strong an attack on AAF policy play into the hands of the United States Navy and other elements that wanted to switch the American effort to the Pacific. Churchill stopped opposing the American course only at the Casablanca Conference in January 1943.

However, some RAF officers, notably the assistant chief of staff, Sir John Slessor, were optimistic about the Americans' plans. The American's first missions to targets in France and the Low Countries were mostly within the range of British fighter escort. But their apparent success, or at least low losses, and high claims of destroyed German fighters converted some British officers who had been skeptical earlier. In December 1942 Harris blithely predicted that the British and American heavies, operating together in daylight, could wipe out the enemy fighter force.[7] By then not even Eaker was that optimistic.

In the summer of 1942 the Eighth was not ready to strike a major blow against Germany. On August 25 Spaatz issued a list of specific targets, all in occupied Western Europe, including aircraft plants and repair depots, marshalling yards, and submarine installations. In September Spaatz agreed on a broad joint directive with the British; they would continue to supply most of the Eighth's fighter support until the Americans could take over the job. Targets would be picked in consultation with the RAF's assistant chief of staff for operations. The need to support the North African invasion and the worsening situation in the Battle of the Atlantic swung the Eighth's operations increasingly toward attacks on the submarine bases in France.

Washington's thinking was increasingly influenced by the U-boat threat and a growing concern with the "intermediate objective" of beating the Luftwaffe. After all, if the bombers did not reach their targets, they were not going to accomplish anything else.

In response to the President's request for an estimate of what the Allies would need for "complete air ascendancy over the enemy," the AAF developed AWPD-42, a new version of AWPD-1, in September. The new plan was influenced by an optimistic assessment of the Eighth Air Force's first missions. AWPD-42 estimated that the Germans might still defeat the Soviets; this might release half the Axis forces engaged in the east. To win air superiority and cripple the Germans, it would be necessary to smash seven target systems, comprising 177 targets. In order of priority, this included 11 fighter assembly plants, 15 bomber assembly plants, 17 aircraft engine plants, and 20 submarine yards—every production center for those items. Following them were 38 transportation targets, 37 electric power targets, 23 oil production targets, 14 aluminum plants, and two rubber plants. It was expected that repeat attacks would be needed on some, but not all, of these targets. Assuming that the bombers could defend themselves, an average circular error in bombing of 1,000 feet (which was twice as good as the Eighth had yet achieved); that it would be possible to mount five or six operation a month (which was overoptimistic in winter, at least); and that there would be an average attrition rate of 20 percent a month, it was estimated that the job could be done by a force of 2,965 heavy bombers, which should reach full strength on January 1, 1944. A third of the targets should be smashed by then; the rest should be dealt with in the first four months of 1944, making possible an invasion in the spring. The RAF was counted on as just a supporting force.

Some of AWPD-42's emphases were echoed at the Anglo-American conference at Casablanca in early 1943. There, the Combined Chiefs of Staff stipulated that the aim of the strategic air offensive was to prepare and support an eventual invasion; it would not be a substitute for it. The directive issued on January 21 reflected fear of the U-boats, which had led the Allied leaders to give the Battle of the Atlantic first charge on all resources, and the navies' demands that the strategic bombers help out in the war at sea. The directive to the Allied bomber forces in England stated that "Your primary object will be the progressive destruction and dislocation of the German military, industrial and economic system, and the undermining of the morale of the German people to a point where their capacity for armed resistance is fatally weakened." Within this framework, the primary objectives, "subject to the exigencies of weather and of tactical feasibility" were in order of priority:

1. Submarine construction yards
2. The aircraft industry
3. Oil plants
4. Other targets in enemy war industry.[8]

But the directive specifically stated that those priorities were not rigid; the submarine bases in France, and attacking Berlin, were also of "great importance."

It might be necessary to bomb northern Italy to support landings in the Mediterranean. (It had been decided that after the conquest of North Africa the Allies would take Sicily, at least, as part of an effort to knock Italy out of the war.) The bomber commanders were to take every opportunity to attack Germany by day, keep up the pressure on German morale, impose heavy losses on the German day fighter force, and contain German fighter strength away from the Russian and Mediterranean theaters. Portal was responsible for the "strategical direction" of the American bombers as well as his own, but Eaker would decide their tactics and techniques. General Marshall had insisted on this, foreclosing any possibility that the British would order Eaker to switch to night attacks.[9]

The Casablanca directive was not a masterpiece of clarity. It contained so many qualifications that it did not clearly settle what targets even the Americans would attack. It left Harris many loopholes to continue a practically independent course of general area attack against Germany; he freely misquoted the directive to further strengthen his position.

Many later criticized the Allies for pursuing the strategic air offensive and trying to counter the U-boats by ineffectively bombing bases and construction yards. They rightly insisted that it would have been wiser to send more four-engine bombers to escort duty in the Atlantic, where they could have achieved more at that time than by bombing Germany. Converted Liberators or similar planes could have quickly closed the "air gap" in mid-Atlantic, where the U-boats were scoring their successes. This criticism is correct, but the RAF and the AAF were not *immediately* responsible for the failure to deal with the U-boats. To be sure, only a few more Liberators were needed to close the gap, as became clear when FDR finally intervened on March 18 to secure more United States Navy Liberators for the task. In fact, the persistence of the air gap in 1942–1943 may have been due merely to maldistribution of the already available Liberators, for which the navy was responsible. It had 112 Liberators in the Pacific, but *none* in the vital Atlantic area.[10]

It should be noted that without the demands of the strategic air offensive there would have been no four-engine heavy bombers for antisubmarine work. Victory in the Battle of the Atlantic was an accidental byproduct of the commitment to strategic bombing, a point many later critics have failed to note.

THE EIGHTH AIR FORCE BEGINS OPERATIONS

On August 17, 1942, the Eighth Air Force launched its first small heavy-bomber mission. A dozen B-17Es of the 97th Bomb Group, escorted by RAF Spitfires, attacked the repair shops in the Rouen-Sotteville marshalling yards. Only half the bombs fell in the target area. A few Messerschmitt 109s went for the bombers, but they neither inflicted nor suffered damage. Two B-17s were slightly damaged by flak; another was damaged, and two men slightly hurt, when it hit an unlucky bird. This was an inauspicious beginning. On August 19 another small force of Fortresses went out on a more important mission, supporting the

Canadian raid on Dieppe. They cratered the Abbeville-Drucat airfield, smashing a hangar and destroying or damaging 16 planes. Small attacks, never by more than two groups of bombers, followed against railroad yards, shipyards, and air bases within the radius of Spitfire escort, which was just 175 miles.

Unfortunately, the British authorities showed little interest in extending the Spitfire's range. It was basically a short-range plane, but it could have been modified to go farther. The British ace and fighter leader, Wing Commander John Johnson, later wrote that "with a little foresight Spitfires could have fought well inside Germany and could have helped the Eighth in their great venture."[11] The Mark 8 Spitfire, which belatedly appeared in August 1943, had additional fuel tanks in its wings and a longer range, but it was never used in Northwest Europe.[12]

The Eighth's slow start was inevitable. Many units were only partly trained. The pilots were inexperienced at flying in formation at high altitudes. Many radio operators could not send or receive code. Many gunners were untrained; some had never even fired their weapons. There were few target-towing planes for gunnery practice. Col. Curtis Le May, the admittedly hard-to-please commander of the 305th Bomb Group, who was about to start the meteoric rise that made him commander of the B-29 force in the Pacific in 1945, deemed that even the Eighth's navigation was inadequate. Men whose experience was in flying over the American West, where isolated buildings and railroad lines provided clear checkpoints, needed time to get used to the crowded European countryside.

Claims of bombing success and claims of enemy planes shot down were not very accurate; Eaker and other senior officers put a good face on things so Eighth would get the support it needed. After the first missions, however, Eaker was not fully satisfied with his equipment. He urged improvements in the B-17 and its accessories, seeking a better oxygen system and oxygen masks (they would never be entirely satisfactory), better heating arrangements, bulletproof glass for the cockpit side windows, backup power systems for the turrets, and replacement of some turret-mounted .50s with 20 mm. cannon—perhaps an early sign of doubt that the B-17, in its existing form, was really the self-defending bomber it was supposed to be.[13]

The Eighth mounted its first big mission on October 9. It sent 108 B-17s and B-24s against a steel plant and locomotive works at Lille (the most important target of this type in France next to the Schneider works), while seven other B-17s flew a diversion. The German interceptors were determined, and the bombing was inaccurate; many civilians were hurt. Four bombers were lost and many damaged. The claims of enemy planes shot down were fantastic. At first it was thought that 56 German fighters (nearly a fourth of all those in Western Europe) had gone down. The British authorities were openly skeptical, receiving the claims with ridicule and even anger. They doubted that that many planes had been in the air. In January 1943 the claims were revised down to 21 destroyed, but in reality, 11 German fighters, at most, had gone down.

Gunnery claims were finally tested against a rigorous system. Enemy planes were counted destroyed only if seen to crash, explode, or fall totally wrapped in flames or if a whole wing or tail had been shot off, or if the pilot had been seen to bail out. To be considered "damaged," a plane would have had to be seen to have parts shot off or be actually on fire. (American observers at first often assumed that German planes that left trails of smoke had been damaged, not realizing that German engines were apt to smoke even when not malfunctioning.) In between, a slippery category of "probable" included those enemy planes that seemed too badly shot up to return to base. Even this system, however, fell down, because there were usually many gunners firing at the same plane and then submitting claims for it destruction. And "destroyed" planes sometimes reached home. Even the gun-camera films that normally served as conclusive proof for the claims of fighter pilots could mislead; in one case an Me-109 photographed as apparently exploding actually survived. Its drop tank had blown up, hiding it in a ball of fire.[14]

On October 21 the Eighth began the campaign against the U-boat bases with an attack on Lorient; this was its first venture beyond fighter escort. Attacks on the submarine bases, interspersed with a few strikes against air bases and transport targets, continued for the rest of 1942. It was already understood that the U-boat pens were immune to existing bombs, but it was hoped that the locks, floating docks, power plants, railroad yards, and warehouses around them could be damaged, hampering the repairs and turnaround of the U-boats.

Between November 1942 and March 1943 the Eighth Air Force sent out more than 100 bombers on just two days. Shortages of spare parts and replacement personnel ate away at it; in February 1943 the Eighth had an average of just 74 planes with crews ready for operations. No replacement crews arrived at all between February and May; for a time Eaker extended a crewman's tour from 25 to 30 missions. In 1943 the chance of an Eighth Air Force bomber crewman finishing a tour of operations was about 34 percent—barely higher than that of the men in Bomber Command. It was true, though, that his chance of surviving the war was better. When a B-17 or B-24 went down, most of the crew usually bailed out; British airmen were less lucky.

Fall and winter weather hampered the Eighth's operations. Only three missions were completed in October, and none at all between October 21 and November 7. When they did fly the crews froze; ice even threatened to choke their inadequate oxygen masks. In terms of losses, the Eighth's initial operations seemed encouraging. Even British observers, who discounted the wild claims of enemy fighters shot down, were impressed by the fact that even when the Germans got at the B-17s the latter survived. But the first missions were misleading. Most were escorted by fighters and aided by successful diversions. The German command was not yet worried about the Americans and had not yet reinforced the day fighter force in the West.

German pilots who had encountered the B-17 were more impressed. Bombers were usually easy targets, but the B-17 (and the B-24) were different. When the Germans attacked from the rear, the normal approach to a bomber formation, they met a terrifying volume of fire. The Fortress had been well designed to counter such attacks and was rugged beyond their experience; it took an average of 20–25 hits with 20 mm. shells to bring one down. The Germans realized that their fighters were not well armed for shooting down B-17s, which called for a different type of armament than that best for fighter-versus-fighter combat. This posed a dilemma that was to be increasingly serious. A fighter weighed down by the heavy, slow-firing cannon best suited for destroying bombers was at a disadvantage against Allied fighters. This had particularly serious results for the Me-109s, which formed most of the German fighter force. Certain peculiarities of its design had made arming the Me-109 a tricky problem all along. Adding more and heavier guns required bulges and gondolas that hurt its performance. In 1942, however, this problem was not yet acute.

Unfortunately, the Germans were not stumped about how to attack the B-17 for long. Oberleutnant Egon Mayer, a fighter group commander, realized that it was vulnerable to attack from the front. In a head-on pass the attacker faced less firepower and had a good chance of hitting the cockpit, engines, and wing tanks. But it took skill to aim properly while closing with the B-17s at up to 600 miles an hour, and coming around for another head-on attack was time consuming. When the bombers left heavy contrails, some pilots even preferred attacks from the rear, using the contrails to slip up unobserved.

Nevertheless, Mayer had uncovered a weak point in the B-17. Even when both top and ball turrets faced forward there was a zone between them covered only by hand-held guns. The latter were difficult to handle in the cramped nose and hard to aim into the wind, and the officers manning them had not had much gunnery training.

Mayer introduced the new tactics when the Eighth attacked the U-boat base at St. Nazaire on November 23. A few weeks later, on January 3, the Germans defending St. Nazaire introduced a new method of directing antiaircraft fire, a "predicted barrage," saturating the area through which the bomber formation was expected to fly instead of trying to follow a target plane continuously.

Coping with fighters and flak posed a not entirely soluble dilemma for the Americans, because the measures best calculated to deal with fighters were the opposite of those best to deal with flak. But fighters were clearly the main danger. More hand-held guns were added to the nose, and calls went out for a powered "chin turret." Pilots were told to make a diving turn into attacking Germans to spoil the enemy's aim and bring the top turrets to bear. But there were limits to the ability of bombers to take evasive action; better formations were needed.

At first the bombers had flown in three-plane flights with a good deal of space between the two flights of a squadron, all planes flying at the same level. But during September 1942 the squadrons began flying a stepped-up group formation. After experiments, Le May worked out the group "combat box" formation, in which both flights and squadrons were staggered so that all top and ball turrets could fire forward. It did not afford even protection; the low squadron was notoriously the most vulnerable. This formation was relatively easy to fly, but it complicated bombing. To deal with this, Le May introduced a practice already used in the Pacific; the whole group would bomb on a signal from the lead plane, which would carry the best available bombardier. Even-bigger formations became desirable; in April 1943 two or three group boxes were combined into a "combat wing" of staggered groups. (The Germans were already assembling fighters in big formations.)

In early 1943 the losses still seemed tolerable. Eaker would have been delighted to receive fighter escort, but he was sure that a force of 300 unescorted bombers could attack any place in Germany with less than 4 percent losses. Unlike Eaker, many subordinate commanders put great faith in the expected YB-40.[15]

INTO GERMANY

Eaker was under pressure to hit Germany itself and wanted to attack the U-boat construction yards there. But the Eighth's operations against Germany would remain sporadic; only 14 missions would be completed against targets there in the first half of 1943. The anti-U-boat campaign remained the focus of its activities; 63 percent of its bombs, in that period, went to countering the submarines.

On January 27 the Eighth bombed Germany for the first time, sending 90 bombers against the submarine yards at Vegesack. Bad weather, however, forced a diversion to the less important target of Wilhelmshaven. Only 55 planes reached this objective, meeting less opposition than expected. Both the bombing and the interception were hampered by the weather, while the German defenders seemed less experienced than those met over France. Three bombers went down, in exchange for seven German fighters. Subsequent missions to Germany were tougher, although they were limited to "fringe" targets on the North Sea coast and the Americans took advantage of the fact that most of the way to the target was over water. That reduced the Germans' warning time, and their single-engine fighter pilots were reluctant to fly far out to sea. On a February 4 mission to Emden, the Americans encountered twin-engine enemy fighters for the first time. These were no match for Allied fighters, but their heavy firepower and great endurance made them a threat to unescorted bombers. Later in the month, when they returned to Wilhelmshaven, the Americans met stronger fighter opposition. And the Germans tried a new trick, air-to-air bombing. Fortunately this never worked very well.

Over the next several months the Eighth Air Force periodically visited German targets, almost all concerned with submarine construction, while it pounded away at the French bases. In March, when not striking submarine targets, it mostly attacked French marshalling yards. From April on, it shifted the "marginal" effort to attacking vehicle plants in France and Belgium. On March 18 it finally bombed the Vegesack construction yards. Careful routing postponed the meeting with enemy interceptors until the last minute, and just 2 bombers of the 97 reaching the target were lost. (A third was scrapped after return.) On this mission new techniques produced the most accurate bombing, and the biggest blow against U-boat construction, so far. The Allies estimated that seven U-boats had been badly damaged and that the yard would be largely out of operation for a year or more. That was grossly optimistic. The completion of one U-boat was delayed by 15 weeks! This illustrated the futility of the anti-U-boat campaign, although the attacks on the yards in Germany hurt the Germans more than the attacks on the French bases. Ironically, the last mission against a U-boat base, on June 28, provided an unexpected recompense for a vast waste of effort, because a 2,000-pound bomb penetrated the concrete bunker at St. Nazaire. This freakish event so perturbed the Germans that they thickened the concrete protecting the bases at the expense of work on coastal defenses.

On April 17 the Americans struck their first important nonsubmarine target in Germany, the Focke-Wulf plant at Bremen. This time evasive routing did not work so well. A German plane spotted the Americans well out over the North Sea, and the interception was skillfully managed. The toughest air battle yet resulted. Of 107 bombers reaching the target area, 16 were shot down. The Germans lost just 5 fighters to American fire; the Americans claimed 62! Despite the opposition, the bombing was accurate, but Focke-Wulf production had already been largely dispersed elsewhere. The heavy losses worried the American command.

During the first five months of 1943, American equipment and performance improved. In March the crewmen began to get body armor—"flak suits." Bombing accuracy crept upward. In February only 20 percent of bombs hitting within 1,000 feet of the aiming point was considered good; by April 30, 40 percent was common. The Vegesack mission saw the introduction of bombing with the use of automatic flight-control equipment—the bombardier controlled the plane during the bomb run through the autopilot. In May the Americans reintroduced the use of incendiary bombs against industrial targets, something they had discontinued after the fall of 1942. It was now realized that in some cases incendiary bombs could do more damage than explosives. At the end of May, YB-40s finally arrived in England,[16] but they failed to provide the solution to the escort problem that was so badly needed.

THE DEFENDERS

Although the Luftwaffe was under continuous pressure, the German fighter force in the West grew, thanks to transfers from Russia and the Mediterranean. It was suffering heavy fighter losses, especially in the south. The fact that many fighters were tied down in the Mediterranean may have been the only thing permitting the Eighth Air Force to penetrate beyond escort range.

During 1942 German aircraft production rose, thanks to rationalization of the use of labor and materials rather than increased priority. The industry was still controlled by Milch rather than by Speer. Even Milch did not see the desperate need for new fighters, while an all-out switch from bomber to fighter production was blocked by insistence on retaliation on the part of Hitler and

Goering. Still, by mid-1943 there would be 810 single-engine fighters and 478 twin-engine fighters (mostly night fighters) in Germany and the West. These defenders were ably led by Gen. Adolf Galland. Nominally just an inspector of fighters, Galland was actually more important than the commanders of Luftflotte Reich and Luftflotte 3. (The latter command controlled the defense of southern Germany as well as of occupied Western Europe.) Despite everything the Allies did, the Germans remained able to replace lost planes.

But one critical factor had begun to turn against the Germans. Their new pilots were not as well trained as their predecessors, or as the Allied pilots they faced. In the summer of 1942 a fuel shortage and the desire to get new pilots as fast as possible had led to a reduction in the hours of training. The number of new pilots grew, but their average number of flying hours fell.[17] But the Luftwaffe was far from the end of its rope, and even unskilled fighter pilots could be deadly opponents for the bombers.

THE VIIIth FIGHTER COMMAND

The Eighth Air Force's bombers were slow to get help from American fighters. After delays caused by design difficulties, P-47C Thunderbolt fighters began arriving in Britain in late December 1942. Their engines and radios were still full of "bugs." The P-47 was a new plane, and VIIIth Fighter Command had to break it in. Clumsy looking, it was so big and heavy that many doubted it could take on the Me-109 and Focke-Wulf 190, its newer stablemate. The 4th Fighter Group's Spitfire veterans, in particular, grumbled that it was a "seven-ton milk bottle" and that evasive action in a P-47 would mean running around inside its roomy cockpit. But once some problems were solved, it proved a superb plane, even better in some ways than the famous P-51 Mustang, discussed in Chapter 7. It was more rugged; its air-cooled engine was more resistant to damage; and with eight .50-caliber guns, it was more heavily armed. Tests showed that it was faster than the Me-109 and FW-190, could outdive them, and could turn with them above 15,000 feet. But it was not good lower down, and its rates of climb and acceleration were poor, as was visibility from its cockpit. Later modifications—paddle-blade propellers and water-injection systems—gave the Thunderbolt better performance, while the redesigned P-47D-25 had a cut-down rear fuselage and a bubble canopy. The P-47's short range was a serious problem. On internal fuel it had little more range than the Spitfire, and it arrived at VIIIth Fighter Command without auxiliary tanks. General Eaker asked the British Ministry of Aircraft Production to build such tanks as early as October 1942, but as late as February 1943 it had not even replied.

During early 1943 the 4th Fighter Group and the rebuilt 78th Fighter Group converted to Thunderbolts, and the 56th Fighter Group reached Britain. That the training system at home was still not running smoothly is suggested by the fact that some of its pilots had not gotten any gunnery training! The 4th and 56th groups began a great rivalry; they became the most successful American fighter units of the war. The men who eventually rose to command them, colonels Donald Blakeslee and Hubert Zemke, were the outstanding fighter tacticians of the war.

The Thunderbolt's radios suffered interference from the engines, which were unreliable. The first P-47 sweep, on March 10, showed that the pilots still could not talk to each other, and the P-47 was withdrawn from operations for a month. Finally, on April 8, Thunderbolts from all three groups, shepherded by RAF Spitfires, began sweeps off the French and Dutch coasts. The 4th Group first clashed with the enemy on April 15, downing two FW-190s for one P-47 lost in combat. But two other P-47s went down because of engine failure; losses for that reason remained high until May. The other groups started slowly; the 56th Group had several fighters shot down but did not score a single kill until June 12. On May 4 the P-47s carried out their first escort mission, to Antwerp. It would be months before they reached Germany.[18]

THE COMBINED BOMBER OFFENSIVE

The Eighth's effort was about to be geared to a more detailed and somewhat different plan from that envisaged at Casablanca. Hoping to find a way to do decisive damage in Germany by striking only a few targets; in December 1942 the Army Air Force formed the Committee of Operations Analysts (COA) to pick the best industrial objectives. COA sought to analyze the whole enemy economy, determine the enemy's minimum requirements and production capabilities, and identify the locations and characteristics of targets. It conferred with British analysts and, when information was lacking about Germany, sometimes used comparisons with American industries, though not necessarily correctly. In its report, submitted on March 8, 1943, COA concluded that destroying some 60 specific targets would "gravely impair and might paralyze the Western Axis war effort." It did not set explicit priorities, but listed targets in what seemed to be a descending order of preference: aircraft production, ball bearings production, the petroleum industry, grinding wheels and crude abrasives (that was later dropped on British advice), nonferrous metals, and synthetic rubber plants. It overestimated the amount of natural rubber the Germans were getting by blockade running, or it might have rated synthetic rubber production a better target. The report's chief influence was its stress on ball bearings. General Arnold was enthusiastic about the report, and about the ball bearings industry as a target.

Ball bearings were vital to all sorts of vehicles and equipment, especially fighters. The Americans estimated that the Germans' stocks of bearings were low and that few could be "gained" even by drastic cutbacks in nonmilitary uses. The Germans could only moderately increase imports from Sweden and Switzerland, while six months to a year would be needed to rebuild the plants if they were destroyed. Redesigning equipment to reduce the use of ball bearings would take an equal amount of time and would have a limited effect. These calculations proved overoptimistic, but were not baseless. Speer had already warned Hitler on September 10, 1942, that tank production at Friedrichshafen and the ball bearings plants at Schweinfurt were crucial to the war effort, and Hitler had ordered increased antiaircraft protection for those cities.

Although not treated as gospel, the COA report became raw material for a new strategic plan. The Eighth Air Force and the RAF Air Staff drew up a list of primary objectives—submarine yards and bases, the aircraft industry, ball bearings, oil, synthetic rubber and tires, and military transport vehicles—comprising 76 targets. A committee of American officers and Air Commodore Bufton drew up an operational plan for a "Combined Bomber Offensive," and a more precise order of priorities. Finished on April 12, it warned, "If the growth of German fighter strength is not arrested quickly, it may become literally impossible to carry out the destruction planned." German fighter strength had to be considered "an Intermediate Objective second to none in priority." The plan set an order of priorities:

I. Intermediate objectives: German fighter strength
II. Primary objectives
    A. German submarine yards and bases
    B. The remainder of the German aircraft industry
    C. Ball bearings
    D. Oil (contingent upon attacks against the Romanian city of Ploesti from the Mediterranean)
III. Secondary objectives:
    A. Synthetic rubber and tires
    B. Military motor transport vehicles

U-boat construction was to be cut 89 percent, fighter production 43 percent, bomber production 65 percent, and ball bearing production 76 percent. Half of enemy synthetic rubber capacity and nearly all of enemy tire production (tire plants were regarded as particularly vulnerable to fire) should be destroyed. If Ploesti was successfully struck, the oil installations in the Ruhr should be attacked. The plan called for a real, combined Anglo-American air offensive, rather than the nominal one agreed on at Casablanca, and for the RAF to use any capacity for precision attack it had, while carrying out selective area attacks in support of the plan.[19] It expressed Bufton's outlook, as opposed to that of Harris.

To accomplish its task, the plan estimated that the combined offensive would need a force of 2,702 heavy bombers and 800 medium bombers by March 31, 1944. The mediums would attack German fighter bases and strategic targets within their range; later they would support the invasion of France. In the first phase of operations, from April to July 1943, the Americans would stay largely within escort fighter range, mostly attacking submarine yards, except for attacks on Schweinfurt and Ploesti. In the next phase, from July to October, deep penetration would begin, largely against fighter plants. Attacks on additional target systems should begin in October. The U.S. Joint Chiefs of Staff accepted the plan for a combined bomber offensive with little debate on May 4.

The plan was a departure in several respects. It made the ball bearings industry a major target, because an attack on ball bearings would hurt enemy armaments production in general and fighter production in particular. Ball bearings to some degree replaced synthetic rubber as a "small" objective, concentrated in a few plants, destruction of which would disrupt the whole enemy war effort.

But the plan was modified before being presented to the Combined Chiefs of Staff at a Washington conference in May, when the aim of combining the British and American efforts was soft pedalled and the stress on selective attack weakened. By securing these changes the British leaders forestalled a serious debate on air strategy. The Combined Chiefs of Staff readily approved the plan and ordered a major attack on the Ploesti oil refineries. Operations from Britain remained under Portal's direction.

The Americans had not forced a showdown over air strategy. This was unfortunate but probably inevitable; their own achievements, so far, had been slight. It remained up to the British as to whether there might yet be a real combined offensive, for the RAF leaders still disagreed among themselves. But Harris won the argument and got the directive he wanted. The specific objectives of the offensive were now for the Eighth Air Force alone. Bomber Command would engage in "the general disorganization of German industry," although its actions were to be "designed as far as practicable to be complementary to the operations of the Eighth Air Force."[20]

The Abortive Offensive of June–October 1943

In April 1943 four new B-17 groups reached Britain. They became operational in May. The 92nd Bomb Group, which had arrived in 1942 but had been relegated to training duties, returned to operations. In May and June seven more B-17 groups and four groups of B-26 medium bombers arrived. The Eighth Air Force was now ready to go beyond fringe areas.

A mission on June 11 to Bremen and Wilhelmshaven, far beyond escort range, showed that attacks on Germany were not going to get easier. A force of 252 bombers, the largest yet dispatched, found Bremen overcast. Only 8 bombers went down, but the fierce fighter attacks disrupted the bomb run, and the attackers missed the U-boat construction yards. In an attack on Bremen and Kiel two days later, the force sent to Kiel met the toughest opposition yet seen, losing 22 bombers. The larger force attacking Bremen lost four B-17s, while a smoke screen prevented accurate bombing.

On June 22 the Eighth made its first attack on a major objective in Germany that was not related to aircraft and submarines. Curiously, in view of its relatively low priority, this was an almost entirely isolated, and very effective, blow against synthetic rubber production. Surprise (the Eighth had only penetrated deep inland thrice before), diversions, and clever routing that led the Germans to think for a time that the Americans were heading for the North Sea coast, contributed to the success of the attack. Of the 235 bombers dispatched, 183 planes (including 11 YB-40 escort Fortresses) reached the synthetic rubber plant at Hüls, which made 30 percent of Germany's synthetic rubber. After the attack the plant was shut for a month, and its recovery was not finished for six months. The Germans were worried; their reserves of rubber were reduced to one and a half months' requirements.

The attack on Hüls showed the vulnerability of the synthetic rubber plants, if the Americans could get at them. The Strategic Bombing Survey later estimated that three to five more major attacks on Hüls would have shut it permanently.

There were probably just three other synthetic rubber plants in Germany, a small pilot plant at Leverkusen and two other large plants, one at Ludwigshafen, further up the Rhine, and the other at Schkopau, which unfortunately was far to the east. An attack on Schkopau, which produced 30 percent of Germany's synthetic rubber, would require a flight far beyond fighter range. But there was no attack on Schkopau, or even a followup on Hüls, because rubber was not rated as all that important a target. Even the Hüls attack had involved a costly penetration beyond fighter range. The attacking force had lost 16 Fortresses (one a YB-40), nearly 10 percent of its strength, while a diversionary attack on Antwerp had cost another 4 planes, plus another scrapped after return to England. The bombers had claimed 47 German planes, while the fighters escorting the Antwerp force claimed 7.[1] More flights beyond fighter range, to Hüls and similar targets, lacking the element of surprise, could be expected to be more costly.

THE ESCORT PROBLEM

Eaker had worried for some time about the cost of going beyond fighter range. He had ceased to be an enthusiast for the self-defending bomber idea. As he had suspected, the YB-40 did not help. Its proponents had not thought the problem through. Despite their firepower and protection, YB-40s were no match for enemy fighters, and once the standard B-17s dropped their bombs, the heavier YB-40s, laden with more guns and armor, could not keep up with them.

The real answer was to extend the range of the fighters. A full solution would require a new fighter; the P-47s range was inherently limited. But it could be improved by something any escort fighter would need: effective drop-tanks. Efforts toward getting them, however, were slow. As noted earlier, the Ministry of Aircraft Production was at first unresponsive, but it eventually proved far more helpful than did the Air Material Command at home. Eaker did get a supply of 200-gallon paper "belly" tanks from the United States in March 1943, but they had been designed solely for ferrying fighters at low altitudes. Clumsy and poorly shaped, they caused considerable drag and tended to leak if loaded and left standing for several hours. Worse, they could not be used over 23,000 feet. At normal combat altitudes drop-tanks had to be pressurized, and to draw fuel from them the P-47s themselves had to be modified. While the VIIIth Fighter Command's able Air Technical Section worked on the P-47, it also, with the help of British engineers, designed a 108-gallon metal drop-tank. The tanks were successfully tested in May, but a steel shortage prevented the British from producing them immediately and as a substitute the British offered a 108-gallon paper tank developed for their own use. Production snags delayed the appearance of the paper tank until September. The Air Material Command in the States had been asked for tanks of comparable size, but moved sluggishly. The Fifth Air Force, in Australia, like the Eighth, had to get local help.

Finally VIIIth Fighter Command obtained 200-gallon paper tanks from the U.S. which were introduced on July 28. Only half-filled, they were used to climb to 22,000 feet and were usually dropped on crossing the enemy coast. Even this extended the P-47s' radius of action from 190 to 260 miles. Finally, in August, so-called 75-gallon metal tanks (they actually held 85 gallons) arrived from the United States; they were introduced in combat before the end of the month. These tanks extended the P-47's radius to 340 miles. The British began supplying 108-gallon paper and metal tanks the next month; when properly used the British tanks eventually gave a radius of 375 miles. Using both "75"-gallon and 108-gallon tanks, the Eighth flew its first mission with escort all the way to a German target on September 27.

To cover the bombers, the fighters had to maintain a high speed, costly in fuel, while weaving back and forth so as not to get ahead of their charges. The escort task was normally accomplished in relays. Some fighter units accompanied the bombers on the first part of their journey, then turned back, while more units rendezvoused at a prearranged point, to cover the rest of the mission to the limit of their range. The planning of the rendezvous points was aided by the British radio-intercept service; its "eavesdropping" on the German fighter pilots told the Americans where the Germans themselves were assembling to attack.

Eaker had repeatedly stressed the need for drop-tanks and escort fighters, but all-out action on these was not taken until after Assistant Secretary of War Robert Lovett returned to the United States from a visit to Britain in June 1943. He stressed the need for more replacement crews, more forward-firing guns on B-17s, and better training in gunnery and formation flying. P-38s and P-51s would be needed for escort. Work on an improved version of the P-51 had been underway for some time, but only now was it given priority.

Much of what happened in the latter half of 1943, would be determined by the availability, or rather the lack of, drop-tanks and long-range fighters. The range limitation was all the more agonizing because American and RAF fighter pilots were well able to handle their German counterparts. After initial reverses the Americans learned how to use the Thunderbolt's good characteristics and to avoid situations in which its relatively poor rate of climb and acceleration put it at a disadvantage. They learned that it was desirable to stay well above the bombers; then they could pounce on Germans going for the Fortresses and Liberators, aided by the P-47's terrific diving speed. The Germans seemed addicted to bad tactics; once in a tight spot, they tried to get away by diving. That worked well against the Spitfires and early-model P-38s, but was suicidal against P-47s, P-51s, and later-model P-38s. The Allies, with their advantages in numbers, longer training, and better planes and fuel, were already inflicting steady heavy losses on the Germans. The latter's fighter losses in the West had already begun to rise sharply in March; initially this probably reflected increasing engagements with British Spitfire 9s, which had overtaken the FW-190A and Me-109G in performance. In July 1943 alone the Germans lost 335 single-engine fighters in the West, nearly half the force available at the start of the month.

An important implication of these heavy losses was, or seemed to be, that if bombing of German factories choked off replacements, the whole enemy fighter force would wither away in just four months, leaving the Allies with complete air superiority. Unfortunately, such hopes were based on an overestimate of the destructiveness of bombing and an underestimate of the ability of German industry to recover from attack.

Eaker and his bomber commanders thought that VIIIth Fighter Command could have done better than it had. They blamed its commander, Gen. Frank Hunter, for slowness in getting the bugs out of the P-47 and getting new fighter groups into action, and they disagreed with him about escort tactics. Hunter favored sweeping well ahead of the bombers, while the bomber men wanted very close escort—too close, in fact. They also blamed Hunter for not getting more range out of the P-47s. He had been reluctant to use drop-tanks at all, and then had favored dropping them at the earliest possible moment. Although many of his pilots thought he was out of touch with operational realities, he appreciated the fact that they wished not just to get rid of the clumsy belly tanks but to use up the fuel in the internal tanks behind their seats as soon as possible. Those tanks were the most dangerous to them if they were hit. This was entirely natural, but the bomber men, just as naturally, took a different view of the risks. On August 3, to the relief of both fighter pilots and bomber commanders, Hunter was replaced by the abler William Kepner.[2]

"BLITZ WEEK"

After the Hüls mission, bad weather prevented attacks on Germany. The Eighth bombed U-boat installations, airfields, and aircraft plants in France. In late July the weather cleared. As the RAF began the Battle of Hamburg, the Eighth Air Force launched a series of operations later called Blitz Week, with much heavier and more continuous attacks, deeper in enemy territory than before, largely against aircraft and naval targets.

On July 24 the Eighth paid the first of its few visits to Norway, sending 309 bombers to attack U-boat bases at Bergen and Trondheim, and an industrial target at Heroya. It was a long flight; the Trondheim attack meant a round-trip of 1,900 miles and was the longest mission yet carried out by the Eighth Air Force. Since the defenses were weak, the B-17s could bomb from lower heights and with greater accuracy than usual. The U-boat bases were assigned to the 4th Bombardment Wing, which had late-model B-17Fs of longer range. The Trondheim port area was severely damaged. The force sent to Bergen found it covered by cloud and did not attack. The 1st Wing's older Fortresses struck aluminum, magnesium, and nitrate plants at Heroya. They were jammed together on a small island, and the B-17s bombed from just 16,000 feet with tremendous effect. The nitrate plant was shut for three and a half months. The metals plants, which were not yet finished, were badly damaged, and the Germans decided that they were not worth rebuilding, given the difficulty of defending them. One B-17 crash-landed in Sweden, and another was junked after returning home, but not a single man was hurt, while a major industrial target was wrecked.

This, however, was an isolated blow against the enemy's light metals industry, a concentrated, vulnerable, and important target system.

The attack into Norway was a good start for Blitz Week, but nothing afterward equalled it. On July 25 the Eighth Air Force and RAF Bomber Command made one of their few attempts at cooperation. The Eighth tried to follow up the RAF's first great area attack on Hamburg with an attack there on the Blohm and Voss U-boat construction yards and the Klockner aircraft engine plant, while another force attacked Kiel. The Kiel attack caused much damage to U-boat yards and a German naval base there and sank a newly launched U-boat and an old cruiser.

Clouds and smoke from the fires set by the RAF obscured Hamburg, however, protecting the Klockner plant. The attack damaged the Blohm and Voss yards and did considerable damage to the industrial area south of the Elbe, but at a high cost. Of 127 B-17s going to Hamburg, 15 were lost even though diversionary routing had fooled the Germans about the Americans' objective for a time. The interception was determined; even the single-engine fighters pursued the withdrawing Americans well out to sea. In all, 19 B-17s went down, and another went to the scrap heap. The Germans were known to have lost at least 6 fighters. A return to Hamburg the next day, and a blow against rubber and tire plants at Hannover, proved costly but successful, although smoke still handicapped the attackers at Hamburg. A small force of only 92 planes, of which 16 were lost, left the Hannover plants burning furiously. Ironically, while the lack of close cooperation with the RAF at the strategic level was bad, too-close cooperation at the tactical level had proven harmful.

After a day's rest, the Eighth launched its deepest penetration yet. Despite bad weather, it struck the Fieseler works at Kassel and a plant building FW-190s at Oscherleben, just 90 miles from Berlin. Only 28 planes managed to reach Oscherleben and find a hole through the clouds, but they cost the Germans four weeks' production there—a total of 50 FW-190s. The price was heavy losses in a terrific air battle, despite the first use of drop-tanks by Thunderbolts. Meeting the withdrawing Fortresses, the P-47s drove off the pursuing German fighters. The Germans had scored an ominous success. For the first time, they scored hits with new 210 mm. air-to-air rockets. These clumsy spin-stabilized missiles, fired out of bulky tubes, were not too accurate, but they outranged the bombers' guns. A single hit could destroy a bomber. On July 29 the bombers reverted to coastal targets, successfully striking Kiel and the Heinkel plant at Warnemunde, which was building FW-190s. On July 30 the Eighth returned with one massed force to hit the Fieseler plant and another factory at Kassel. Again, after a tough fight, Thunderbolts saved the bombers from heavier losses as they surprised the pursuing Germans.

That ended Blitz Week. Although the weather was reasonably good the next day, after six big missions in a week, the Americans were in no shape to attack again. The men were exhausted; although it was midsummer, many had suffered frostbite, and anoxia when ice formed in oxygen tubes. Eaker had driven his men as far as they could take it, or farther; the men who had survived suffered a high rate of mental breakdowns. Blitz Week had also been costly in other ways. The Eighth had lost 88 B-17s in action; their crews were now dead or prisoners. And 17 other B-17s were being scrapped; besides this, 10 P-47s and 2 B-26s had been lost in action or junked. Eaker's operational bomber strength had been reduced to under 200 planes. He had lost 8.5 percent of the planes that had actually attacked the targets. That was not a rate that could be stood for long.

The Germans were improving their defensive methods. They were introducing 30 mm. cannon as well as rockets. The growing number of day fighters were spreading over all of Germany, including the previously almost undefended south. Well stocked bases were everywhere, so that fighters could rearm and refuel and fly a second or even third sortie against deep-penetrating bombers.[3]

But Arnold would not tolerate waiting for full-length escort before striking again deep into Germany, and Eaker himself was unwilling to let German fighter production grow unmolested. Deep penetrations would go on, in the hope that careful planning would keep losses down until long-range fighters were available, while the bombers struck critical targets.

Meanwhile, B-24 units that Eaker had parted with earlier were trying for a "decisive" blow.

PLOESTI

On August 1, 1943, as the Eighth Air Force was preparing to attack Schweinfurt, an American force in the Mediterranean theater carried out another costly operation, the famous low-level attack on the oil refineries at Ploesti. This operation had certain affinities with the attack on the Ruhr dams. It was an attempt to wreck a vital installation with a single attack at low level, by heavy bombers accustomed to operating far higher.

Ploesti was the main source of natural petroleum in Axis Europe; it supplied about a fourth of Germany's fuel. It was especially important as a source of fuel for the Eastern front. The idea of attacking Ploesti had been alive since 1940, but the German conquest of Greece and Crete had prevented action. Some Soviet bombers had struck Ploesti in 1941 before the Soviets were driven far to the east, beyond easy range. The British were hard pressed and short of bombers, but nevertheless considered an air attack on Ploesti, perhaps in conjunction with a raid by a paratroop force. The extreme distance from Allied bases and other problems forced them to put the idea aside repeatedly.

An American force carried out the first Western attack on Ploesti in June 1942. The attack was the byproduct of an abortive scheme to bomb Tokyo from bases in China. A small force of B-24s, en route to China via the Atlantic Ocean and Africa, was diverted to Egypt when the deteriorating situation in China made it unlikely that an attack could be launched there. The force was then ordered to bomb Ploesti, in the hope of interfering with the German summer

offensive against the Soviets. On the night of June 11–12, thirteen B-24Ds left
Egypt. Twelve reached the Ploesti area at dawn, only to find it blanketed by
cloud. They bombed on "estimated time of arrival" over the Astra Romana
refinery, the biggest in Europe, doing no damage, and landed all over the Middle East. One plane was lost in a crash, and four others were interned in Turkey.
This first blow by U.S. air forces against the European Axis preceded the Eighth
Air Force's first strike by several weeks. The results did not encourage a return
to Ploesti, but the force became the nucleus of the United States Ninth Air Force.
It operated as a small tactical air force in the North African and Sicilian campaigns, supporting the British advance from Egypt in the same way the Twelfth
Air Force supported Eisenhower's advance from the west. The Ninth finally
acquired two B-24 groups, which bombed airfields, ships, and transportation
targets. Like the heavy bombers of the Twelfth, they made an important contribution but played no part in the strategic air campaign proper.[4]

The looming end of the North African campaign, and the establishment of
a heavy bomber force on bases in Libya, revived the prospect of an attack on
Ploesti. It was discussed by the Combined Chiefs of Staff at Casablanca. Ploesti
was a tough target; the major refineries were widely dispersed. In March Col.
Jacob Smart, of General Arnold's advisory council, suggested a low-level attack
by 200 planes based in Libya. This would allow great accuracy against the most
vital points in the refineries and, it was hoped, would let the attackers, main-
taining radio silence, reach Ploesti unobserved. The Balkans were primitive and
spottily occupied, and air defenses, at least outside Ploesti, were weak. The enemy
would not expect such a deep penetration. Hugging the ground, the bombers
would offer only fleeting targets to enemy flak, and the usual fighter tactics would
be ineffective. This scheme did not arouse universal enthusiasm, but it gradually
edged out a rival plan for a high-level attack from Syria.

At the Washington conference in May, the Combined Chiefs decided to attack Ploesti, which, it was thought, would be especially helpful to the Soviets.
General Eaker, although he later turned against the Ploesti plan, had also argued
that it was necessary to hit Ploesti before striking the Germans' synthetic oil
plants. The Combined Chiefs ordered two B-24 groups, temporarily transferred
from the Eighth Air Force to Africa to support the invasion of Sicily, to attack
Ploesti. The new 389th Bomb Group, scheduled to leave the United States for
England, would join them as an additional "loan."[5]

The Ninth Bomber Command withdrew all five of its B-24 groups from operations on July 20 to prepare for Ploesti. Auxiliary tanks were installed to provide
fuel for the 2,700-mile round-trip; the Norden sights were replaced by simple
low-altitude bombsights, and many planes were reengined. To "discourage"
enemy flak gunners, extra guns were installed in the B-24s that would be in
lead flights, and crewmen who would not otherwise be occupied in the attack
were given submachine guns to shoot out the windows. The crews practiced
low-level flights and attacks on a dummy Ploesti in the desert, and studied
elaborate relief models of the target area.

The plan was to have all five groups fly in column, led by the 376th Bomb Group. It would be followed by the 93rd, 98th, 44th, and 389th Groups. Crossing the Mediterranean west of Greece, they would turn northeast, climbing to 10,000 feet to pass over Corfu and the Albanian coast, which was backed by high mountains. Past the worst of the mountains, they would descend to cross the Danube below 5,000 feet. On reaching Pitesti, the 389th Group would peel off to fly to its target, the Steaua Romana refinery at Campina, well north of Ploesti and the other targets. The other four groups would fly to Floresti, then turn southeast for the final run to Ploesti, dropping to attack height, between 100 and 300 feet, and splitting into six forces, each assigned a single refinery. After bombing, the B-24s would rendezvous to exit from the Balkans via Corfu.

That was the plan. . . .

It might have been different had the Western powers had a truer picture of the defenses. But their intelligence was astonishingly bad, considering that many Romanians (not to mention Romanian Jews) were pro-Allied and the Allies had many potential contacts; the oilfields were largely owned by Western interests. The Allies were reluctant to fly reconnaissance missions lest they tip off the enemy that something was planned. Enemy air strength was believed to include about 100 Me-109s (some Romanian), 30 Me-110 night fighters, and some obsolete Romanian-built fighters.

The effective Axis air strength may have been slightly overestimated, but on the ground the enemy was far stronger than the Allies supposed. Ploesti's defenses had been carefully prepared by a Luftwaffe general, Alfred Gerstenberg. There were 250 or more guns, four-fifths of which were German manned, and hundreds of machine guns. There was far more camouflage than the Allies expected. Gerstenberg had had a trunk pipeline laid between the refineries, so knocked-out units in one plant could be quickly replaced by intact units in another.

On August 1, 177 B-24s headed out over the Mediterranean. Another crashed on takeoff. They were commanded by Brig. Gen. Uzal Ent, who flew with the 376th Group's commander, Col. Keith Compton, but as the result of a last-minute switch, not in the lead plane. The mission was already less than a complete secret. The force maintained radio silence, but the German intercept service had picked up a routine signal between ground stations, warning Allied commands in the theater that an operation was on.

Near Corfu, things began going wrong. As the force started climbing, the lead plane went out of control and crashed. The backup lead plane then aborted its mission. Then, as the B-24s approached the Pindus range, they encountered towering clouds. The 376th and 93rd Groups climbed further, to 16,000 feet, to get above the clouds. But Col. John Kane, the commander of the 98th Group, elected to fly through them. He knew that many of his planes had no oxygen, not having expected to need it. (They were already overloaded.) The force had split into two sections, which lost sight of each other. The two high-flying lead groups got the benefit of a tail wind and pulled farther ahead of the three groups behind Kane. With radio silence, such a situation was hard to avoid. The enemy, however, repeatedly spotted the Americans, and Kane's planes were shot at over Albania. A German radar in Bulgaria detected the Americans, and ancient Bulgarian biplanes tried to intercept them; they sighted the B-24s but could not overtake them.

The two lead groups pushed on. The 376th Group's leading planes were passing the town of Targoviste en route to Floresti when Ent broke radio silence. He, or someone else aboard his plane, mistook Targoviste for Floresti. Visibility was bad thanks to haze, and the two places looked alike—each had a castle and a valley running southeast with a railroad line in it. Believing the lead planes were mistakenly passing Floresti, Ent ordered a turn southeast. Several pilots warned that this was a mistake, but when Ent flew on down the Targoviste-Bucharest railroad line, all but one followed him. The lead plane ignored Ent and, all alone, took the right course. Badly damaged by flak, it bombed the Colombia Aquila refinery—not its planned target—and belly-landed.

Fifteen minutes later, with Bucharest in sight, Ent ordered a turn north. He had probably known earlier that he had blundered, for the run from Floresti to Ploesti was supposed to take four minutes. But with visibility limited, he probably wanted to be absolutely sure of where he was. This was prudent, but what happened later suggested that Ent, a normally able man of undoubted courage, had become confused. Colonel Compton later said that Ent was seeking the Astra Romana refinery (assigned to Kane's 98th Group), but other pilots of the 376th Group thought he intended to attack the originally planned target, the Romana Americana refinery, from the south, or even take them all the way around to Floresti to get on the planned approach route. Ent, who was later paralyzed in an accident and died a few years after the war, never gave a full explanation.

Ent's planes met a storm of fire on the way north. Flak guns emerged from hiding places in haystacks and railroad cars. Machine guns and even small arms shot at the B-24s. Ent sheered east of Ploesti and the ring of refineries—and guns—around it. He came near the Romana Americana refinery, but the enemy fire was so great that Ent gave up. He ordered the 376th Group to attack "targets of opportunity." Strangely, he then sent a signal, "Mission successful," to Libya. Most of his planes bombed nearby marshalling yards and storage tanks, or even open fields. One flight leader, Maj. Norman Appold, led some planes around to the northeast to bomb the Concordia Vega refinery, originally assigned to the 93rd Group. The 93rd, meanwhile, had gone straight north from Bucharest and attacked the nearest refineries, Colombia Aquila and Astra Romana. It lost 11 planes over the target, including the group commander's.

Meanwhile, Kane's force was on the way. Kane, too, was confused. Wrongly thinking that he had passed the "lead groups," and that they had been slightly off course when last seen, he actually turned west at the Danube for a time in the hope of meeting them. Then he resumed course. At Pitesti the 389th Group broke off for Campina. But like Ent, Colonel Jack Wood was confused by deceptively similar valleys. He was lost for a short time, but got back on the right track. The Steaua Romana plant proved to be just as ferociously defended as the main target, and 6 of the 29 planes went down in the target area. But they did a terrific job of bombing. Steaua Romana was thoroughly smashed.

The 98th and 44th Groups turned right at Floresti. The Germans, alerted, had run a flak train onto the Floresti-Pitesti rail line. As the B-24s came into sight, the sides of the cars dropped and shells streamed up at the planes as the train tried to follow them. American gunners blew up the locomotive, but several B-24s were so badly damaged that they had no prospect of getting home. Fighters attacked the Americans, and Romanian-manned Stukas even tried to dive-bomb the B-24s as they hurtled south, but flak was their deadliest foe. The 98th and part of the 44th Groups reached the Astra Romana refineries only to find that they had already been bombed, causing tremendous confusion to the new attackers. They ran into a hell of flak, attacking fighters, and exploding oil installations. Kane's group suffered particularly badly, losing 21 of its 41 planes. But the attacking groups did a good job. Most of the 44th Group's planes were assigned to hit the Creditul Minier refinery at Brazi, well southwest of the other targets. It, too, was thoroughly smashed, for the loss of only 2 planes.

Only two groups left the Balkans in some sort of formation. The American force was badly scattered as it was jumped by German and Bulgarian planes on the way home; 8 planes landed in Turkey; others reached bases all over the Eastern Mediterranean. In all, 54 B-24s had been lost and many more damaged; 310 men had been killed, and 54 of those returning to Allied bases were wounded. About 150 men, many injured, were prisoners in Romania and Bulgaria. (Later the Turks graciously let the 79 men interned in Turkey "escape.") The Ploesti force had suffered losses that, as a proportion of the force involved, put even the Eighth Air Force's worst disasters in the shade. Five men were awarded the Medal of Honor.

The Germans apparently lost at least six fighters; the Bulgarian and Romanian losses are unknown but probably totalled no more than nine planes. The attack had not knocked out Ploesti with one blow, although that had not really been expected. It was a classic example of the weakness of even the cleverest plan, if it is based on tricks and relies on absolute precision of execution without any margin for error. The idea that radio silence would save the force from discovery once the Balkan coast was crossed was unrealistic and contributed to its disorganization. Bad luck and the loss of the original lead planes dogged the mission. The wrong turn at Targoviste, and Ent's strange behavior after turning north from Bucharest, hurt the mission, but his mistake was a natural one.

Nevertheless, it should be noted, three of the five groups actually executed the original plan, although hampered by the ragged earlier attacks on some of their objectives. And they did much damage. The Colombia Aquila, Steaua Romana, and Creditul Minier refineries were actually more heavily damaged than expected; the last was knocked out for the duration. Had the whole force acted according to plan, it might have done more damage than the planners had hoped. As it was, the attack eliminated about 40 percent of Ploesti's refining capacity for four to six months, but the enemy already had that much spare capacity. The Germans also lost some important specialized products—lubricating oils and paraffin wax—from Steaua Romana and Creditul Minier. But they swiftly brought in 10,000 slave laborers, and speedy repairs and the activation of idle undamaged units prevented a serious loss of supplies. The destruction effected did help eliminate the "cushion" of idle machinery that had existed earlier, so when the steady high-altitude attacks began in 1944, they had immediate effect.[6]

THE SCHWEINFURT-REGENSBURG MISSION

In early August the Eighth Air Force rebuilt its strength. Bad weather allowed only one mission to Germany. The planners had plenty of time to ready the great double blow against Regensburg and Schweinfurt on August 17.

That operation grew out of the confluence of two originally separate plans. While the Washington authorities were anxious to start hitting the ball bearings industry, Eaker thought that a direct blow against enemy fighter production—the most immediate threat to Allied bombers—should come first. The main Me-109 plants, at Regensburg in Bavaria and Wiener Neustadt in Austria, which made 500 of the 650 Me-109s built every month, had not yet been attacked. Even before Blitz Week, an elaborate coordinated assault had been planned. The Ninth Air Force's B-24 groups would strike Wiener Neustadt from the south, as soon as possible after Ploesti. On the same day, Le May's 4th Bombardment Wing, with its long-range Fortresses, would bomb Regensburg, while the 1st Wing carried out a diversionary operation. The dual assault from north and south would allow surprise blows against both Messerschmitt plants, splitting and confusing the Germans. Further, Le May's force, instead of returning to England, would fly to bases in North Africa, further confusing the enemy and meeting less opposition than on a conventional withdrawal. Le May's force would also bomb on the way home from North Africa. After that, Schweinfurt would be attacked as early as possible.

But it became apparent that weather suitable for both the Eighth and Ninth Air Forces was unlikely. Finally, the Ninth was told to go ahead alone, and it struck Wiener Neustadt on August 13. Of 101 bombers put up, 65 bombed the target, taking the Germans by surprise. Only 2 bombers were lost. The attack did only moderate damage but led the Germans to begin a difficult dispersal of their production facilities.

Meanwhile, the planners had decided to combine the Regensburg and Schweinfurt missions. Ten minutes after Le May's force left for Regensburg and Africa, the 1st Bombardment Wing would take off for Schweinfurt. It was hoped that the 4th Wing would attract most of the enemy's fighters. The Eighth's heavies would be aided by a mass of diversionary operations.

No one imagined that this would be an easy mission. The unprecedentedly deep penetration alarmed the crews at the briefings. Many gunners took along extra ammunition. This was a rare "maximum effort." Normally, bomber groups put up only three of their four squadrons at a time, letting one squadron rest (and insuring that a group could not be wiped out in one day.) For this mission, all four squadrons went up; the "extra" ones formed special "composite groups."

The plan promptly went awry. Low clouds hung over the American bases, especially the 1st Wing's, on the morning of August 17. They promised to be short lived, but would make mass takeoffs and climbing to altitude dangerous. The clouds posed a dilemma for the American commanders, who were under pressure to get on with the long-delayed mission. The Regensburg force had to leave early, so it could land in Africa while there was still daylight. Le May was ready to go. The clouds over his bases were not so bad, and he was rightly confident that his pilots were trained well enough to cope with them. Gen. Frederick Anderson, the head of VIIIth Bomber Command, let Le May's wing take off after an hour and a half, while holding Gen. Robert Williams's 1st Wing, which finally left three and a half hours after the 4th Wing. The Americans thus had the worst of it in two ways. The German fighters that intercepted the 4th Wing would have time to land, refuel, and get ready to meet Williams's planes. But the Allied fighters that escorted the 4th Wing would not have enough time to return to base and reinforce the planes that would escort the 1st Wing on the initial stages of its journey.

Le May took off with seven groups and 146 planes; several aborted before reaching the Netherlands. The Germans were eager, and struck even before the Thunderbolts of the 56th and 353rd fighter groups left the bombers at Eupen, in Belgium. Some 300 German fighters were ready for action, deployed in depth, and there were constant attacks. Night fighters stalked behind to catch crip-ples. The Germans fired rockets and tried air-to-air bombing, but most of the damage was done with conventional attacks by single-engine fighters. By the time the force reached Regensburg, the Germans had largely exhausted their fuel and ammunition. Only some test pilots from a local factory defense unit harassed the bombers as they settle into their bomb run.

Because of the target's importance, the B-17s bombed from relatively low, 17,000 to 20,000 feet; fortunately, Regensburg was not particularly heavily defend-ed by flak. In spite of the heavy losses, the bombing was very accurate, destroy-ing many workshops and storerooms, and a hangar and finished planes on the factory airfield. But the most important single building, the final assembly shop, was not hit. Le May's force reached Africa without much further trouble. It had had 24 planes shot down. He found the African bases in poor shape, which discouraged future "shuttle missions" there.

The Germans had expected the force that hit Regensburg to return to England, and were preparing for another great battle. They had one, but not quite as they expected. Just as they realized that Le May was going south, they detected a second force coming from England. The 1st Wing, nine groups of bombers comprising 230 planes, had finally taken off for Schweinfurt as the 4th Wind neared Regensburg. Its target was not quite so far, but it would have to fight all the way there and back. The bombing plan had one unusual feature, for an American attack. If smoke hid the three factory targets, the last four groups, carrying incendiaries, were to bomb the center of Schweinfurt. That way they would hit housing and kill some skilled workers.

The 1st Wing remained unlucky. After crossing the Dutch coast, it encountered a thick cloud layer. The commander of the 1st Air Task Force (the leading half of the wing) chose to go under it at 17,000 feet. This contributed to the failure of the 4th Fighter Group, one of the two groups that were to escort the force on the Antwerp-Eupen leg of the route, to rendezvous on time—it only joined the bombers just before it had to leave. The 78th Fighter Group, which managed to rendezvous, was overstretched. This cost at least one bomber; the Germans once again struck even before the Thunderbolts turned back. The decision to fly at 17,000 feet may have been unfortunate for other reasons. Flak was deadlier, and the German fighters, flying at their best altitude, were able to use the clouds as cover. They slammed repeatedly into the Americans, concentrating on the leading groups. Survivors of the Schweinfurt mission were unanimous in regarding it as their worst experience of the war, except possibly for those who also went on the second mission, two months later.

The Germans once again had to let up as the bombers neared the target, but they had disrupted the Schweinfurt force more than they had the 4th Wing. The approach to the target had been altered at the last minute to allow for the changed position of the sun later in the day, and the attack was made from a less familiar angle. The bombing was inaccurate; the last four groups were unable to see the factories, but were so disorganized that they did not hit even the center of the city. After more fierce fighting the 1st Wing was met by the 56th Fighter Group east of Eupen. The fighter group had squeezed 15 extra miles of range out of the clumsy 200-gallon tanks, and it jumped the pursuing Germans. Three Thunderbolts went down with their pilots, but a dozen German fighters were shot down, probably saving several bombers. Along with the rescue of six B-17 crews from the sea, this was almost the sole merciful occurrence of the day. The Schweinfurt force had lost 36 Fortresses. In all, of 376 B-17s, 60 had gone down and 11 had to be scrapped. Seven Allied fighters were lost. The Americans alone had lost 601 men: 102 killed, 381 prisoners, and 20 interned in Switzerland, while 38 fell in enemy territory but managed to evade capture. The Germans had lost about 47 planes, but only 16 men killed. Only about 21 planes had fallen to the bomber gunners, who claimed to have shot down 288!

The Regensburg attack did a lot of damage to Me-109 production, and it paid an unexpected dividend: it destroyed the fuselage jigs and acceptance gauges for the Me-262 jet fighter. But the attack was not the crushing blow that had been hoped for. The Germans recovered many machine-tools even though the buildings they were in were smashed. More tools were rushed from the Skoda works, and the factory was dispersed, first to "shadow" workshops in nearby towns and then to forest clearings. Production recovered and even increased.

The Schweinfurt attack was a comparative failure. Only one of the three major plants was seriously damaged. Although many machines were moved from the badly hit Kugelfischer plant to a branch facility, there was no major effort to disperse the industry. Fearing that it would cost too much production, Speer gambled that the Allies did not really recognize the ball bearings industry's importance. However, he did secure still greater antiaircraft defenses for Schweinfurt, and he took steps to increase production elsewhere.[7]

BREATHING SPACE AND BUILDUP

The Eighth attacked aircraft factories and air bases in France and the Low Countries and at Watten, in France, smashed a huge bunker designed to house V-2 rockets; the concrete was still wet, and it was wrecked beyond repair. Some of its operations were part of an elaborate but unsuccessful attempt to make the Germans think the Allies intended to land in France, provoking an air battle. Bad weather delayed a return to Germany.

On September 6, three weeks after the Regensburg-Schweinfurt mission, 338 B-17s set out for the SKF ball bearings plant at Stuttgart, while B-24s flew a diversion over the North Sea. Poorly planned and conducted, the mission failed. Over France the force hit such heavy cloud that it should have turned back. Only one wing saw the target; some units overshot, while others used up fuel circling and seeking a hole in the clouds, which inhibited bombing but not the German fighters. Between German attacks and lack of fuel, 45 went down and 10 were written off after landing. Of the B-17s that were lost, 12 managed to ditch, and Air Sea Rescue pulled 118 of their men out of the sea, which prevented a disaster not far short of the Regensburg-Schweinfurt mission. Some men were more shaken by the waste and bungling over Stuttgart than by the earlier and more famous battle.[8]

During September VIIIth Bomber Command was reorganized. The old 1st Bombardment Wing became the 1st Bombardment Division and the B-24 units became the 2nd Bombardment Division, while the old 4th Wing became the 3rd Bombardment Division. Each Fortress division was subdivided into three newly formed combat bomb wings, each of which, when enough units arrived, would consist of three groups. The Eighth Air Force received much new equipment. It began getting the new B-17G, the ultimate Flying Fortress. Most important of its many improvements was a remote-controlled "chin" turret under the nose, to deal with head-on attacks. (Chin turrets were also installed on B-17Fs that were used as "lead ships.") The B-17G's waist positions were staggered and enclosed with Plexiglas panels, making life easier for the waist gunners, who all too often had been freezing and without room to work. Later B-17Gs had a Cheyenne tail turret, powered and with better sights. But few, if any, now thought that any improvement would enable the bombers to defend themselves.

In August and September the Eighth received fighter reinforcements. Drop-tanks, though too few were available, were extending the fighter's range. But escort was still limited to northwestern Germany. Two of the five new fighter groups had P-38H fighters whose range theoretically allowed escort out to 450 miles, but they lacked enough planes, and equipment problems meant that the 55th Group did not become operational until October 15. The 20th Group was not ready until the end of 1943! It was already suspected that the P-38, due to its lack of acceleration and other problems not yet fully known, was not really the solution to the escort problem.

The Eighth found a partial solution to another problem, bad weather, which often prevented successful visual attacks on Germany and did so in all of September. Experiments with bombing on Gee had not worked; the Americans borrowed H2S equipment from the British while developing their own version, H2X. A pathfinder group was formed to use both systems; its bombers would lead other formations. On September 27 the American pathfinders led their first operation against Emden; this was also the first mission to a German target that was escorted all the way. The target area was an important port, giving a good H2S picture. Two forces, comprising 305 B-17s, were sent out, each led by two H2S planes. The lead wings bombed on signals from the Pathfinder planes, which dropped smoke markers to guide the following wings. The results were mixed; half the H2S sets failed, and the markers vanished before the last wings of each force could bomb. Another attempt on Emden would be made on October 2.

The wings that bombed on signal had achieved a circular error of half a mile to a mile, but dropping on markers had been wildly inaccurate, producing an average error of over five miles. More and better radar was needed, but even with it, this sort of bombing would be no more than a poor way to keep up the pressure on Germany when visual bombing was impossible. Crewmen referred to such attacks as "women and children's day."

Strangely, the Eighth Air Force made little use of Oboe. In early 1943 the British did not want it risked over Germany in planes that were a lot more likely to be shot down than Mosquitos. Later experiments were plagued by equipment failure, while the limited range of Oboe probably discouraged more effort to make it work. Even in late 1944, with more and better equipment and far more experience, over half the radar missions failed. One advantage of such missions, however, was that the Germans were reluctant to send their pilots, who now were not usually instrument trained, through solid overcast. They eventually formed two special "bad weather units," Jagdgeschwader 300 and 301, of pilots who could be trusted in such conditions.[9]

A SECOND BLITZ WEEK

On October 4 a mission to Frankfurt and the Saar was foiled by bad weather. Then better conditions allowed a series of missions reminiscent of Blitz Week, culminating in the horrifying second attack on Schweinfurt. On October 8 the Americans attacked the aircraft plant at Bremen and the U-boat yards there and at Vegesack, using Carpet, a jammer to deal with German gun-laying radar, for the first time. As soon as the P-47s turned back there was tough opposition, and 30 of the 399 bombers dispatched were lost.

This was followed, on October 9, by an unusual mission deep into the Baltic by 378 B-17s and B-24s. As a diversion to attract the Luftwaffe, one force attacked an aircraft plant at Anklam, while other forces struck further east, at the Focke-Wulf plant at Marienburg in East Prussia, the U-board yards at Danzig, and the Polish port of Gdynia. The diversion succeeded, at a high cost; the Anklam force lost 18 of the 106 bombers that reached the target. (The other forces lost 10 planes in all.) There was little flak at Marienburg; the B-17s bombed from just 11,000 to 14,500 feet with great accuracy, using an effective new weapon, the M47A2 napalm-filled bomb. Smoke screens foiled the attack on Danzig and hampered the one on Gdynia, which nevertheless did severe damage. Overall, the mission was a remarkable success, but it was to a relatively lightly defended area.

The next mission, on October 10, was also unusual. While the B-24s flew a diversion, 274 B-17s went to Münster to disrupt rail and waterway traffic, not by hitting transportation facilities but by bombing the residential center of the city to kill the railroad workers. Bomber Command never aimed so frankly at killing German civilians as the Eighth Air Force did at Münster. It was a strange choice of targets in other ways; transportation was not a high-priority target at this time, and even a destructive isolated attack would not hurt Germany's flexible rail system. (As we shall see later, however, attacks on a few targets, one near Münster, could have wrecked the German *waterway* system.) Münster was deep in Germany, and the Eighth was likely to meet strong opposition. Morality apart, the mission was of doubtful wisdom.

It was a nightmare. Plans to provide escort all the way to Münster miscarried. The 56th Fighter Group, which was to take the bombers to the target, joined the Fortresses late and had to leave early; 200 German fighters then piled into the leading combat wing. Twin-engine fighters, and even bombers, fired rockets and large-caliber cannon, while single-engine fighters attacked head-on, destroying all 12 planes of the leading 100th Bomb Group. Then the Germans hit the 390th Group, flying the high position, and destroyed half its planes. The battle lasted until the withdrawal escort arrived. In all, 30 bombers were lost and 3 written off. Two groups of the relatively unhurt second task force, forced off the bomb run at Münster by mistake, completed the disaster. Trying to hit an airfield at Entschede in the Netherlands as a "target of opportunity," they accidentally killed 155 Dutch civilians. It was not one of the Eighth Air Force's better days.[10]

SCHWEINFURT II

Weather and the need for rest prevented operations for three days. The Eighth had already lost 88 bombers, as many as in the whole of the first Blitz Week.

Now it had to return to Schweinfurt, the hardest target of all. Photographs had shown that repairs there were proceeding rapidly. Eaker had put off the dreaded day, hoping to have some P-38s to sweep in front of the bombers most of the way to Schweinfurt. But the P-38s were not ready. There would be no escort most of the way, but the mission was carefully planned to take the maximum advantage of mass, while making it hard for the same German fighters to hit more than one bomber division on a single sortie. The 1st Bombardment Division would lead the attack, and the 3rd Division would fly a parallel course slightly farther south and 30 minutes behind it. Near Aachen their courses would diverge; the 3rd Division would fly south for a time before turning sharply east to Schweinfurt. The 2nd Division's B-24s would fly farther south, and come in to the target right behind the 3rd Division. If the factories could not be seen, they would hit the center of the city.

Morale was already low; the men received the news that they were going to Schweinfurt with shock. Some returned to barracks to change into their best uniforms, expecting to need them in the POW camps or to be buried in them. Gunners took aboard extra ammunition, sometimes so much that their officers ordered some of it removed; the planes were already overloaded.

Weather hampered the force. Just 29 of the 60 B-24s got into formation, too few to enter enemy territory, so the 2nd Division flew a diversion over the North Sea. Many Fortresses aborted; 383 took off, but only 291 set out across the English Channel.

Small forces of German fighters went for bombers of both divisions before the escorts left; the Thunderbolts destroyed 13 fighters, while losing two planes themselves. (Three more P-47s were junked after return.) Over the Rhineland, between Aachen and Düren, the P-47s turned back. Then the main German attacks on the 1st Division started. Stukas staggered above the B-17s to drop time-fused bombs, but fighters, aided by some rocket-carrying bombers, were the main enemy, in the most furious air battle of the war. The Germans used the same tactics as at Münster, concentrating on a single formation at a time. Single-engine fighters, some using rockets, mostly attacked from head-on or just off to the side. Twin-engine fighters and bombers came in from the rear. Standing out to one side to avoid the tail guns, they fired rockets and blasted away with heavy cannon. On this mission they left crippled planes to the single-engine fighters; their aim was to disrupt the formations. The Germans concentrated on the 1st Division; the 3rd's turn apparently confused them, and it suffered less.

Despite terrible losses, about 228 planes reached Schweinfurt, bombing with remarkable accuracy. Then the Germans hounded the B-17s right back to the coast, as weather prevented the arrival of the withdrawal escort. Over Europe, 60 bombers went down, and another 5 crashed in England; a dozen more had to be scrapped. Of the men, 605 were missing or dead, and 43 wounded. Morale at American bomber bases hit rock bottom.

As after Ploesti, the extent of the losses caused widespread questions. President Roosevelt held an embarrassing press conference, notable for its obfuscations.

General Arnold claimed, "The opposition isn't nearly what it was, and we are wearing them down." The wild claim that the enemy had lost over 700 planes in the first half of October was played up. (The Americans had claimed 186 on October 14 alone, when the actual German losses were 43.)

But the men in England knew better. Schweinfurt had shown that unescorted attacks deep into Germany were not even tolerable as occasional enterprises in the interim before the Eighth received long-range fighters. Unlike the August 17 mission, this one had been as well planned and executed as such an operation could possible be; after hours of the fiercest imaginable attack, the bombing had been better than could have reasonably been expected. One or two more Schweinfurts could break the Eighth Air Force. It never again ventured in strength beyond fighter escort. Small ball bearings plants in France and Italy were hit, but the Allies did not strike Schweinfurt again until late February 1944.[11]

This was a good thing for the Germans. The factories at Schweinfurt had been badly damaged; more incendiaries had been used than in the first attack, and fires raged. The flames did more damage to tools than anything but a direct hit by HE bombs would have done. The Americans, analyzing reconnaissance photographs and receiving pleasant reports from Swedish sources, were optimistic. Speer, in a near panic, appointed Philip Kessler, his most trusted associate, commissioner of ball bearings production. The Germans belatedly dispersed the industry and sought a porcelain substitute for metal bearings in nonprecision machinery.

After the war Speer estimated that armaments production would have been crucially weakened after two months and brought to a standstill in four if the Allies had made an all-out, continued attack on the ball bearings industry. His views have been widely cited and sound impressive, particularly since they were an indictment of his own failure to disperse the industry earlier. The immediate cause of the defeat of the ball bearings campaign was the American inability to continue the attacks and Harris's refusal to take part. But there is a good reason to think that Speer exaggerated, and that Allied analysts had been overenthusiastic about ball bearings as a target.

It soon became apparent that the damage to the ball bearings plants was less than the Americans and even the Germans themselves had supposed. The cleanup at the factories showed that perhaps just 10 percent of the machines were total losses. And the plants were so well organized that they could continue some production even after heavy damage. And most important, the Germans found that they were not so short of ball bearings as they had supposed! Kessler instituted a rigid system of controls, to insure that every bearing was found and properly used. Under his system it was discovered that the industries using them had six to twelve months' supplies of almost all types.

Additionally, the Allies had overestimated the time needed to replace the specialized machines needed by the ball bearings industry—it took four months instead of nine. The Germans received more help from Sweden than the Allies had expected. The Swedes had promised not to increase their exports of ball bearings beyond a certain monetary value, but they adjusted their exports to give the Germans exactly the types of bearings they needed most. Moreover, the Germans were able to redesign machinery to reduce the use of ball bearings much faster than the Allies had expected, and they substituted plain bearings for ball bearings far more easily than had been supposed.[12]

Ball bearings as a target system had proven a false trail, and the fortunes of the Eighth Air Force had reached their nadir.

The Struggle for Air Superiority, November 1943–April 1944

The Eighth Air Force soon recovered its strength. A flow of replacements and new units, better trained than earlier arrivals, made it stronger than ever. The Eighth had grown from 20 complete heavy bomber groups in October to 25 by the end of 1943. VIIIth Fighter Command grew to 12 groups. The groups themselves were being strengthened, so that instead of putting up three squadrons of 16 planes each, some groups were starting to fly two separate, A and B groups, each of three 12-plane squadrons, more manageable than the standard 16-plane units.

Moreover, the Eighth was getting support from other forces. During October the Ninth Air Force headquarters arrived from the Mediterranean. It would control the U.S. tactical air forces supporting the cross-channel invasion; in the meantime it would support the Eighth. The Eighth's B-26 units were transferred to it, and in November it received three fighter groups from the States; one, the 354th, would play a particularly important part in the struggle for air superiority over Germany. On November 1 a new strategic air force, the Fifteenth, under General James Doolittle, was formed in the Mediterranean. Based at Foggia, in Italy, it would support the Eighth, attacking aircraft plants in southern Germany and in Austria, Hungary, and Romania. It took over the heavy bombers and some of the fighters of the Twelfth and Ninth Air Forces, starting its existence with 6 heavy bomber groups and just 4 not fully equipped fighter groups. The plan was to build the Fifteenth up to a force of 21 heavy groups (15 diverted from the Eighth) and 7 fighter groups by April 1944.

High hopes were entertained for the Fifteenth. General Arnold's headquarters hoped it would split the defending German forces, encounter better weather conditions during the winter, and hit some targets that were inaccessible, or not easily reached, from England.

Eaker and the British were less enthusiastic. They held that most of the objectives within the Fifteenth's radius of operations—Ploesti was an outstanding exception—could be hit by the Eighth, and warned that the weather over Germany, not over the bombers' bases, was the critical factor. And the Alps would be a serious obstacle to the return of damaged planes. These views proved well founded; even the weather over Italy proved worse than expected. Base facilities in Italy were inadequate, and their improvement was slow. The Fifteenth was not established in the Foggia area until the end of December. It made only a few attacks, mostly against Wiener Neustadt, before 1944. Then its buildup picked up speed; three B-24 groups arrived in the Mediterranean every month from December through February.

In practice, the overwhelming burden of the struggle continued to rest on the Eighth Air Force, and particularly its fighters. The Eighth had long had priority over other theaters for long-range fighters, but many of the latter had been allocated to reconnaissance units. The first P-51B Mustangs were slated for the Ninth Air Force, not the Eighth, but after Schweinfurt, the Eighth's priority became absolute. From October to December all new P-38s and P-51Bs would go to England. The British agreed that the RAF squadrons scheduled to receive Mustangs would escort the Eighth.[1] But as the climactic struggle for air superiority began, there were terribly few long-range fighters.

The Luftwaffe's victory had been decisive, yet conditional. It had stopped the Americans from attacking well inside Germany, and it was growing in strength, but its own losses had been heavy. In the West alone it had lost 248 single-engine fighters (16 percent of the force) in August, 276 in September, and 284 in October. In all theaters together, it usually lost 30 to 40 percent of its fighters every month, while its fighter production was under attack. Some Luftwaffe officers were worried. Gen. Hubert Weise, who commanded the defense of central Germany, presciently suggested on November 6 that at least some twin-engine day fighter units be reequipped with single-engine planes. But as late as February 1944 most German officers did not believe that Allied fighters would fly east of Brunswick. And the Luftwaffe's equipment and tactics had become increasingly oriented toward attacking unescorted bombers, not dealing with Allied fighters.[2]

THE BATTLE OF BREMEN

The heavy bombers stayed on the ground for some days after Schweinfurt. Then attempts to hit nonferrous metals plants at Düren, within P-47 range, were foiled by weather and the failure of Oboe equipment.

Overcast persisted over Germany. In their inadequate cold-weather gear, bomber crewmen shivered through a miserable fall and winter. There was no visual bombing of Germany for the rest of 1943; until mid-February 1944 the Eighth depended on bombing by radar.

The next mission typified the fighting of the next few months. On November 3 the Eighth introduced H2X, the three-centimeter American version of H2S. It sent 566 bombers, the largest force yet put in the air, to Wilhelmshaven; 539 reached the target. They were escorted all the way, the 55th Group's P-38s supplying escort in the target area. Only 7 bombers and 3 fighters were lost; the P-38s downed 3 German fighters. H2X worked well, and the bombs damaged a shipyard.

But that sort of target no longer had a high priority. During November and December the Eighth flew to ports and a few inland industrial areas, selected because they promised a good picture on the H2X screen and lay inside escort range, rather than their intrinsic importance. Bremen alone was attacked six times; some spoke of the late 1943 operations as the Battle of Bremen. The limitations were unfortunate, for the Eighth's striking power was growing. By late December it was sending over 700 bombers on a single mission.

Only on some missions to France and Norway did the Americans actually see a target. On November 16 they went to Norway, bombing the molybdenum mine and refining plant at Knaben, which had been damaged by RAF Mosquitos on March 3. It was the enemy's biggest source of molybdenum, vital for steel alloys, which Speer would say had been a good target. But the Allies did not hit the plant hard and often enough to end production, and German metallurgists, with some difficulty, got around the shortage of molybdenum. The bombers also attacked the plant at Rjukan, which produced heavy water for nuclear research. It had been rebuilt after Norwegians working for the British wrecked it. The bomber attack was not too successful, but the Nazis moved the plant to Germany.[3]

Weather had reduced the Americans to a not very effective form of area bombing that did little harm to the enemy war effort. But they cut into the enemy's air strength. General Weise's fears were borne out spectacularly over Emden on December 11; Thunderbolts of the 56th Group massacred 14 of 30 attacking Me-110s. The bombers were well protected, although sometimes at a high cost to the escorting fighters, which were often pitifully few by the time a distant target was reached.

While doing a remarkable job of protecting the bombers, the P-38s, which formed the target-area escort on distant missions, suffered tremendous operational difficulties. The P-38's cockpit was inadequately heated, and the windshield often frosted up. Pilots even suffered frostbite. The P-38's engines were subject to an almost endless series of woes. Half or more of the P-38 losses in the winter of 1943-1944 were due to mechanical problems.

At first sight this was puzzling, for the Lightning had piled up a fine record in the Mediterranean and the Pacific. But conditions in other theaters were very different from those in Northern Europe. After the pilots had realized that the P-38, like other Allied planes, could not match the very maneuverable Japanese fighters in a dogfight, they found it superior in almost every other respect. They easily outdived Japanese planes, without going into a very fast or steep dive, and they rarely flew above 25,000 feet. Conditions in the Mediterranean were not too different. There the German fighters, usually escorting their own bombers and transports or covering convoys, rarely flew very high. Most combat took place below 20,000 feet, where the Lightning was better in most respects than the FW-190 and Me-109. Operations at 30,000 feet or more, in the cold and damp of a European winter, were something else.

Even when it functioned properly, the Lightning was not well suited, in its current form, for high-altitude escort in Europe. At 30,000 feet its acceleration and rate of roll were poor. Moreover, it suffered from "compressibility" in a fast dive; the Germans could dive away from American pilots, who were rightly afraid that compressibility would tear their planes apart. The twin engines, which gave pilots in the Pacific security against engine failure on long overwater flights, were a drawback over Germany. The ability to fly on one engine proved of little use; when one engine was hit, it caught fire, and the pilot had to bail out.

At least some of these faults were corrected, albeit slowly. Later-model P-38Js had adequate cockpit heaters and windscreen defrosters, better electrical and engine-cooling systems, and bigger fuel tanks. P-38J-25s and P-38Ls, which arrived still later, had hydraulically boosted ailerons and electrically operated dive flaps. They could take on Me-109s and FW-190s even at high altitude. At least some of these improvements, particularly the cockpit heating and dive flaps, could have been made much earlier.[4] But by the time the Lightning was improved, it was no longer needed. The Eighth and Ninth air forces were converting to another plane without its problems, and one much easier to build: the P-51 Mustang.

THE P-51

The P-51 developed in an unusual way. In 1940 the British had asked the North American Aviation Company to build P-40s for them. North American's president demurred, suggesting that his engineers could quickly develop a much better plane. Accordingly, North American's Edgar Schmued designed a fighter that somewhat resembled the Me-109 (which led to unfortunate mistakes in combat) but incorporated the novelty of laminar-flow, low-drag wings and an aerodynamic cooling scoop under the fuselage. The first "NA-73" was rolled out just 127 days after the British gave the go-ahead—an amazingly short period of development. Tests showed that it was fast at low altitude and handled well. But its inadequate Allison engine did not deliver enough power at high altitudes to make it a match for German fighters. Deliveries to the British, who dubbed it the Mustang, began in November 1941. They used it for strafing and reconnaissance. The Mustang had a remarkably long range; it attacked targets in Norway and well inside Germany.

The British gave the fifth and tenth Mustangs built to the AAF for testing, but the Air Material Command showed little interest. General Eaker, however, flew a Mustang in December 1941 and thought it a good plane despite its poor high-altitude performance. He commended it to Spaatz and Arnold. Arnold overruled the Air Material Command and ordered Mustangs procured for the AAF as P-51As. Some were later modified as reconnaissance planes and as A-36 dive-bombers.

As far as the AAF was concerned, the Mustang remained of secondary importance. When the need for a new long-range escort fighter became clear in 1942–1943, the Air Material Command concentrated on another plane, the General Motors P-75. Huge, and clumsy, it was composed of subassemblies used in other fighters, hastily slapped together. This made it easy to build, but fighter specialists deemed it hopelessly unstable and unmaneuverable.

Some people wondered what the Mustang would be like with a better engine, like the Rolls Royce Merlin that powered the Spitfire. In May 1942 Rolls Royce itself obtained several Mustangs in which to try out the Merlin. Testing did not start until October and was not entirely satisfactory; and American pilot who tried the modified Mustang thought its directional stability poor. But British officials, including Churchill himself, urged the Americans to look into it, as did Thomas Hitchcock, the influential assistant military attaché of the U.S. Embassy in London.

The Packard car company had been making Merlins in the United States since September 1941. North American's own engineers finally tested Packard Merlins in Mustangs in November 1942. They found that the engines overheated; the radiators had to be modified. As the need for longer range was stressed, more fuel tanks were added behind the pilot and in the wings. At first even the North American engineers doubted that the P-51 could take the added weight, but tests with tanks filled with water showed that it could. The AAF ordered 2,200 of the Merlin-powered P-51Bs, but Arnold did not give the Mustang all-out priority until after June 1943, possibly fearing that it would interfere with production of the proven Thunderbolt. Nor were all P-51Bs allotted to the Eighth Air Force until October. But these were just the last of a series of unnecessary blunders made with the Mustang. Arnold later admitted that the fact that it was not available sooner was the AAF's own fault. It seems likely that, had the AAF shown more interest in the Mustang and tried Packard Merlins in it as soon as they became available, the Eighth Air Force would have had P-51Bs by early 1943.

Belated or not, the P-51B was a remarkable plane. Its profile and big fuel tanks, and the low fuel consumption of the Merlin—half that of the Pratt and Whitney in the P-47—gave it tremendous range. On its internal tanks alone it could fly 475 miles and back; with two 75-gallon tanks under the wings it had a radius of 650 miles; and with two 108-gallon tanks its radius leaped to 850 miles, making missions to any part of German-held Europe possible. It was faster than the existing models of the Me-109 and FW-190 in level flight, and outclimbed both. It could easily outdive the FW-190, and overhaul the Me-109 in a prolonged dive, and could outturn the Me-109 and, usually, the FW-190.

The first P-51Bs reached England in November 1943 and equipped the Ninth Air Force's 354th Fighter Group, which was assigned to escort duty with the Eighth. It flew its first mission, a fighter sweep, on December 1, and escorted bombers to Amiens on December 5. On December 11 the 354th took the bombers to Emden, and on December 20 it was engaged in a major battle over

Bremen. The P-51s and P-38s of the target-area escort stopped the German twin-engine fighters from getting at the bombers, although three P-51s were lost, for 3 enemy planes downed.

The Mustang still had some bugs in its engines and propellers. Its drop-tanks sometimes failed to feed, and there was a shortage of spare parts. Its guns often jammed, especially when fired while the plane was in a tight turn. Nevertheless, a new P-51 group, the 357th, would become operational in February, while the 4th Group was also converting to Mustangs.

Along with the arrival of the P-51B, other factors were improving the position of VIIIth Fighter Command. Another P-38 group, the 20th, finally became ready, while the P-47s received improved propellers, and water-injection systems for their engines. Plans were also afoot to extend the P-47's range. A bigger belly tank, carrying 165 gallons, gave it a radius of 425 miles, and there were plans to modify it so it could carry a 108-gallon drop-tank under each wing, providing a radius of 475 miles. (Later, in the Pacific, Thunderbolts flying to very distant targets carried a 310-gallon tank under one wing and a 165-gallon tank under the other, but such extravagant loads proved unnecessary in Europe.)[5]

The Mustang did not, by itself, as is sometimes supposed, save the Eighth Air Force from defeat or secure air superiority over Europe. In fact, the coming battles for the air over Germany were fought mostly by Thunderbolts. The extension of the P-47's range and the improvements to the P-38 would probably have secured the same result, albeit more slowly and at a higher cost in lives and equipment, even had the Mustang never been built. But the new plane was a fortunate gift from a combination of British-government and private initiative, even if the AAF was slow to use it.

DAMAGE ASSESSMENT, 1943

Up to the end of 1943, the Allied bomber offensive, or perhaps "offensives" would be more accurate—had not done fatal or crippling damage to the Nazi war economy. The weight of attack had not been great enough. Lack of enough bombers; the British concentration on general area attack (a type of offensive that at any rate had been largely unavoidable until the latter half of 1943); erratic target selection; and the lack of escort for repeated attacks on targets deep in Germany had all contributed to this unsatisfactory result. The Allies had simply not hit any critical point in the enemy war effort hard enough. They had not prevented a massive rise in Nazi war production; they had merely made the rise smaller than it would have been otherwise.

Germany's failure to mobilize fully for war had left an unused cushion of machinery and manpower that was only now being rationally harnessed to the war effort. This achievement was largely due to Albert Speer. Hitler's appointment of his architect as minister of armaments production in February 1942, to succeed Fritz Todt, who had been killed in an air crash, had seemed to be a frivolous action, but it greatly prolonged the life of the Nazi regime. The jungle of competing authorities and personal rivalries of the Nazi leaders was not destroyed but was tamed; Speer could count on the backing of Hitler and, for a time, Joseph Goebbels, one of the smarter Nazi leaders.

Following policies originated by Todt, Speer revitalized an already existing system of committees and directorates that had been set up to organize German industry for the war effort, and he established a centralized planning apparatus. But he avoided the bureaucratic excesses of most "planned" economies and did not suppose that he could control everything that went on in a complex industrial economy. Instead, most decision making devolved to the committees or "rings" dominating each industry. Central planning operated to set priorities, and as a board of appeal. Speer and his assistants cut through red tape and encouraged rationalization, standardization, and the application of the latest mass production methods, in which German industry had been somewhat backward. The price of this was inadequate statistics, and Speer did not always gear production efforts to the real needs of the war effort or even to other items being produced. But by the end of 1943 he had increased the overall production of weapons and equipment by about 50 percent over the level when he had taken over. This figure was higher in some crucial sectors; tank production rose from 600 per month in late 1942 to 1,250 a month a year later.[6]

Allied air attacks, especially those of the British, had begun to have an effect, but only in certain sectors, and repair work had been quick. The Germans got around any shortages. Ruhr steel production was cut about 8 percent, but the stocks of steel in the hands of producers tided them over. The areas attacked largely recovered.

The Allies had struck serious blows at individual industries, however. The American attacks on fighter plants in the summer of 1943 had cut production by 25 percent and forced a limited amount of dispersal, which cost more production than the bombings themselves. The dispersal made the industry more vulnerable when the German transportation system was attacked in 1944. But the fighter force was nevertheless able to replace its losses and even expand.

Bombing, primarily during the Battle of Hamburg, cost the Germans about 30 U-boats in 1943, but these losses came almost entirely after the Battle of the Atlantic had already been decided at sea. The attacks did cause the Germans to build the new Type 21 and Type 23 U-boats in pieces inland. Only final assembly took place at the traditional construction yards. This probably delayed their arrival in service, and made this industry, also, more vulnerable to the attack on transportation later.

The development of other new weapons—the V-2 and new types of aircraft—was hampered by Allied air attacks. Overall, however, the Allies may have reduced the growing German output of armaments by about 5.5 percent. Speer later put the figure, dubiously, at 9 or 10 percent, but the inadequacy of surviving German statistics make all estimates rough.[7]

While the Allies had correctly estimated the damage to the Ruhr and Hamburg, they had overestimated the damage to Berlin, while underestimating the Germans' ability to recover. Moreover, they were confused by the fact that they had overestimated German war production in 1940–1942 and supposed that it had long ago been pushed to the maximum possible level. Eaker and Portal concluded, late in 1943, that 10 percent of the enemy's "war potential" had been destroyed. What was actually going on in Germany was not understood until after the war. That the war crazy Nazis had failed to fully mobilize until after they had effectively lost the war was something too fantastic to be believed. It was still generally thought that German morale might crack; in fact, contrary to what is sometimes claimed, it did decline under the bombing, but there was no question of its breaking. Increasingly, much of the task of production was carried out by slave laborers, mostly from Eastern Europe, and their "morale" was immune from attack; they had never had any to start with.

The Allied air forces had thus failed, though perhaps by a narrow margin, to strike a decisive blow. Not only had they clearly failed to fulfill any hopes their commanders had had to defeat Nazi Germany without an invasion, something the top Allied leaders had never expected, but they had failed to fulfill the 1943 plan for a combined bomber offensive. In terms of war production, the enemy was stronger than ever.

Nevertheless, the Allies had struck a major blow by forcing the Germans to divert gigantic efforts to defense against air attacks and repairs; 1–1.5 million workers were devoted to cleaning up and rebuilding. While most of these workers were slave laborers, an irreducible minimum of German skilled workers were needed for repair work. The effort devoted to air defense was considerable; by late 1943 the Germans had deployed 8,876 88-mm. guns and 24,500 light and medium guns to defend the Reich, all of which would have been useful in ground operations—the 88 was the best antitank gun of the war. Antiaircraft guns cost about twice as much labor as ground weapons of comparable caliber. The Germans had also deployed 7,000 searchlights, and both the heavier guns and the lights had their own radar sets. A third of the optical industry, and half of the electronics industry, was devoted to air defense work. The Germans now had some 1,650 fighters, the vast majority of all they had, in Germany and the Western-occupied countries to defend against the strategic bombers. They had also been provoked into investing in futile retaliatory efforts, like the development of the V-weapons and a renewed bomber offensive against London, the Little Blitz.[8]

COMMAND ARRANGEMENTS AND STRATEGY, 1943–1944

The looming invasion of France, American dissatisfaction with the course of the strategic air offensive, and the need to coordinate the heavy bomber forces, now striking from Italy as well as from England, forced changes in the command arrangements and strategy governing the bomber effort.

To control the Allied Expeditionary Air Forces, which was the name of the tactical air operations for Operation Overlord, a headquarters was activated on

November 25. Its commander, Air Marshal Sir Trafford Leigh-Mallory, was disliked and distrusted by many British officers, and by most Americans other than Eisenhower. Leigh-Mallory would control the British Second Tactical and U.S. Ninth air forces. His precise authority beyond that, however, was not absolutely defined.

American officers feared that Leigh-Mallory would intrude on strategic operations excessively. They wanted an inter-Allied headquarters, to control all strategic air forces operating against Germany, including RAF Bomber Command, an idea the British opposed. To coordinate their own operations and limit Leigh-Mallory's influence, the Americans formed the U.S. Strategic Air Forces in Europe (USSTAF) on January 1. This was actually the old Eighth Air Force headquarters, renamed and put under General Spaatz, and it controlled the Eighth and Fifteen air forces. VIIIth Bomber Command disappeared; its headquarters became the new headquarters of the Eighth Air Force, under General Doolittle, a man whose contribution to the development of aviation would be hard to exaggerate. Gen. Nathan Twining took over the Fifteenth. Eaker went to the Mediterranean to head the newly established Mediterranean Allied Air Forces. He and others considered this a sort of demotion, but it is now known that Eaker's transfer was instigated by Eisenhower. He had nothing against Eaker, but preferred the air commanders who had served him well in the Mediterranean. They continued to serve him well in 1944 and 1945.

The Americans pressed for the revision of the directive of June 1943, against weakening British resistance. In mid-February the Combined Chiefs of Staff issued a new directive governing the strategic air forces. Their overall mission remained the "progressive destruction and dislocation of German military, industrial, and economic system, the disruption of vital elements of lines of communication, and material reduction of German air combat strength by successful prosecution of Combined Bomber offensive from all convenient bases."[9] There were no phrases about attacking enemy morale, the convenient loophole through which Harris had wriggled before. The primary objective was the German air force; attacks on fighter and ball bearings production shared an equal first priority. Second priority, under this objective, went to "installations supporting the German fighter force."[10] Attacks on V-weapons (Crossbow) had third priority, followed by attacks on Berlin and other industrial areas, when weather was unsuitable for operations against the primary objective. Allied forces in the Mediterranean would strike cities, transportation targets, and other objectives in Southeastern Europe, when conditions for operations against the German air force or in support of operations in Italy were impossible. (The Allies hoped to encourage the Axis satellites, especially Romania, to get out of the war.) Compared to the directive of June 1943, this proved short lived. The Combined Bomber Offensive had only a few weeks to run. Operations designed to directly prepare for Overlord would be needed.[11]

NEW POLICIES

By January 1944 it was clear that the decisive battle for air supremacy would not be long delayed. Doolittle made important changes in policy, at least two of which were not calculated to make him popular with bomber crews. He extended their tours from 25 to 30 missions and agreed with General Kepner's recommendation to cut the fighters loose from the bombers. As a rule only a third of each fighter group need stay near the heavies; the rest could attack and freely chase the enemy on sight. It proved a wise decision. Escort tactics were modified in other ways. Instead of joining the bombers at a predetermined point and flying along with them until relieved by another unit, each group would patrol an area through which the bombers passed. And once an escort group finished its task, it could go down and strafe enemy targets, especially airfields. Although strafing proved expensive—German light flak was very dangerous—it cost the enemy many planes at crucial moments and disrupted the German practice of landing after a first interception to refuel and rearm for a second sortie.[12]

PREPARING FOR "BIG WEEK"

As far back as November the Americans had planned a massive new attack on the German aircraft industry by both the Eighth and Fifteenth air forces. The RAF agreed to join by launching area attacks on the cities in which the aircraft plants were located. The plan was expected to be costly and needed a week of clear weather over Germany, as well as reasonable weather over England and Italy. But the weather over Germany remained miserable for almost all of the first seven weeks of 1944. Until late February the Eighth was able to carry out just two visual missions over Germany, and one of these was partly abortive and the other a lucky accident. The Fifteenth Air Force was tied down, hitting nearby targets in support of the Anzio beachhead, which was in grave danger from a German counteroffensive.

The Eighth continued radar bombing. Some radar missions were effective; the IG Farben chemical plant at Ludwigshafen was damaged twice. And the fighter escort did better. In November and December the P-51s and P-38s of the target-area escort had often been hard pressed to defend their charges and sometimes suffered lopsided losses themselves to the Germans. In early 1944 the bombers still suffered dreadfully sometimes, but even small forces of American fighters usually inflicted disproportionate losses on the attackers.

On January 11 conditions in Germany seemed promising for visual attack, and the Eighth put up 663 bombers. While the 1st Bombardment Division's B-17s would bomb the Oschersleben Focke Wulf plant and a Junkers plant at Halberstadt, the other two divisions would hit aircraft components and assembly plants that were building the Me-110s around Brunswick. If weather hid the targets, Brunswick itself would be bombed. With long-range fighters still few, only the 1st Division would be escorted all the way to the target. The Germans were expected to concentrate against it. Its target were farthest in, and it might seem to be going to Berlin. The other divisions would have to fend for themselves as they neared Brunswick.

The meteorologists had been overoptimistic; as the bombers flew into central Germany the weather deteriorated. The 2nd and 3rd Divisions were recalled, but the 1st was so close to its target that it was allowed to proceed. The commander of the 3rd Division's leading wing decided he too might as well go ahead, and he ignored the recall signal. Weather had interfered with the rendezvous of the escort (this was before the change in policy), and only one P-38 squadron and the 354th Fighter Group accompanied the 1st Division. The Germans reacted violently, and the biggest air battle since Schweinfurt resulted. The P-51s had rendezvoused late and were short of gas, and most left shortly after the bombers reached Oschersleben and Halberstadt. The Germans inflicted heavy losses on the bombers, although failing to disrupt a very accurate attack. In all, 60 bombers went down for 39 German fighters, even though the fighter-versus-fighter clashes were thoroughly in the Americans' favor. One Mustang pilot, Maj. James Howard, a Flying Tiger veteran, turned in a remarkable performance. Separated from the rest of his unit, he found himself the sole escort for a whole B-17 wing. He broke up attacks by 30 Me-110s and shot down four, despite having jammed guns. The Oschersleben mission, with its heavy losses, was hardly an Allied success, but on top of the Battle of Bremen it should have warned the Nazis that they would be in big trouble when the escorts became more numerous, and that the writing was on the wall for the twin-engine fighters. If anything, they were even more vulnerable to single-engine fighters than the B-17s.

Then the weather closed in. For two weeks the Americans could not strike Germany at all; then they resumed radar bombing. When the weather proved worse than expected, an attempted visual mission to Brunswick on January 30 had to fall back on H2X. Two groups passing Hannover saw a hole in the clouds and sensibly seized a chance to bomb the rubber plant there. This and the Oschersleben mission were the only visual attacks on German targets between October 14, 1943, and February 20, 1944.[13]

BIG WEEK

On February 19 the USSTAF's meteorologists finally predicted a stretch of clear weather suited for visual attacks on aircraft and ball bearings targets. Their colleagues at the Eighth and Ninth Air Forces disagreed, not without reason, but Spaatz decided the Eighth should start Operation Argument. (Weather over the targets assigned to the Fifteenth did not allow the Italy-based force to join in.) As it was, the mission of February 20 was the largest yet mounted. Sixteen combat wings of bombers, over 1,000 planes, took off; 878 completed their missions. A massive escort force was put up by seventeen Eighth and Ninth Air Force groups (thirteen P-47, two P-38, and two P-51 groups) and sixteen RAF squadrons. Despite the massive number of fighters, the escort at the far end

would be thin, and as on January 11, the Americans took the gamble of sending part of the force unescorted. The 3rd Bombardment Division's six combat
wings would cross Denmark to strike aircraft plants at Tutow in northeast Germany and Poznan in Poland, without fighters. Ten combat wings from the other
two divisions would attack nine targets around Brunswick and Leipzig in central Germany; these ten wings had all the escort, and their flight was timed to
prevent the enemy from concentrating against the 3rd Division.

The Germans did not attack the northern force heavily, but because of clouds
the gamble nevertheless did not pay off. Tutow had to be bombed on radar,
and the force slated for Poznan went to Rostock instead. The central German
targets were mostly in the clear, and the aircraft plants around Leipzig were heavily bombed. The German fighters reacted strongly, but all the bomber forces
together lost only 21 planes (5 more were written off), while the escort claimed
the destruction of 61 German fighters, for the loss of only 4 American fighters.
Another Me-110 unit was massacred, as 18 of 24 planes were shot down. That
night the RAF joined the assault with a selective area attack on Stuttgart, of
the sort Bottomley had sought for so long.

On February 21 the Eighth launched another all-out effort (weather kept the
Fifteenth on the ground again) against six Luftwaffe installations and two plants
at Brunswick producing parts for Me-110s. Cloud forced the Eighth to bomb
Brunswick on radar, and the factories were not hit; 16 bombers went down and
another 7 were written off, while American fighters claimed 33 German fighters
for 5 of their own lost.

But the prospects for visual bombing over the next few days looked good,
and the operation went on. It was decided to strike Schweinfurt and aircraft
plants in the central area, and the Fifteenth would finally join in by attacking
Regensburg. It operated without escort.

Yet again, the weather interfered with the Eighth's operations. Only the 1st
Division hit some of its primary targets, damaging two plants building Junkers
88s. This third day's mission proved costly. The Germans struck the American
force *before* it was deep in Germany, in an area where the escort was thin, destroying 41 bombers of the Eighth and 14 more of the Fifteenth. The Eighth's escort
fighters again claimed a lopsided 59 Germans for the loss of 11 American fighters.
Bad weather gave the Eighth Air Force a break on February 23, while the Fifteenth made a small attack on a ball bearings plant at Steyr, in Austria.

On February 24, after four months, the B-17s returned to Schweinfurt, as B-24s
struck an Me-110 plant at Gotha. It was hoped that these attacks, and one by
the Fifteenth Air Force on Steyr, would attract the enemy fighters and let five
wings hit the targets in northeast Germany that had been saved by weather
on February 20. The ploy worked, at heavy cost to the forces attacking Gotha
and Steyr, but weather again forced an attack on Rostock. The targets at Gotha
and Schweinfurt were hit hard, but ball bearing production there had already
been dispersed. The Eighth lost 44 bombers of 505, and the Fifteenth lost 17
of a force of just 87. American fighters claimed 38 German planes for 10 of their
own lost. That night Bomber Command finally struck Schweinfurt.

On February 25 the weather allowed a last day of concentrated effort. The Eighth attacked the ball bearings plant at Stuttgart and aircraft plants at Augsburg, Fürth, and Regensburg; the Fifteenth struck another plant at Regensburg. The Germans concentrated on the Fifteenth's bomber force, which had no escort in the target area, downing 33 of its 176 planes, while the Eighth lost 31 bombers of the 754 dispatched and junked another 3. The Eighth's escort claimed 26 German planes for 3 missing in action and 2 more damaged beyond repair. The bombing was very accurate, and more concentrated against single-engine fighter plants than previous attacks. Then the weather closed in; Big Week was at an end. When the Eighth next visited Brunswick on February 29, it bombed on radar.

The Eighth and Fifteenth Air Forces together had lost 226 heavy bombers and 28 fighters, and about 2,600 men. The RAF had lost 157 bombers, while dropping 9,000 tons of bombs on Schweinfurt, Augsburg, Steyr, and Leipzig. The Eighth had dropped 10,000 tons of bombs, nearly 4,000 of which fell on aircraft plants.

The attacks on ball bearings production simply failed, for reasons already discussed. The results of the attacks on the aircraft industry were more complex. The United States Strategic Bombing Survey later estimated that the Big Week attacks on aircraft plants cost the Germans about two months production, suggesting that the Germans lost 2,500 planes, including 500 shot down in the air. At least 1,000 planes (possibly more), finished but not yet tested, were destroyed at the factories, while another 1,000 were never built at all. But the Germans' energetic recovery measures paid off. They found that even in buildings that were completely wrecked, tools and equipment had survived under fallen girders and rubble and could be recovered. They salvaged 160 damaged Me-109s from the ruined Erla plant at Leipzig. Moreover, the attacks as carried out (rather than as planned), fell disproportionately on plants making the twin-engine fighters, the value of which was now in sharp decline.[14]

The Germans hastily began a more radical policy of dispersing the aircraft industry, into a mass of small targets almost immune to economical direct attack. This policy was costly in labor and rendered the industry even more vulnerable to the disruption of transportation which began later in 1944. The attack on the Messerschmitt plant at Augsburg further delayed the development of the Me-262 jet fighter. All this gave a definite, if delayed, value to the Big Week bombings. Although the Army Air Force's official historians later argued that the bombings had denied the Germans many hundreds of planes at a crucial moment before the invasion of France, in fact the Germans replaced the lost planes. During the whole first half of 1944 the number of serviceable aircraft in the Luftwaffe fell only slightly. It would seem that the bombers would have been better occupied striking other targets.

But the Germans could not replace good pilots. The true value of Big Week was the destruction of German planes, and pilots, in the air. The heavy bombers served as the anvil on which the escort fighters hammered the Luftwaffe fighter force. The effectiveness of the Mustang is suggested by the fact that the 354th Group, the only unit with much experience with it, claimed 46.5 German fighters for only 3 Mustangs lost during Big Week.

Actual German losses are unclear; their records were jumbled, and a variety of figures can be extracted. In January they had lost 307 fighters (day and night) in the West alone, and 292 fighter pilots, or 12.1 percent of the total available at the start of the month, in all theaters. In February they probably lost at least 355 day fighters alone, and a total of 225 pilots and crewmen in combat over Germany. Other figures for that month suggest that combat losses in February may have been as high as 533 planes in the West alone, including 65 night fighters, with 434 total fighter pilot losses from all causes in all theaters, of 17.9 percent of the total pilot force at the start of the month. Whatever the real numbers were—and pilot losses were probably more carefully recorded than losses of planes, something at which the Luftwaffe was sloppy—the Germans were losing a massive proportion of their trained men. After Big Week they no longer always resisted American attacks all-out. Some attacks were almost ignored, while others were fiercely opposed.[15] Outside "Greater Germany" the Nazis did not seriously contest attacks, save on Ploesti.

BERLIN

Big Week was just the opening blow of the climactic struggle for the air. During March and April the Eighth Air Force alone attacked aircraft and ball bearings targets in Germany on 27 days; when the weather there was impossible, it hit V-weapons sites and airfields in France in preparation for D-Day. The Fifteenth Air Force, which still had no Mustangs, was unable to strike Germany and Austria during March; in April it concentrated mainly on the Ploesti refineries.

In March the Americans' operations focused for the first time on Berlin. They were anxious to smash the Erkner ball bearing plant and several plants producing complete planes and engines, and electrical components for planes and vehicles. The Americans were conscious of the prestige and morale factors involved in striking at the enemy capital; these insured that the Nazis would fight over Berlin and enable the Americans to grind them down before D-Day.

Spaatz was eager to get going; on March 3 and 4 the Eighth set out under conditions that were not really suitable. The March 3 mission proved entirely abortive, and on March 4 most of the force turned back. Just 30 B-17s reached Berlin and bombed on radar. They were covered by only a bit more than one group of badly scattered Mustangs, but the Luftwaffe missed a chance to crush a weak American force. The weather proved a worse enemy; 24 American fighters did not return. The Germans were not, however, reluctant to fight. They had readied four special "high-altitude" groups of lightened Me-109s with special engines to tackle the escort fighters, enabling the logier standard Me-109s and FW-190s to get at the bombers.

On March 6 the weather was finally suitable for an attack on Berlin; 730 bombers set out, and 672 reached Germany, accompanied by 801 fighters. For the first time, some P-47s carried two 108-gallon drop-tanks. The Americans planned to hit the Erkner plant, an engine plant, and an electrical equipment plant. It proved the costliest mission, in terms of absolute losses, ever mounted by the AAF in Europe. Over 400 German fighters intercepted. The Nazis took the extreme step of throwing many precious night fighters into a day battle, something they had recently avoided.

As the Americans passed Dümmer Lake and entered central Germany, the Germans hit the leading 1st Division hard. As the battle moved east, the German controllers perceived that the middle of the American bomber stream, the 3rd Division, was weakly escorted, and they moved to exploit this. Small forces of fighters tied down the American fighters covering the van and rear of the 3rd Division; then a hundred-odd German fighters swarmed all over the combat wing in the middle. Between fighters and unusually heavy losses to flak, the Americans lost 69 bombers and 11 fighters over Germany; 6 more bombers and 3 fighters were junked after returning to Britain. An incredible total of 347 bombers suffered some sort of damage. Moreover, overcast and scattering of the bomber formations rendered the attack a failure; the primary targets were not hit. But the Germans had suffered heavy losses too; some 66 fighters went down, and 36 pilots and crewmen were killed. Although the American losses in absolute terms were worse than those over Schweinfurt, they were inflicted on a much bigger force.

The Eighth returned to Berlin on March 8, sending 623 bombers escorted by 891 fighters. The Germans reacted less strongly than on March 6, but they found a weak spot again. This time the leading combat wing was poorly covered; 37 bombers and 18 fighters went down. However, the escort alone claimed 79 German planes in the air and another 8 on the ground. Conditions for bombing were much better, and the Erkner plant was wrecked.[16]

The weather, none too good in early March, was even worse for most of the rest of the month. Later missions to Berlin and other targets bombed mostly on radar. Only on March 16 and 18 did the weather permit visual attacks on aircraft plants in southern Germany. The Germans strongly opposed these missions and suffered heavy losses.

After the 4th Fighter Group massacred another twin-engine fighter unit over Augsburg on March 16, the Germans employed them only in close conjunction with single-engine fighters. One group of "heavy" fighters would be closely escorted by two groups of Me-109s, and FW-190s. But this dangerously restricted the freedom of action of the lighter planes, and assembling the large formations that the Luftwaffe had become accustomed to throw against the bombers had already proven dangerous. It consumed fuel and flying time, and the gathering formations could be seen a long way off. American fighters, now ranging far from the bombers, often interrupted their assembly with fatal results. Allied tacticians thought that the Germans should have used small formations and left it up to their ground controllers to insure that the fighters arrived at the right place and time.

In March the Germans lost at least 357 day fighters downed, along with 94 night fighters, and over 300 German fighter pilots were killed over Germany alone. On all fronts from all causes during March, the Germans lost 511 fighter pilots, or 21.7 percent of the total at the start of the month. And several of those killed were among the Luftwaffe's ablest pilots.[17] The hammering of the Luftwaffe continued through April, as the weather improved. The aircraft industry continued to be the main target, as the Eighth revisited many of the plants in central and southern Germany that had been hit during Big Week, as well as Schweinfurt. Strong escort allowed attacks on aircraft plants in northeastern Germany as well. An attack on Marienburg, which had required a tricky and costly diversion in 1943, now involved no unusual risk.

When weather prevented the bombing of Germany, the fighters went alone on mass strafing missions against airfields and other targets. This was effective but costly; the Americans lost many more fighters to flak during strafing than to air combat. Few of their aces were shot down by German fighters, but many wound up behind barbed wire after one strafing pass too many.

To flush out the Luftwaffe, the Eighth struck Berlin twice in April; the second mission to the capital provoked the reaction the Americans wanted. But the Nazis began replacing the twin-engined fighter units with the Sturmgruppen, equipped with heavily armed and armored FW-190A-8s. They were sluggish and unmaneuverable, so each Sturmgruppe was covered by at least two groups of standard fighters. The drawbacks of such big formations have already been noted, but the FW-190A-8s were less vulnerable than their twin-engine counterparts and were deadly if they got at the bombers. When this happened, a single group of Allied bombers could suffer losses as bad as any over Schweinfurt, in minutes rather than hours. But the Luftwaffe only occasionally achieved a success of this sort.

After April, direct support of the coming invasion absorbed most the efforts of the British and American strategic air forces. March and April 1944 had seen the bitterest air fighting of the war. The Allies had broken the power of the Luftwaffe. The Eighth Air Force had played the most important role in this costly victory. In April it suffered its heaviest losses in the whole war; 512 planes (361 heavy bombers) had been lost and 65 more junked after returning to England. But more and more the losses were due to flak rather than fighters. By May 1944 the Germans no longer regularly intercepted Allied attacks, and when they did fight, some of their pilots seemed utterly incompetent.

Victory in the air had not been gained by bombing German factories; fighter production actually rose. After Big Week, Milch had willingly yielded control of production to Speer, while fighters finally gained overriding priority over bombers. Hitler refused to stop bomber production completely, but he even considered sending 100,000 Hungarian Jews to work as slave laborers in the fighter plants, instead of to Auschwitz. Speer saved him from this distasteful expedient, resorting to the same techniques that had saved ball bearing production. He appointed one of his assistants, Karl-Otto Saur, to head a special "fighter staff."

A member of the staff was permanently attached to each existing factory, even as dispersal to hundreds of sites, many hidden in forests, was hastened. Blast walls were placed around vital machinery, and all wood and other combustibles were removed from the plants. Over 100,000 more workers were gathered for repair and dispersal work; flying repair crews rushed to plants that had been bombed. The normal work week (for the German workers) was increased from 50–60 hours to 72 hours, and more in an "emergency." They received extra welfare services, food, and clothing in recompense.

Acceptances (not production) of new single-engine fighters reached 3,031, a peak for the whole war, in September 1944. Since acceptances lagged behind production, actual production must have peaked in July or August. In the whole of 1944 the Germans built 25,860 single-engine fighters, compared to only 9,626 in 1943. The figures may be misleading, since there is good reason to think that some of the "new" fighters were actually serious damaged planes that had been rebuilt in the factories. Nevertheless, even with this discount, more fighters rolled off the assembly lines than ever before.

The bombing of aircraft plants did hurt the introduction of new types of planes, however. The effect of the Allied attacks on jet production has already been noted. An attack on the Dornier plant at Friedrichshafen on March 18 wrecked the tooling-up of the Dornier 335, a very fast propeller-driven fighter of radical design; it never appeared in combat. Other attacks delayed production of the Tank 152, the planned successor to the FW-190.

It was not planes, but pilots, or at least adequately trained ones, that were lacking. The loss of pilots, on top of an inadequate training program, defeated the Luftwaffe. April 1944 had seen the loss of another 447 pilots, no less than 20.1 percent of those available. Already under strain in 1943, the Germans had nearly doubled the number of new fighter pilots being trained, but only at the cost of reducing the hours of training—and rushing inadequately trained men into combat. There, they inevitably suffered heavy losses against the better trained Allied pilots. Then their replacements, rushed through even faster, arrived even less well trained. A vicious downward spiral developed. From the spring of 1944 the German pilot force was composed of two disparate elements: a slowly declining core of extremely skilled veterans, far more experienced than almost any Allied pilots, and a mass of poorly trained new men, who rarely survived for long. To the end the Luftwaffe had plenty of planes, but on the increasingly rare occasions when it came up to fight, it stood little chance of success.[18]

Even after World War II, air combat, or at least fighter-versus-fighter combat, retained, for some, an aura of chivalry. Even many people who had no use for such ideas tended to see it as a relatively impersonal fight of machine versus machine. Fighter pilots tended to think of themselves as shooting at another plane, not at another man, and in the Western world, unlike the Japanese, most of them followed an unwritten law against firing at parachutes. But in blunt fact, victory over an opposing air force was gained by killing the opposing pilots. As General Sherman once said, "War is cruelty, and you cannot refine it."[19]

The Strategic Air Offensive and the Normandy Invasion, February–June 1944

The late winter and spring of 1944 was crowded with decisions and events powerfully affecting the strategic air offensive against Germany. The Americans, now supported by Bomber Command, had continued to attack the German aircraft and ball bearings industry and had won control of the air over Europe. In April and May they started a decisive offensive against enemy oil production, despite command changes and the diversion of much of the air effort to preparations for the invasion of France. All along, the aim of the strategic air offensive had been to pave the way for an invasion, but now it shifted to actions that promised a quick pay-off that would help the coming campaign. It did not change entirely, because General Eisenhower reposed great trust in Spaatz, accepting his suggestion that an offensive against enemy oil should begin in the midst of the preparations for D-Day. Nevertheless, there was a considerable reorientation of the strategic bombing effort, to attacks on airfields, V-weapon sites, and the railroad system in France and Belgium.

As the shift occurred, at the same time that the Americans were winning control of the air during the day, the British had suffered a shattering defeat at night. After the Nuremberg mission it was clear that without a radical change, Bomber Command could not continue attacks deep inside Germany. The independent area offensive had failed. The shift to targets in France and Belgium in support of Overlord hid the defeat, but it forced Bomber Command to belatedly develop, or perhaps discover, a capability for attacks on precision targets, something Harris had always denied was possible. In a short time the RAF was bombing more accurately at night than the Americans could even on a clear day, making area attacks obsolete. After the spring of 1944 the British could join the Americans against precise targets that were vital to the enemy war effort, and they could often hit them more effectively than the Americans could. But as we shall see, they did not always do so.

COMMAND ARRANGEMENTS AND PLANS

It had been apparent for some time that the strategic air forces had to be at Eisenhower's disposal. But how he would control them was a contended issue. No one wanted to trust Leigh-Mallory, the tactical air commander, with the heavy bombers as well. Churchill was willing to let Eisenhower control all the strategic air forces through his deputy supreme commander, Air Marshal Sir Arthur Tedder, but other British leaders regarded Bomber Command as a last "independent" arm of British action, and wished it to remain so. The Americans were insistent, and a nominal "compromise" reached on March 22, 1944, gave them what they wanted. The strategic air forces came under Eisenhower's direction, while Tedder would perform the actual task of coordinating them. Spaatz's USSTAF came directly under Eisenhower.

The formal transfer of control over the strategic air forces took place on April 14, but Eisenhower had begun informally exercising his powers at the end of March. Already, on March 10, the Ninth Air Force had shifted from support of the Eighth to preinvasion tasks, save for its Mustangs, which continued escorting the heavies. On April 1 the demands of the invasion received priority for all the Allied air forces.

This did not immediately cause a drastic change in the Eighth's operations. Eisenhower was sensible to the argument that missions to Germany were the best way to smash the Luftwaffe. Events vindicated this view. While the Eighth Air Force destroyed hundreds of planes in the air and on the ground in Germany itself, the tactical air forces' attacks in France were rarely intercepted; few planes were found on French bases.

On April 17 Eisenhower's directive to Spaatz and Harris left "the destruction of German air combat strength" their immediate first objective. Their other main mission was to disrupt the enemy's rail communications, "particularly those affecting the enemy's movement toward the 'Overlord' lodgment area." The first priority for Spaatz's operations went to enemy fighter and ball bearing production; second priority went to installations supporting the German fighter force, followed by the German bomber force and its supporting installations. The enemy railroad system was the secondary objective. The directive to Sir Arthur Harris was, at least at first sight, vague.

In view of the tactical difficulties of destroying precise targets by night, RAF Bomber Command will continue to be employed in accordance with their main aim of disorganizing German industry. Their operations, will, however, be designed as far as practicable to be complementary to the operations of the USSTAF. In particular, where tactical conditions allow, their targets will be selected so as to give the maximum assistance in the aims of reducing the strength of the German Air Force and destroying and disrupting enemy rail communications.[1]

A list of such targets was issued to Harris, who, if the Luftwaffe had not made it too hard, might have tried to climb through the loophole offered by the first phrase. As it was, he did launch some area attacks on cities not too deep in western Germany. But most of his efforts went to the Transportation Plan, the attempt to smash the French and Belgian railroad system.[2]

THE TRANSPORTATION PLAN

How best to use the heavy bombers to support Overlord was a controversial matter. The prime problem of the invasion was that only a limited force could be put ashore on D-Day. The Germans, using roads and railroads, could reinforce their troops in Normandy faster than the Allies could strengthen their beachhead. The German reinforcements had to be stopped, or at least slowed. One major element in achieving this would be deception measures. Once the Allies were ashore, they would try to convince the enemy that the landing in Normandy was just a diversionary attack and that the main invasion was still to come in the Calais area. But the Allied air forces also had to do everything possible to interfere with the movement of German forces and supplies to the real battlefront.

The original plan for the Normandy invasion, formulated in 1943, had assumed that enemy transportation would be attacked through simple "interdiction." Allied planes would cut the railroad lines and destroy the bridges leading to the battle area just before the invasion. But crucial figures doubted that this would be enough. In December 1943 Solomon Zuckerman, who had been Air Marshal Tedder's scientific adviser when Tedder commanded Eisenhower's air forces in the Mediterranean, had analyzed attacks on the enemy railroad system in Sicily and Italy. He concluded that bridge busting and line cuts would be costly in bombs and not a reliable means of interrupting transport. Instead, attacks should be aimed at marshalling yards and repair depots, bigger targets, where every bomb was likely to do damage. Rolling stock and locomotives, as well as vital yard space and facilities, would be wrecked, delaying movements and preventing recovery.

After returning to Britain Zuckerman had become an assistant to Leigh-Mallory. They and Tedder supported the Transportation Plan, calling for attacks on railroad centers in France and Belgium—estimates of how many would range from 33 to 101. It would have to start 90 days before the invasion and would require massive tonnages of bombs, estimated at 45,000 tons, much of which would have to be delivered by the heavy bombers. (The bridge busting and line cutting would also be done, largely by the tactical forces' fighter-bombers and light and medium bombers.) Just before the invasion, lines leading to Normandy would also be hit. Leigh-Mallory's staff estimated that the Germans used as much as two-thirds of Western Europe's railroad capacity for military traffic, so attacks on rail centers should quickly hurt them.

This plan did not command universal admiration. Even before it was formally proposed, Harris predictably argued that it was wrong to divert Bomber Command from the task of smashing German cities and give the Germans a breathing space. In a humbler vein, he declared that his force could not bomb accurately enough to deal with the railroad centers. On February 15 Harris and Spaatz jointly objected to the plan. Harris now suggested that interdiction would be effective. Spaatz argued that the proposed action would divert his bombers from Germany and endanger the winning of air superiority, because the Luftwaffe would not be heavily engaged before D-Day.

Unlike Harris, Spaatz had a new strategic alternative in mind. In January the Combined Chiefs of Staff had expressed interest in attacking enemy oil production. Spaatz and Portal had then opposed this as premature; they preferred to go on attacking German fighter production. But on February 28, right after the Big Week attacks, Spaatz's planners and the Economic Objectives Unit of the U.S. Embassy in London concluded that the USSTAF should turn its attention to oil. Spaatz decided that the arguments of the planners and the embassy unit were sound. On March 5 he urged Eisenhower to give an attack on oil first priority; attacking the Luftwaffe should get second priority; rubber and tire production third; and attacks on German railroad centers fourth—when weather prevented attacks on other targets. An all-out attack on synthetic oil plants in Germany and the oil refineries in southeastern Europe would cut Germany's gasoline supply in half in six months. Line cutting and bridge busting would stop the Germans from reinforcing and supplying Normandy. Privately, Spaatz thought the invasion neither necessary or desirable, although he would do his best to support it. He remarked, later in March, that the invasion could not succeed, but said, "I don't want any part of the blame. After it fails, we can show them how we can win by bombing."[3]

The tide, however, was against him, even though other opponents assembled formidable arguments against the Transportation Plan. They included Churchill, the chief of the Imperial General Staff, the British Joint Intelligence Committee, and the Ministry of Economic Warfare. Many agreed with Spaatz that interdiction would be more effective, and noted that wrecking the whole French and Belgian railroad system would hamper the Allies at a later stage. British railroad experts estimated that German military traffic used only a fifth of the system's capacity (the real proportion was a third), so that capacity would have to be reduced by more than 80 percent before the enemy would be hurt. Railroad centers were the worst place to try to interrupt service, because in such places many lines had to be cut to block traffic, and repairs would be easier than out in the country.

Some, notably in the Economic Objectives Unit, questioned Zuckerman's analysis of operations in Sicily and Italy. They believed that the reduction of traffic into Sicily had resulted mainly from attacks on the ferries across the Straits of Messina, not from bombing marshalling yards, and that other results of bombing such yards had been exaggerated. Moreover, later experience in Italy was showing that bridge attacks were more effective, and less costly in bombs, than Zuckerman and Tedder had supposed. (Unfortunately, the evidence on this point was still inconclusive when the decision on the Transportation Plan had to be made.)

Last but not least, Churchill and the War Cabinet were horrified at the civilian deaths that attacks on rail centers would cause. An early estimate suggested that there would be 160,000 French and Belgian casualties, one-quarter of which would be fatal. And Churchill thought that the Germans were using just a tenth of the rail traffic and could easily get around any trouble caused by the bombing.

But proponents of the plan had a formidable list of arguments, and Eisenhower was unlikely to overrule both his deputy and the tactical air commander. General Lewis Brereton, the Ninth Air Force commander, backed them rather than Spaatz. Tedder and Leigh-Mallory pointed out the danger of waiting to start in on the enemy's transportation system until just before the invasion; among other things, it gambled too much on good weather.

Harris had to reverse his position; Portal and others had become suspicious of him and on March 4 had ordered him to carry out experimental attacks on six French marshalling yards, as well as a precision attack on the tank engine and transmission plants at Friedrichshafen. The success of these attacks, which will be discussed later, showed that Bomber Command could participate in the Transportation Plan, and both Portal and Harris came to support it.

The decision finally came down to Eisenhower on March 26. Spaatz made the case for the oil plan, arguing that the Luftwaffe would fight to defend oil installations, but not rail centers, and that smashing oil would hurt the enemy more. He did not stress the argument that interdiction would do the better job than attacks on rail centers. But the experts admitted that even a successful attack on oil would not hurt German military capabilities before D-Day. Ike was impressed by the potential of an oil attack and agreed to consider it when the first critical situation in Overlord was past. Although many present doubted that the Transportation Plan would be effective, Eisenhower commented that it was only necessary to show that there would be "*some* reduction, however small, to justify adopting the plan, provided there was no alternative."[4] So he favored it; he later told General Marshall that he saw no other way for the air forces to help the invasion.[5] But he remained aware of Spaatz's argument that an attack on the German oil industry would force a battle on the Luftwaffe and at least leave the way open to adding interdiction attacks at a later stage. Spaatz kept the oil alternative before him.

Churchill continued opposing the Transportation Plan, although it was revised to require bombing only 74 rail centers and estimates of probable civilian losses were reduced to 10,500 killed and 5,500 seriously injured. Eisenhower's insistence and FDR's refusal to overrule the military commanders ended Churchill's opposition, but not his conviction that the plan was wrong. The Ninth Air Force had attacked some rail centers as early as March, even before the plan was approved, but opposition on the part of Churchill and the War Cabinet delayed attacks on some targets. Many rail centers were alloted to the strategic air forces. Bomber Command received 39 targets and the Eighth Air Force 23, including some in western Germany. The Fifteenth Air Force was initially assigned targets in southern France and Germany, but the German targets were finally dropped;

attacks on the railroads in Southeastern Europe were substituted. Spaatz was to slyly use this to start the oil campaign. Bomber Command bore the main brunt of the Transportation Plan.[6]

NIGHT PRECISION BOMBING

Bomber Command's surprising ability to handle this task stemmed from the convergence of two different developments. The long-standing efforts by 617 Squadron to develop the ability to attack small targets bore fruit, as it became apparent that the regular Oboe marking technique could be refined to allow far greater accuracy than Harris had imagined. Ironically, Bomber Command matched and surpassed the AAF in accuracy just as it became possible for the Americans to go anywhere in Germany—and as the German night defenses made it dangerous for Bomber Command to attack the enemy homeland.

For some months, 617 Squadron's efforts against precision targets had not been particularly successful. In September 1943 an attempt by eight Lancasters to smash the Dortmund-Ems Canal with delay-fused 12,000-pound blockbusters failed. Attempts to destroy the Antheor viaduct in southern France failed despite the use of a very accurate new bombsight. But Squadron Leader Leonard Cheshire, the able and very brave commander of 617 Squadron, persisted. Nine of his Lancasters made a very accurate attack on a V-weapons site in France on December 16, using Oboe Mosquito marking and bombing from 12,000 to 15,000 feet with the new Stabilized Automatic Bombsight. Although the bombs just missed the target, which was tiny, this episode should have shown what could be done with Oboe. Cheshire, however, now swung to the other extreme— low-level instead of high-altitude marking. He and Squadron Leader H. B. Martin, a veteran of the Dams attack, observed that a low-flying plane could mark a target for a force flying much higher and demonstrated this in January 1944. Martin realized that marking by dive-bombing would be even more effective. The new technique was perfected in a series of small attacks on French factories in February and March. On the night of February 8–9, Cheshire dived his Lancaster to 200 feet to drop incendiary bombs on the Gnome-Rhone aircraft engine plant at Limoges. Then eleven other Lancasters smashed the factory with six-ton bombs.

The Limoges attack was the first of a dozen attacks on French aircraft, explosives, and bearings plants. All but one of the targets was wrecked; only one bomber was lost in 350 sorties. This was a remarkable record even though the targets were lightly defended. The attacks showed the terrific effect of the British blockbusters, which were far more effective, pound for pound, than the AAF's lighter bombs. Cheshire realized that the Lancaster was not well-suited for low-level marking, and sought Mosquitos for the job.

Meanwhile, the main force had begun the experimental attacks on French marshalling yards. By the end of March all the designated yards had been hit, using the conventional Musical Parramatta marking technique. The results were excellent; Bomber Command could be trusted to wreck the rail centers without too great harm to people nearby. In the fifteenth attack on marshalling yards, against Aulnoye on April 10–11, the use of a master bomber was reintroduced, by the main force in what was called "controlled Oboe." After Oboe-guided Mosquitos marked the target, the master bomber checked them, steered the force to the best markers, and if necessary corrected or supplemented the markers dropped on Oboe with differently colored markers of his own. The first 15 attacks together showed an overall average bombing error of 680 yards for the 55 percent of the bombs that were considered "effectively aimed"—this excluded bombs carried by planes that had aborted, as well as duds and bombs dropped far from the target due to gross errors. That was close to what the Eighth Air Force was achieving in good visibility.

Cheshire was developing an even better technique. On April 5–6, using a Mosquito, he acted as master bomber for an attack on an aircraft plant at Toulouse. He dropped a red spot fire on it from a shallow dive. Then two Lancasters dropped more markers from higher up; 140 Lancasters from 5 Group smashed the factory. (As a result of this, 5 Group was promptly given more Mosquitos and two Lancaster squadrons transferred from the Pathfinders.) The average bombing error fell to 380 yards. Then, when offset marking was reintroduced, it was cut to 285 yards with the fully developed "5 Group visual," or dive-marking technique. This incorporated "proximity marking" by Oboe Mosquitos and lighting up the target area with flares before the dive-marking Mosquitos pushed over.

At first it was not certain that the attacks on French targets, whether using Oboe or dive-marking techniques, showed what could be done in Germany. The French targets were all, at first, lightly defended. The attacks on them were made from lower levels than was normally possible over the Reich: 12,300 feet for Oboe-guided attacks and 7,500 feet for attacks using 5 Group visual. The latter tactic, especially, needed perfect visibility and a dangerously long stay over the target. But it was decided to try it in Germany.

A first attempt to use dive-marking there, in an attack on Brunswick on April 22–23, misfired. The Mosquitos marked well, but communications broke down and haze led to the inaccurate dropping of skymarkers, which misled many bombers. Moreover, this night saw the introduction of the J-bomb, a badly designed 30-pound liquid-filled incendiary, a British counterpart to the napalm bomb. The J-bombs were often duds, but when they went off, they sprayed spectacular jets of flame that hid the markers. Things went better over Munich on April 24–25. Cheshire led Mosquitos down through heavy flak to mark the marshalling yards, which were wrecked. This kind of success was not invariably repeated; an attack on the bearings plants and marshalling yards at Schweinfurt on April 26–27 was less accurate, and the bombers suffered heavily from fighters.

The next night Bomber Command finally struck Friedrichshafen, nearly two months after Harris had been ordered to hit it. A force of 323 bombers (under half the number sent against Nuremberg a month earlier) dropped 1,234 tons of bombs on the place. Since the target was unusually far south and on the rim of the Germans' defensive system, the defenders were slow to react, although they did down 18 Lancasters. This, the sole attack by Bomber Command's main strength on that city during the war, proved the most damaging attack ever made on German tank production. Although in moonlight, the Friedrichshafen attack used standard pathfinder marking and showed how accurate British bombers could now be, even without dive-marking and beyond Oboe range.

Cheshire's contributions were not finished; he devised a better formation for bombing in daylight and, borrowing a Mustang from the Americans, showed that it was even better for dive-marking than the Mosquito.

Bomber Command could now hit German targets accurately but could not go deep into Germany regularly with reasonable losses. Trips as far as Brunswick, Munich, and Schweinfurt were atypical in this period. Most of its few ventures into Germany were no deeper than the Ruhr, and only in the most favorable conditions. Its new tactics reversed the process of concentration that had been underway since 1941. Instead of concentrating in a single massive bomber stream, several forces attacked different targets. (The practice of splitting the bombers among several targets would have been forced in any case by the need to strike many targets in France, targets that required only relatively small forces.) The Germans could not get at the whole of Bomber Command at once, although they could inflict heavy losses on part of it, as they tended to do once the new tactics were understood.

A real answer to the night fighter was still in the future. Harris secured three more fighter squadrons for 100 Group's covering operations, but this was not enough to counter the Luftwaffe. An improved version of the Mandrel radar jammer was ready, but was held back for use on D-Day. Bomber Command mostly hit French targets; in the period of April–June 1944 only 17 percent of its bombs fell on Germany. Even so, it sometimes suffered heavily. In May the Luftwaffe pushed night fighters forward into France. On the night of May 3–4 the Germans downed 42 of 362 bombers sent to Mailly-le-Camp, and on May 10–11, 12 bombers of 89 attacking Lille were lost.[7]

IMPLEMENTING THE TRANSPORTATION PLAN

Bomber Command delivered 46,000 of the 71,000 tons of bombs dropped on rail centers. The Eighth Air Force hit some French marshalling yards in late April; on May 1 it finally joined the railroad campaign on a full scale, dropping 13,000 tons of bombs. The heavies were assisted by dive-bombing P-47s. By D-Day, 51 of the 80 rail centers on the final target list were believed useless.

However, there were already substantial doubts that the rail center bombings were the main cause of the paralysis of the enemy's supply system. Spaatz's in-sistence that bridge busting and line cutting by smaller planes would be more effective than bombing railroad yards represented a genuine conviction, not just a way to deflect participation in the Transportation Plan, and others agreed with him. An experimental attack on several bridges by RAF Typhoon fighter-bombers on April 21 did not destroy them but left them unusable for a time; this strongly suggested that such attacks would be effective. The headquarters of Bernard Montgomery, the British general who would be commander of the ground forces on D-Day, urged trying to destroy more bridges. Leigh-Mallory was strongly opposed, but the Americans proved him wrong. On May 7 medium bombers and dive-bombing Thunderbolts successfully attacked several bridges, after which even Leigh-Mallory was convinced.

Two rings of interdiction were to be established across the rail routes into Normandy. The first would cut all bridges across the Seine and Loire, while an outer ring would be established east of Paris. To avoid tipping off the enemy to the invasion site, the Allies concentrated on the outer ring first. Most of the Seine bridges waited until the last two weeks before D-Day, while the Loire bridges would be hit only after the invasion. The destruction of the Loire bridges had an additional benefit; after the breakout from Normandy, it enabled Gen. George Patton's Third Army to dash far to the east without much attention to its southern flank.

Experience showed that B-26 attacks from medium altitude were more effective than the fighter-bombers, although the latter proved useful in finishing off damaged bridges and blocking tunnels. The Eighth's heavies attacked the Seine bridges on June 4, but the Ninth Air Force did most of the work. Only 4,400 tons of bombs were needed for bridge attacks, far less than against marshalling yards. Fighters of the tactical and strategic air forces helped to strangle traffic by attacking trains. These "Chattanooga Choo-Choo" missions, begun on May 21, concentrated on France and Belgium, but ranged as far as Poland. Napalm bombs were not yet available for fighter-bombers, but dropping belly tanks on stalled trains and setting them on fire helped persuade French train crews that working for the Germans was bad business as well as unpatriotic. Over 50,000 Germans and slave laborers were brought in, in an increasingly futile attempt to keep trains rolling; even so, daylight runs were sharply reduced even where the lines were not cut. By June 9 rail traffic in France had fallen to just 38 percent of the February level. Under continued pounding it fell off still more, and in the most critical areas it was even worse. German troops had to detrain far from the battle area, forcing costly and time-consuming road marches.

The evidence strongly suggests that it was the bridge-busting campaign, not the bombing of rail centers, that wrecked the Germans' transportation efforts. Although some German officers were worried even before the interdiction strikes began, the immediate effect of the attacks on rail centers was to eliminate French civilian traffic from the railroads. Until the bridges were smashed, the German Army, at great cost, was still able to keep enough trains rolling to supply its vital needs and move troops. Bridge busting, largely carried out by medium bombers and fighter-bombers, was responsible for isolating the Normandy battlefield. The campaign against rail centers was thus a tragic mistake. It killed up to 12,000 civilians and was to hamper the Allied supply system at a later stage in the campaign. The bombs dropped on marshalling yards proved worse than useless. Much, if not all, of the 59,000 tons of bombs expended by the heavy bombers could have hit German targets, with staggering effects on the enemy.

Unfortunate though it was, however, the Transportation Plan was not an avoidable mistake. It was never likely that Eisenhower would override Tedder, Leigh-Mallory, and Brereton. He could have forgone the plan only had he been certain that interdiction would do the job, and certainty about this was impossible at the time. Since the interdiction campaign could not start until just before D-Day, while the rail center attack had to start much earlier, Eisenhower could not afford to wait to see if the cheaper interdiction program worked. Had the evidence from Sicily and Italy been rightly interpreted, things might have been different. But the very fact that until March 1944 attacks on the enemy transportation system in Italy had been directed against marshalling yards, in accordance with the Tedder-Zuckerman policy, prevented the development of corrective data.[8]

OTHER PRE-INVASION OPERATIONS

In Germany the strategic air forces hit camps, fuel and ammunition dumps, and airfields in France to prepare for D-Day. The immediate results of the airfield attacks were small. The Luftwaffe was in Germany, and energetically repaired its installations. But when it tried to move planes to France after D-Day, it found the deterioration of its German bases under heavy bombing a big handicap. During May the Eighth Air Force and Bomber Command joined in attacks on the enemy coastal radar system and began pounding coastal batteries.[9]

THE BATTLE AGAINST THE V-WEAPONS

As far back as late 1943 the strategic air forces had become involved in a costly struggle related to the task of preparing for the invasion: the struggle against the V-weapons. The Nazis had persisted with plans to launch an area offensive of their own with wildly inaccurate—and in the case of the V-2, costly—missiles.

As early as May 1943 the Allies had observed the construction of the first of seven "large sites" in the Calais and Cotentin areas related to secret weapons. Six of these huge concrete structures were intended to store V-1 and V-2 missiles and to act as launching sites for the latter. A seventh, at Mimoyecques (Calais), was to house a third V-weapon that was a superartillery piece, a "high-pressure pump gun." It was designed to fire a special finned projectile, boosted by a series of charges detonated in a very long barrel. This was potentially far more dangerous to London than the V-1 or V-2, but it is uncertain whether the Nazis could have gotten it working properly in time for use in the war.

The Allies promptly attacked the large sites, and in November they spotted the first of 96 "ski sites." Some correctly suspected that these were ramps for launching V-1s, but the extent of the threat was hard to gauge. Some feared that the rocket's warhead might be as big as ten tons. Nor could the Allies be sure that the missiles would be merely area-bombardment weapons. And while the V-2 was hopelessly inaccurate, the V-1 could conceivably have been fitted with a radio-control system and used against precision targets—in fact the Nazi Air Ministry had planned this at an early date, only to drop the idea when higher authority wanted just revenge attacks on London. Some among the Allies regarded the construction sites in France as a decoy to draw the Allied air effort from important targets. Others feared that they were designed to house even deadlier things; poison gas or biological weapons were among the least fantastic guesses. The Eighth Air Force and, on a much smaller scale, Bomber Command, joined the tactical air forces in pounding the large sites and ski sites.

They were damaged, but the results did not seem commensurate with the effort. Although tests on duplicate ski sites, and an actual attack by Ninth Air Force Thunderbolts, showed that low-altitude strikes by fighter-bombers were far more effective on these objectives than the heavier planes, the British insisted on using the latter.

Even if at unnecessary cost, the Allies seemed to have dealt with the ski sites, while Ninth Air Force bombers had damaged Mimoyecques; the Germans abandoned half the site. But the Germans had merely given up on the ski sites and shifted over to a simpler launcher. These smaller "modified" sites, as the Allies called them, were more easily built and camouflaged, were simpler to repair when damaged, and were much more difficult targets. Although the British heard of them in February, none were identified in photographs until April 27. They did not seem to pose an immediate threat, and there was not much air effort to spare for them in the month before D-Day.

From December to early June the Eighth Air Force alone had lost 49 planes and dropped 17,600 tons of bombs in attacks on V-weapons targets. This was a high proportion of the 154 planes lost and the 36,200 tons of bombs expended in the campaign. Probably much of this effort was wasted. While the Germans had hoped to start V-1 attacks early in 1944, it is likely that factors other than attacks on the ski sites caused the delay. The British attack on Kassel in October 1943 forced the movement of some production facilities; other area attacks reduced production. The first 2,000 V-1's built were faulty, and were scrapped. The attacks on the French railroads also slowed preparations for the V-1 offensive.

The Allies were content with having prevented German secret weapons from interfering with the invasion, although as it turned out, neither the V-1 nor the V-2 would have been accurate enough to effectively attack the ports from which the invasion was mounted. The Allies thought the danger over, when the modified sites opened fire on London on June 12.

Although not a major threat to the war effort, the V-1s killed many civilians, and as repeatedly noted earlier, no government is likely to tolerate attacks on its capital without reacting violently, whatever the military wisdom of the attacks or the counteraction. The British were upset; they had hardly expected renewed attacks on Britain at this late date. There was wild talk of using gas against the launching sites or even of killing German civilians in reprisal. Eisenhower agreed to a major offensive against V-weapons sites. On June 16 he gave the V-weapons campaign higher priority than anything but the immediate requirements of the battle in France. In practice, it received higher priority than attacks on the French transportation system, dumps, and airfields. The Eighth Air Force and Bomber Command struck launchers and supposed storage facilities.

An enormous effort was expended on V-weapons targets in the summer of 1944, including over a quarter of the tonnage of bombs dropped by the Eighth Air Force and Bomber Command in July and August. But much of this effort was misdirected by the British Air Ministry. It insisted on hitting the old ski sites, which it was known were not being used; the large sites, the purpose of which was still uncertain; and eight "storage sites" for V-1s, which the Germans had in fact abandoned in May in favor of three underground depots in caves and tunnels. Low-level attacks on the real launchers were neglected. Finally, 5 Group, using the new Tallboy deep-penetration bombs designed by Wallis, hit the underground storage depots and the large sites; the latter were abandoned after these attacks. These may have been the most effective attacks against the V-weapons.

Spaatz considered attacks on the launchers and large sites with conventional weapons a poor idea. He urged knocking out the power system in the Calais area, believing that this would paralyze both the large sites and the storage sites, and favored hitting the large sites with radio-controlled "war weary" heavy bombers, packed with ten tons of TNT or napalm. (Some of these missiles were finally sent against the large sites in early August, but by then the British had already dealt with them effectively.) Spaatz preferred to concentrate conventional heavy bombers on gyrocompass plants in Germany and any large storage depots that could be identified in France. But he was largely overruled. Some attacks were made on targets believed to be connected with V-weapons in Germany itself, but these attacks were costly and had little effect.

The V-1 was largely defeated by defensive measures. Many of the fastest fighters—notably Tempests, Meteor jets (see Chapter 9), and a whole wing of RAF Mustangs—were kept in England to stop the V-1s. Many of the V-1s that got through the fighters were shot down by skillfully redeployed antiaircraft guns, aided by effective new radars and gun directors and proximity-fuzed shells. Finally the armies overran the launching areas. The Nazis kept up a small-scale assault with air-launched V-1s fired by bombers; later, long-range V-1s were launched from the Netherlands. Meanwhile, the Germans fired older-model V-1s at the port of Antwerp and some other target on the Continent, hoping to interfere with Allied supplies. These killed many Belgians, but did the Allied war effort little harm.

The main V-1 offensive had hardly stopped when V-2 attacks on London began on September 8. (Later the V-2 was also used on Antwerp.) The rocket, fired from mobile installations in the Netherlands, needed no elaborate launcher and was not so vulnerable to active countermeasures. Fighter Command occasionally hit V-2 launch sites, but they were not suitable targets for the heavy bombers.

The counter-V-weapons campaign was a costly and not too successful commitment for the Allied strategic air forces. They had delayed and reduced the German attack, but after the bombing of Peenemunde in 1943, the delay and reduction was mainly from the indirect effects of area attacks or attacks on other objectives, rather than those deliberately aimed at the missile threat. The Allies had often struck targets that were irrelevant. They apparently did not know enough about the V-weapons to concentrate their efforts against vulnerable points in production; the factory making the V-2's fuel pumps, for example, would have been a good target. But it is arguable that an all-out attack on the production of liquid oxygen, which the Allies knew the V-2 needed, and the gyrocompass plants (as Spaatz wanted) would have rendered the missiles ineffective. And if the bombs expended on the V-weapons targets had been devoted to attacks on oil production, they might have done more to stop the V-weapons than any direct attack.

The V-1 more than paid for itself by causing the British to invest tremendous efforts in defensive measures and by diverting Allied bombs from more important targets. Curiously, the cheap, slow V-1 cruise missile proved more effective than the spectacular and costly V-2 rocket. The V-2 could not be intercepted and was rarely caught on the ground. But for those very reasons, the British could only grit their teeth and endure them. The deaths of British civilians were tragic, but of less than no help to the Nazis. The V-2s, however, unlike the V-1s, were a costly drain on German resources and unjustified by any diversion of the resources of the Allies.[10] The V-2 was a great step toward the conquest of space, but as a weapon it was a bust. After World War II, many of the men involved in its development wound up working in the American aerospace effort. But without intending to, in a sense they had really been working for the Western powers all along.

SUPPORT FOR THE LAND CAMPAIGN

The struggle against the V-weapons was not the only "diversion" required of the strategic air forces. For months after D-Day, immediate support of the armies in Western Europe took precedence over strategic attacks on Germany, and this must be appreciated if the true nature of the strategic air war is to be understood. Between June and August 1944, because of the demands of the land battle and the attacks on V-weapons sites, only a little over a third of the bombs dropped by the American strategic air forces and only a sixth of those dropped by Bomber Command fell on targets in Germany. Despite this, as we shall see, they struck decisive blows against the German war effort.

The effects of the operations of the heavy bombers, and their escort fighters, in support of the armies are often hard to distinguish from those of the Ninth and Second tactical air forces, but were undoubtedly considerable. In turn, the liberation of France aided the strategic air campaign. By destroying the German early-warning system and enabling the British to push forward their electronic guidance systems and countermeasures, it helped change the balance of strength at night. And large numbers of German fighters were sucked into the battle for France, further undermining what remained of the air defense of Germany itself.

On D-Day the Eighth Air Force's fighters joined the other Allied air forces to protect the landing, but its operations over Germany had already insured that the German reaction to D-Day would be belated and far weaker than anyone had expected. While Bomber Command attacked ten major coastal batteries, over a thousand American heavies tried to drench the beach defenses with bombs. But overcast forced bombing on H2X, and to avoid hitting the landing craft nearing the beaches, the bomb release was delayed. As a result, the bombs fell well behind the defenders. Attacks on "transportation choke points" in the city of Caen and elsewhere proved more successful, helping to delay the 21st Panzer Division's counterattack against the British, the only serious German countermove on D-Day.

After D-Day the strategic air forces returned to isolating the battle area. The heavy bombers interdicted the Loire crossings, which were far from the mediums bombers' bases. The Eighth's fighters joined the tactical fighters in attacking every daylight movement. Bomber Command wrecked the German bases for motor-torpedo boats and other light craft at Le Havre and Boulogne, smashing a threat to the cross-Channel supply route. The Eighth Air Force conducted a different sort of special operation; on June 25 it carried out the first of four massive air drops of supplies to the resistance forces in southern France.

The pre-invasion attacks on French airfields now paid off. As nearly a thousand planes rushed from Germany to France, they found the bases there overcrowded and in poor shape. "Ultra" and lower-level code breaking disclosed the destinations and arrival times of the reinforcements and helped the Allies ambush them as they came in to land. The transfer of German fighters westward merely threw the outnumbered, deteriorating force against the massive tactical air forces as well as against the Eighth.

Despite the failure of the attacks on D-Day, the Allies persisted in using the heavy bombers against German defenses in the field. The British particularly stressed what became knows as "carpet bombing" in support of their offensives in Normandy. Sometimes this achieved remarkable results, but it could be dangerous to Allied soldiers if a mistake was made. Attacks on towns in the Germans' immediate rear—Caen was an especially bad case—sometimes killed many French people. The Eighth Air Force's attack on July 25, the most effective carpet bombing of the campaign, showed both the effectiveness and the danger of such operations. After an abortive attack the day before, in which some American soldiers were killed by bombs that had fallen short, 1,507 heavies joined the mediums in plastering the battle area to blow a hole for the breakout from Normandy. The Germans were so well dug in that few died, but their tanks and guns were shattered or even half-buried in fields plowed up by bombs. But some bombs fell on the Americans, and more than a hundred were killed.

Similar attacks remained a feature of major Allied offensives, although some observers doubted that they were usually worthwhile. They especially disliked attacks on towns and cities just behind the German front, arguing that by the time Allied troops arrived, a smashed town was a tougher defensive position than one still intact, and the blocked roads and streets hampered Allied movements more than they hurt the retreat or supply efforts of the Germans.

During August, as the Allies broke out of Normandy, the Eighth extended its attacks on transportation eastward, while Bomber Command smashed enemy fuel storage depots in the forward area. To stem the Allied advance, the Germans rushed their painfully rebuilt reserve of nearly 800 fighters to France. Huge numbers of these were shot down, caught on the ground, or landed in areas the Allies were overrunning. General Galland estimated that the dissipated reserve destroyed only 25 Allied planes, for the loss of 400 German fighters. To keep the ground forces supplied, some 200 B-24s were used as transports for nearly a month after August 28. The strategic air forces also supported the attempt by airborne troops to grab a bridgehead over the lower Rhine at Arnhem. Bomber Command and the Eighth Air Force bombed flak positions to protect the unarmored, low-flying troop carrier planes; over the next few days American heavy bombers dropped supplies to the airborne troops. On September 18 a force of 107 B-17s carried out an even farther-reaching operation to supply the Polish resistance forces fighting in Warsaw. But that operation was too late to do much good.

When the British were defeated at Arnhem, Eisenhower concentrated on opening the sea route to Antwerp and preparing an autumn offensive in the Rhineland. The capture of the German-occupied islands and peninsulas in the Antwerp approaches was aided by Bomber Command, which smashed the dykes protecting most of Walcheren Island from the sea.

Both Patton's secondary offensive beginning on November 9 and the main Rhineland offensive in the north beginning on November 16 were strongly supported by the Eighth Air Force. On November 16 some 1,191 American heavy bombers were joined by 1,188 RAF heavies, as well as the mediums and fighter-bombers, in the biggest air attack of the whole war. But it was not as effective as that of July 25. In a month of fighting, the Americans advanced less than ten miles.[11]

The Germans checked the fall offensive without much interference with their own preparations for a winter counteroffensive, and they scraped up their last resources for the coming attack in the Ardennes. This, and their defensive successes on the ground, were all the more remarkable because the last resistance in the air was crumbling. And so was the whole basis of their war effort.

Decisive Offensives I: Oil, May 1944–September 1944

Up to the spring of 1944 the strategic air offensive had not struck a decisive blow against Germany. It had done much damage; it had forced the Nazis to commit enormous resources to repairs and defense; it had slowed work on new weapons, and it had defeated the Luftwaffe. But it had not critically hurt the German economy, or even seriously interrupted production of a vital item. This was not clear at the time; the Allies overestimated the damage done. Nor had the Allied leaders expected Germany to collapse under strategic bombing; they had viewed it as a softening-up process for an invasion and were content with the apparent results.[1] Nevertheless, it had fallen short of the aims set for it.

But all of this now changed, even though the strategic air forces were largely committed to supporting the invasion and the fight against the V-weapons. Although Bomber Command was in a difficult position, the Americans could now go anywhere in occupied Europe and had enough bombers to strike at the decisive targets: the enemy's oil production and transportation systems. Now the Americans were strong enough to take them on even while other tasks had priority.

On D-Day the Eighth Air Force reached its final complement of 40 heavy bomber groups (2,100 planes) and 15 escort fighter groups (nearly 1,000 fighters.) The equipment of the heavy bomber units did not change much during the rest of the war, save for the conversion of five B-24 groups to B-17s and the addition of still more planes to each group. But formations were altered to improve bombing accuracy and reduce losses to flak. The superiority of American fighters grew even more marked. The new P-51D, with a cut-down fuselage, bubble canopy, and heavier armament, was arriving. It eventually equipped 14 of the Eighth's fighter groups. Only the 56th Group retained later models of the P-47, with bigger drop-tanks. Fighter pilots got G-suits to cope with tight turns and pull-outs, and superior gyroscopic gunsights.

THE GERMAN OIL INDUSTRY

An attack on oil production required hitting many targets; the Allies listed 81 targets when they started the campaign and wound up attacking 135, although most of those later added to the list were minor storage sites, while 90 percent of production was concentrated in 54 large refineries and synthetic oil plants. Until 1944, apart from the escort problem, the USSTAF had not had enough bombers to deal with the oil installations, while Bomber Command at least had not been supposed to have the accuracy to help out.

Germany's oil situation had actually improved in late 1943 and early 1944. Synthetic oil production had grown, along with that of natural crude oil from the new Austrian fields. Italy was no longer a drain, and after taking over most of Italy in September 1943, the Germans had found big fuel reserves there. Bad winter weather had restricted consumption. So German fuel reserves had actually risen. Stocks of aviation gasoline alone rose from 280,000 tons in September 1943 to 574,000 tons in April 1944. Still, if production were halted, that would only be enough to keep the Luftwaffe going for three months. In March 1944, before the Allied oil offensive began, the Germans produced or imported 968,000 tons of oil products: 341,000 tons made in Bergius and Fischer-Tropsch plants; 201,000 tons made in other synthetic plants; 191,000 tons domestically refined from natural crude oil; 49,000 tons produced in occupied countries; and 186,000 tons imported from Hungary and Romania. Aviation gasoline comprised 180,000 tons of this total.

The refining of crude oil was concentrated in several areas: in northwest Germany at Hamburg and Hannover, at Vienna and Budapest near the Austrian and Hungarian oilfields, and of course at Ploesti. The Nazis had a surplus of refining capacity, so a good deal of destruction would have to be done before the amount of fuel refined was cut.

The Nazis mainly relied, however, on synthetic fuel production, using several different processes. This was concentrated around coalfields in the Ruhr, in central Germany around Leipzig, in Upper Silesia, and in the areas of Czechoslovakia bordering central Germany and Silesia. That the targets, although numerous, tended to be grouped together would help the Allies, allowing a single mission to hit a whole set of targets without dangerously dispersing the fighter cover.

Eighteen plants (six were rather small) using the Bergius hydrogenation process were the most important sources of fuel. They provided no less than 35 percent of all Germany's liquid fuels and 90 percent of its aviation gasoline. They also made *treibgas*, a mixture of propane and butane that was an important substitute for automotive gasoline. Merseburg-Leuna, near Leipzig, and Poelitz, near Stettin, were particularly important, each producing 600,000 tons a year; these two plants carried on nearly a third of the Bergius production. Merseburg-Leuna, in particular, would become all too familiar to the men of the Eighth Air Force. The Eighth attacked it no less than 20 times; Bomber Command, joining in later, mounted three missions against it. The hydrogenation plants were not only important for fuel. They produced nitrogen, methanol, and other materials essential for making synthetic rubber, explosives, artificial fertilizers, and lesser chemical products.

Nine Fischer-Tropsch plants (six in the Ruhr), were less significant, producing low-grade fuels. More than 80 small benzol plants used a by-product of coke ovens in a third process to grind out modest quantities of low-grade truck fuel and small, but increasing, quantities of aviation gasoline. The Germans also made some fuel by distillation from coal tars. The importance and vulnerability of oil targets thus varied widely. The bigger Bergius plants were the core of the enemy's fuel supply. Fortunately they covered a large area (Merseburg-Leuna sprawled over 757 acres) and were easily found. Standing well outside built-up areas, they were easy to see even on H2S and H2X screens and were vulnerable to bomb damage.

Natural oil refineries were smaller and less vulnerable, but were especially important for some purposes. They made all of Germany's lubricating oils and a disproportionate amount of its diesel and motor fuel. The benzol plants were small, scattered in dense urban areas (especially in the Ruhr) and hard to find. The Allies were never fully informed of their locations, but they were nevertheless vulnerable to RAF area attacks.

The Allies did not fully understand the enemy oil industry and did not see its connection with rubber, explosives and fertilizer production. They overestimated the amount of fuel produced by the crude-oil refineries and the Fischer-Tropsch plants, and hence the total enemy fuel production, and also the size of Germany's reserves. This might have made oil seem a less attractive target than it really was, but luckily they also overestimated German fuel consumption. The various errors cancelled each other out.[2]

THE START OF THE OFFENSIVE

Fortunately, Eisenhower had the greatest respect for Spaatz (who regularly cleaned out other Allied leaders at poker) and, even while overruling him on the Transportation Plan, had been impressed by the potential of an attack on oil. He was also mindful of Spaatz's advice that attacks on the oil plants would force the Luftwaffe to fight, weakening it before the supreme trial of D-Day. Spaatz kept this before him, while he acted effectively, if almost surreptitiously, to get the offensive against oil started in the Mediterranean. His weaker southern arm, the Fifteenth Air Force, was committed to attacking transportation targets in southeastern Europe. This afforded a way to get at the Ploesti refineries without a formal order or a quarrel over priorities. Each major refinery there had a small marshalling yard associated with it. Restricted by weather, commitments in Italy, and a lack of escort fighters, the Fifteenth Air Force had not been very active in the strategic air war since Big Week, but it was now getting some Mustangs. On April 5, while a larger force hit the Bucharest marshalling yards, 146 B-24s and 90 B-17s bombed the railroad yards at Ploesti, with intervalometers set to space the bombs widely, enlarging the bombing pattern so that some would hit the refineries instead of the nominal targets. Thirteen bombers were lost, but the attack did much damage, as did further attacks on April 15 and 24.

By the time of the April 24 attack, Eisenhower had approved an outright attack on oil as a measure to defeat the Luftwaffe. On April 19 he gave Spaatz permission to strike oil targets in Germany, on the next two days that offered good visual bombing. Conditions were not suitable until May 12. Then the Eighth dispatched 886 bombers, escorted by 980 fighters from the Eighth and Ninth Air Forces, against the synthetic oil plants in central Germany. The two leading combat wings attacked an aircraft depot at Zwickau to deceive the enemy about the real objective. The Americans expected a tough fight, and they got one. The force going to Zwickau ran into heavy opposition, as 200 enemy fighters plowed into the incoming bombers. A force of 50 twin-engine fighters, and more single-engine planes, jumped the bombers as they returned home. The Americans lost 46 heavy bombers and 10 fighters, while the Germans are known to have had 28 pilots killed and 26 wounded. Despite the heavy loss of bombers, the attacks were effective; 1,718 tons of bombs fell on Merseburg-Leuna and five other oil targets, knocking out several plants completely for a time.

An attack on oil targets in Silesia misfired the next day; bad weather forced a diversion to targets on the Baltic coast. Preinvasion tasks and weather delayed a return to oil targets until May 28; by then the targets hit earlier were recovering. The Eighth sent out a record force of 1,282 bombers, but only about two-thirds reached their primary targets, against strong opposition.

The next day, while the rest of the force hit aircraft plants, 224 B-24s of the 2nd Division hit the Poelitz plant for the first time. For some weeks thereafter the Eighth concentrated on supporting the Normandy invasion, but the Fifteenth Air Force pounded the Ploesti refineries on May 5, on May 31, and on D-Day itself.

Decoded messages encouraged persistence. On May 16 the Allies decoded a message from the Luftwaffe high command that disclosed that flak batteries were being shifted from other targets to the synthetic oil plants at Poelitz and Blechhammer. On May 21 a message from the Naval high command to Naval Gruppe West was decoded. It warned that oil production was failing. This, and photoreconnaissance pictures, helped lead the British Joint Intelligence Committee to the welcome conclusion that continuing the campaign would produce a crippling effect within three to six months. The day after D-Day, a message sent by the Luftwaffe high command to the 1st Parachute Army on June 5 was decoded that gave dramatic proof that the Luftwaffe was already short of fuel and allocations were being revised and reduced.[3]

BOMBER COMMAND JOINS IN

On June 3 the Air Staff asked Harris to attack ten synthetic oil plants in the Ruhr (which produced 30 percent of German synthetic oil) as soon as the situation in Normandy allowed. The Ruhr oil plants remained the special, though not exclusive, province of the RAF; it only hit oil plants elsewhere in December.

Harris was unenthusiastic about the oil plan. He estimated that destroying the ten plants would require 32,000 tons of bombs, a relatively large amount. (The Eighth Air Force actually dropped only 5,166 tons in the whole first month of its campaign against oil.) But he could not reasonably refuse to take part. On the night of June 12–13, 271 Lancasters carried out an ordinary Oboe-directed attack on the Reich's third-largest Bergius plant at Gelsenkirchen; no master bomber was used. Seventeen planes were lost. The attack caused heavy damage; decoded signals showed that the Germans expected the plant to be out of action for months. On June 16–17 a similar attack on a plant at Sterkrade had less dramatic results at much higher cost. Attacks on two more plants, on June 21–22, using variants of the 5 Group visual technique, failed outright, thanks to solid overcast and fierce opposition. Except for the initial attack, Bomber Command's first venture against oil since 1941 had gone badly. Of 832 bombers dispatched, 93 had been lost, despite aid from improved jamming.[4] If this went on, Bomber Command would do little to help Spaatz, and that at an intolerable cost. (It might have made more sense to send Bomber Command to the refineries at Hamburg and Bremen, which involved a less deep penetration of enemy defenses.) But as it turned out, there were not one, but two ways out of this dilemma.

The first, in which the Air Staff had been interested for some months, was to return to daylight operations. In April, Bottomley had suggested that with escort Bomber Command could hit targets in France, the Low Countries, and western Germany in daylight. This would take advantage of American successes during the day and allow more accuracy against small targets. He conceded, however, that the poor armament and limited ceiling of British bombers would prevent a full-scale day offensive against German targets. Harris was at first violently opposed, deeming the problems cited by Bottomley prohibitive, but in mid-June he began day attacks on nearby French targets. The bombers flew in loose "gaggles," covered by Spitfires. After an Oboe-guided pathfinder plane marked the target, each bombardier sighted and dropped his bombs individually under the direction of a master bomber. German fighters rarely reached the bombers, and the latter proved surprisingly tough targets; the wild corkscrews used to evade the enemy at night worked against the day fighters too. In July a new technique, Oboe- or G-H-formation bombing, was introduced. Small formations of bombers followed a lead plane equipped with Oboe or G-H; when the leader bombed on electronic guidance, the rest of the formation let go as well. When a bigger formation was used, the leader fired a puff of smoke; the van of the force bombed on the leader, but those in the rear bombed when they drew even with the smoke. The 3 Group specialized in the G-H formation technique and became a blind-bombing day force. Oboe remained slightly more accurate; indeed, Oboe-formation bombing seemed to be the most accurate of all bombing methods; it was even better than 5 Group visual at night. Until late August, however, these methods were not used against German targets. By then the prospect for night bombing, too, had improved.[5]

The British did not mount any major operation against Germany at all in the first half of July; they concentrated on supporting the campaign in France. But they had a lucky break. On July 13 a Junkers 88G night fighter, full of the latest equipment, landed by mistake in Britain, giving the British intact examples of the SN-2 radar, Flensburg, and Naxos. During and after the Battle of Berlin, in contrast with their efforts in 1942–1943 (see Chapter 4), the British had been strangely lax or ineffective in countering German electronic devices. They now did what R. V. Jones thought should have been done months before. The Monica tail-warning radar on the bombers was hastily removed, neutralizing Flensburg, and a partial silence was imposed on H2S. It would be used over enemy territory, but only when absolutely needed. This neutralized Naxos and Korfu. (Jones believed that, if taken earlier, these measures alone would have largely frustrated the enemy fighters.) A new form of Window was quickly produced to interfere with the SN-2 radar. The 100 Group soon received Piperack, an airborne jammer for the SN-2, and its Mosquitos were fitted with Serrate IV, which could home in on the SN-2. Other electronic countermeasures devices also came into service: Jostle, an improved device for jamming German fighter communications, and Perfectos, a device that enabled Mosquitos to trigger the IFF recognition signals (Identification Friend or Foe) of German night fighters, betraying their position. From the summer of 1944 the British held an edge in the electronics war that they never lost. The Germans did develop some new devices, but with little effect.[6]

When Bomber Command returned to Germany on the night of July 18–19, it found the going easier. During the rest of July it carried out five successful attacks on oil plants in the Ruhr. Harris also used the improved conditions to revive the area campaign; the other five major operations of the period were area attacks on Hamburg, Stuttgart, and Kiel, by much larger forces then those sent to oil plants. Losses in attacks on Germany fell from over 11 percent to an "acceptable" 3.9 percent. Many of the losses still suffered, surprisingly, were not to conventional night fighters but to a revival of Wild Sow—single-engine fighters without radar, operating on nights with good visibility.

During August the British launched a dozen big night attacks on German targets; losses fell to 3.7 percent that month, although four of these missions were to Stettin and Koenigsberg, very deep in Germany. The British now made more effective use of the Mandrel jammer, and the advance of the Allied armies in France aided them. As the Nazis retreated, their early warning system collapsed and their fighters lost their western bases, giving them less depth in which to operate. And ground-based jamming and electronic guidance systems followed the Allied armies closely. With Oboe and G-H stations near the German borders, accurate bombing deep in Germany became easier. The fuel shortage began to reduce German night fighter operations. British losses at night fell to 2.4 percent in September.

The British official historians, and most later commentators, credited the change in the situation at night mainly to the ground advance and the fuel shortage. But the fact that the greatest drop in the loss rate took place in July, before the Normandy breakout, or before the impact of the gasoline shortage was acute, strongly suggests that the steps taken after July 13 in the electronics war were mainly responsible.

Harris had his own idea of how to exploit the victory at night: more area attacks. Only one night attack was directed against an oil plant during August. However, it is true that two precision attacks were made on the Opel vehicle plant at Russelsheim, which was wrongly thought to be making V-weapons, and that the area attacks on Stettin and Koenigsberg were designed to hamper German supply lines to the Eastern Front.

Bomber Command started day attacks on Germany on August 27 with a successful attack on a Fischer-Tropsch oil plant at Homberg. During September, 11 of 12 major night operations were area attacks—the other opened the campaign against the German transportation system—while 13 day attacks were made on oil targets. Harris launched area attacks during the day as well. Portal did little to control him, unfortunately, for when the RAF did strike oil targets it was very effective. The main burden of the oil campaign fell on the Americans.[7]

THE USSTAF AGAINST THE GERMAN OIL INDUSTRY

The Fifteenth Air Force had continued to hit Ploesti in a specialized campaign that will be treated on its own later in this chapter. The Normandy invasion had forced the Eighth Air Force to leave the oil industry alone for the first half of June, and Spaatz was anxious to return to it. On June 8 he made oil the primary strategic aim of U.S. strategic air operations. The target system was divided up among the various Allied air forces. The Fifteenth drew Ploesti and the natural oil refineries in Austria and Hungary, as well as the synthetic plants in Silesia, Poland, and Czechoslovakia. The Eighth would take on everything in the rest of what had been Germany before 1938, while Bomber Command was allotted the ten Ruhr plants, although the Eighth would sometimes also attack them. Given the difficulties Bomber Command still faced in penetrating Germany, and the desirability of forcing Harris to contribute more to the oil effort, it might have been desirable to split responsibility for the northwestern refineries too.

On June 14 Spaatz restarted the Eighth's campaign against oil in a small way. While nearly 1,300 bombers hammered other targets, 61 B-24s bombed a refinery at Emmerich, near the Dutch-German border, in the Eighth's first attack on natural crude-oil production. On June 15 most of the Eighth was again engaged in France, but 172 B-17s struck refineries at Hannover. On June 18 the Eighth was really unleashed, against eleven different refineries at Hamburg, Bremen, and Hannover. The weather forced the use of H2X, but the attack on Hamburg seemed successful. This was the first of fifteen missions the Eighth would fly against the oil targets in the Hamburg-Harburg area; Bomber Command would fly four. One June 20 the Eighth mounted its largest force yet (1,361 bombers) against Germany, striking the synthetic plants at Magdeburg and Poelitz and refineries at Hamburg, Harburg, Hannover, and Ostermoor. These attacks, especially the 2nd Division's on Poelitz, met strong resistance; 49 bombers and 5 fighters went down over Germany while 3 more bombers never flew again. Despite these exceptionally bad losses, the bombing was effective.

This was the last big mission in June that was concentrated on oil alone. On June 21, while the main force struck aircraft plants, rail centers, and other targets in Berlin, 145 B-17s of the 3rd Division hit the largest of the Fischer-Tropsch plants, at Ruhland. This force then flew to the Ukraine, carrying out the Eighth's first shuttle mission to Soviet bases.

Even with complete air superiority—which, it bears repeating, did not always prevent terrible losses to an individual bomber group—attacks on oil objectives sometimes failed. On June 24 an attack by 340 B-17s on a refinery at Bremen misfired when clouds and smoke screens hid the target. On June 29 the Eighth ended the month with a major mission against aircraft and V-1 plants, and a Bergius plant at Böhlen. But only 81 B-17s of the 179 assigned to Böhlen reached the target; most of the force went after the plane and missile plants. The directors of the air offensive did not yet see that attacks on aircraft plants, or at least those building piston-engine planes, were superfluous if German fuel production was crippled.[8]

GERMAN COUNTERMEASURES

As yet the Eighth Air Force had only devoted sporadic efforts to oil, and Bomber Command had mounted just one really effective mission, but oil production had received a terrific blow. The attacks on oil targets had reduced the more clever Nazis to something close to panic. Speer's only consolation was that he detected a slackening of effort in late June. On June 30 he reported that fuel production within the Reich had fallen drastically. Automotive gasoline production had fallen from 125,000 tons in April to 70,400 tons in June; diesel fuel, from 88,900 tons to 66,300 tons; treibgas, from 37,600 tons to 10,400 tons. He warned Hitler that aviation gasoline production had been reduced by up to 90 percent by June 22. "If it is not possible for us to protect these plants we will be forced to curtail the flow of supplies to the Army in September, which will mean that from that time on there will be a terrible bottleneck which may lead to the most tragic consequences."[9] Fuel consumption had to be economized, and defenses strengthened.

On May 30, following the precedents set during the ball bearings and aircraft campaigns, Speer had appointed Edmund Geilenberg as commissioner-general for emergency measures. Geilenberg had been an able superintendent of weapons production; if he proved less successful than Kessler and Saur, this was not for lack of trying. Apart from attempts at a comeback in the air, immense efforts were put into ground defenses and reconstruction. Priority was given to the ten biggest Bergius plants and the Fischer-Tropsch plant at Ruhland; they were designated *hydrierfestungen* (hydrogenation fortresses). Enormous numbers of guns and smoke generators were jammed around them; The Leipzig area alone was eventually defended by over 1,000 guns. The Germans used more and more heavy guns, up to 128 mm., in massive *Grossbatterien* of up to 24 guns, with fire-control arrangements cross-connected, so that if one fire-control radar failed or was jammed, another could take over. They introduced new incendiary shrapnel shells, to ensure that the fragments would not just rip holes in fuel tanks but set them on fire. Sometimes, as smoke materials ran short (they were largely made at the Merseburg-Leuna plant), the Germans countered the jamming of their radar by switching back to optical range finders.

They camouflaged the plants and built decoys; the Merseburg-Leuna decoy plant was especially successful for a time. Within the actual plants, the Germans installed blast walls and even totally enclosed reinforced concrete "dog houses" for especially vital machinery. Replacement tanks were taken from nitrogen plants. Vast numbers of workers, mostly slave laborers, were mobilized for repair and reconstruction work; by late fall they numbered 350,000—the Nazis were desperate enough to take some Jews from Auschwitz for this force. And 7,000 engineers were released from the Army. Deep shelters were built at the plants, so workers could emerge to fight fires and start work as soon as the bombers left. The work force was put under the SS, inspiring heroic efforts by the German workers and savage measures against the slave laborers.

Nevertheless, it was harder to rebuild as attack succeeded attack. After each blow recuperation took longer, and each time production fell short of the previous peak. The overall structures of the plants were weakened; strained pipes would leak even after distant explosions. In August the Germans began cannibalizing machinery from plants deemed irreparable, to keep other plants going.

They would have found things even harder if not for Allied mistakes. The Allies underestimated the German ability to recover and left too much time between attacks, so the plants usually managed to get in some production before the bombers returned. Overestimating the importance of the Fischer-Tropsch plants, they gave them a higher priority than they deserved. The mission planners did not always choose aiming points best calculated to paralyze the plants, and the average bomb was too small to do much damage. The Americans rarely used bombs heavier than 500 pounds; 2,000 or 4,000 pounders (they could not carry the latter) would have caused more serious damage. RAF attacks were more damaging, since much bigger bombs were used and the attacks lasted longer; there was more chance for fires to spread before the emergency squads got to work.

In 1943 the Germans had decided to move some lubricating oil refineries to Eastern Europe and to build small, dispersed refineries in the Balkans and Poland to replace lost capacity if Ploesti came under attack, but they had not carried out these plans. Elaborate new plans for underground plants and dispersed facilities in Germany itself were developed but could not be executed. Much of the existing and projected underground plant space was slated for missile and plane production; oil plants could not be built quickly, and the work lagged behind schedule. The Strategic Bombing Survey later judged, however, that if they had been started early enough, underground hydrogenation plants near coalfields, and refineries located by oilfields might have supplied "respectable quantities" of fuel despite bombing, at least for a time. Bombing of transportation facilities, however, would eventually have rendered them useless, and Tallboy bombs might have wrecked the plants themselves.

Fuel production and imports declined from 968,000 tons in March, including 180,000 tons of aviation gasoline, to 511,000 tons in June, including 54,000 tons of aviation gasoline. (Allied intelligence estimated a fall from 1,200,000 tons to 670,000 tons.) In July total production fell to 438,000 tons, including 35,000 tons of aviation gasoline, and in August to 345,000 tons, only 17,000 of which was aviation fuel. According to Speer, that month automotive gasoline production within Germany had fallen to 60,000 tons and diesel fuel to 65,000 tons. Nitrogen and rubber production fell precipitately.[10]

THE BATTLE CONTINUES

The Allies were well aware of the German oil crisis, although they underestimated its magnitude and side effects. To make the oil effort more systematic, a Joint Oil Targets Committee was set up in London on July 7, composed of representatives of Eisenhower, Spaatz's command, Bomber Command, the Air Ministry, British intelligence, and the U.S. Embassy's Economic Objectives Unit. Priority was given to the Bergius plants and to crude-oil refineries. Target selection was now aided by specific information from decoded signals, giving details of damage to some targets. There was encouraging news of German worries; on August 12 the Allies learned that two days earlier the Luftwaffe had curtailed all but "absolutely essential" operational activity.[11]

The bombers continued to hit oil targets, but while oil had priority, it was not the only target attacked. The Fifteenth Air Force, while hacking away at Ploesti and starting attacks on refineries at Vienna and Budapest, also devoted much effort to aircraft plants and railroad targets in Austria, Hungary, and the Balkans; support of the Soviet advance was the main aim of the railroad attacks. The Eighth Air Force, for its part, hit aircraft, V-weapons, and tank plants in Germany as well as providing support for the armies. On July 7 the Eighth and Fifteenth together mounted a huge attack on the oil plants. While 1,129 heavy bombers, escorted by 756 fighters, went to Merseburg-Leuna, Bohlen, and Lutzendorf in central Germany, as well as aircraft and ball bearings plants, the Fifteenth sent almost as big a force to the Silesian oil plants. Despite having transferred massive numbers of fighters to France, the Germans intercepted both forces strongly. The Eighth alone lost 37 bombers and 6 fighters over Germany; another 3 bombers and 1 fighter were junked after return. Most of the bombers were lost when a Stürmgruppe hit Liberators of the 2nd Division en route to German aircraft plants; a whole squadron of the Liberators was shot down. But as on every later occasion on which the Luftwaffe tried all-out interception of a strategic mission, it suffered much heavier losses than it inflicted. For the next two months, although there was growing worry about jet and rocket fighters, which had yet to engage in serious combat, opposition from conventional planes was ragged, at least for the Eighth Air Force. The Fifteenth met tougher opposition, especially over Vienna.

The Americans continued to waste effort on the now well dispersed production of piston-engine planes and ball bearings, but there were many missions to oil targets. Merseburg-Leuna alone was bombed six times between July 20 and September 28. Some attacks against oil and aircraft plants in central Germany, and the mission to the Hamburg refineries on August 4, caused the Luftwaffe to come up. The limited forces committed fought hard, but their losses were proportionately as bad as on July 7, while the bombers went relatively unscathed. Only on September 11 did the Nazis have the forces and the will for another massive effort; it too ended disastrously.[12]

PLOESTI

Far to the southeast of the other main targets of the strategic air war, the Fifteenth Air Force, with some British help, waged its own campaign against the refineries and transportation facilities around Ploesti. The British effort, although inconspicuous, was more important than it seemed at the time. Starting in April the RAF's 205 Group had begun dropping mines in the Danube, which carried about a third of the oil produced in Romania to the Reich. The Germans tried elaborate countermeasures, including a squadron of transport planes equipped to sweep magnetic mines from the air. (Ironically, they foolishly grounded the unit as gasoline grew short.) The mines sank many ships and barges and largely halted river traffic. RAF night intruders also strafed and destroyed some oil barges.

The Americans continued a long and difficult campaign against the oil source. General Gerstenberg was still in command at Ploesti and operated as Geilenberg's local counterpart. On May 5, after the oil campaign had been formally approved, the Fifteenth attacked the marshalling yards and oil installations for the fourth time. The Germans tried a large-scale smoke screen but this time it was not particularly effective. An attack on May 18 was partly aborted because of bad visibility, however, and one on May 31 was an outright failure because of the smoke. Despite this, production at Ploesti fell from 370,000 tons, a month before the attack, to 160,000 tons in May.

An attack on June 6 was rated a success, but the Americans were sorely puzzled by the growing effectiveness of the smoke screens, while the Nazis took increasing control of the rebuilding effort from the faltering Romanians. On June 10 the Americans tried a new tactic; 36 P-38s went under the smoke to dive-bomb the refineries while others covered them. Three refineries were hit, but 24 P-38s were lost to intense opposition from fighters and flak, while only ten Me-109s went down. Although this was one of the Germans' few successes in fighter-versus-fighter combat, the loss was a high proportion of the defending force in Romania, and some observers thought there was a slackening of resistance thereafter.

The fighter-bomber experiment was not repeated. Instead, the heavies shifted their attention to other oil and transport installations in Romania. On June 23 and 24 the Fifteenth bombed Ploesti blindly through the smoke. Production in June fell to 75,000 tons. The Fifteenth got ready to launch H2X missions (it had just received the necessary equipment), while it attacked oil installations at Bucharest and at Brasov, north of Ploesti. On July 9 it returned to Ploesti, using H2X for the first time to peer through the smoke screen. The results of this first radar mission were not especially good; they proved better on July 15 but less successful on July 22. On July 28 a new tactic to aid visual bombing was introduced; a master bomber like that used by the British at night flew ahead in a P-38 to see where the smoke screen was thinnest. Instead of being bound to strike a predetermined target, the bombers were directed to those refineries that were most exposed. This worked well, and worked again on July 31.

Smoke and skilled repair efforts had raised overall production in July to 190,000 tons, but this was Gerstenberg's last success. By late July fighter resistance was definitely in decline, while cumulative damage from the more accurate bombing was beginning to shut some refineries permanently. When the Fifteenth returned to Ploesti on August 10, the bomber force could afford to string itself out in a long stream. By the time the later groups arrived, the smoke screen had thinned out.

On August 17–19 Allied attacks cut production to 10 percent of the March level. These last blows were designed more to stop the enemy from carrying off machinery than halt production; the Germans were about to leave Ploesti. On August 20 the Soviets began a major offensive in Romania and swiftly encircled much of the defending force, and Romania jumped over to the Allied side. On August 30 the Soviets entered Ploesti to find a shambles.

The air campaign against Ploesti had lasted just over four months. Despite the early Soviet capture of the area, it had been worthwhile, denying the Nazis at least 700,000 tons of oil products. (Some estimates run considerably higher; the Ploesti campaign results were less thoroughly recorded than other aspects of the oil struggle.) The Americans had also helped the Soviet advance by pinning down fighters and flak in defense of Ploesti and damaging rail installations behind the Axis front.

The Fifteenth had dropped 13,469 tons of bombs on oil installations and related transport targets to achieve this, and its cost in lives and planes had not been small. The Americans had lost 223 heavy bombers, 24 fighter-bombers, and 28 escort fighters, while the RAF had lost 38 bombers at night. Because of the German fighter resistance over Ploesti, Vienna, and some other southern targets, the Fifteenth had had a much higher rate of loss than the Eighth. It lost almost as many bombers in the summer of 1944 as the British-based force, which was twice as big. The men of the Fifteenth sardonically composed a ditty, sung to the tune of "As Time Goes By": "It's still the same old story, the Eighth gets all the glory, while we go out to die. The fundamental things apply, as flak goes by."[13]

THE SHUTTLE MISSIONS

The Americans thought shuttle missions to bases in the USSR would allow attacks on targets beyond the normal range of British or Italy-based planes. They also wanted a precedent for later operations against Japan, using Soviet Far Eastern bases. But ideas about the value of such missions proved greatly exaggerated. (Curiously, the British were not interested in them, although shuttle missions might have let Bomber Command hit eastern targets otherwise out of reach on short summer nights.) The Soviets agreed "in principle" to shuttle bases in October 1943, but showed little interest in getting things underway, and they cut down the size of the project. The Americans finally were allowed to use three bases in the Ukraine.

Although the Soviet personnel they worked with were friendly and cooperative, it became increasingly clear that Stalin had had second thoughts about the whole business. When the bases became operational, it was difficult to get an agreement with the Soviets on what targets to hit. In practice, few shuttle missions were flown, and they had little effect. The Eighth Air Force's first shuttle mission proved disastrous. After bombing the Ruhland oil plant on June 21, six groups flew to the Ukraine with their P-51 escorts. That night, German bombers struck the base at Poltava, destroying 44 B-17s, 15 Mustangs, 200,000 gallons of gasoline, and ammunition and equipment, as well as some Soviet planes. Spaatz later admitted that this was the most effective operation the Germans ever launched against the AAF; it was one of the heaviest losses of equipment, although not of men, ever inflicted on the Eighth Air Force.

The Soviets would not let American units take over the defense of the bases, and they became increasingly uncooperative. The shuttle effort trailed off; it was a minor footnote to the strategic bombing offensive.[14]

A LUFTWAFFE RESURGENCE? THE THREAT OF JET AND ROCKET FIGHTERS

The Allies knew that the Germans were developing planes powered by turbo-jets and rockets. New fighters, faster than anything the Allies would have for some time, might threaten Allied air supremacy. Fears about Nazi jet fighters persisted until nearly the end of the war, but a strong German jet fighter force never materialized.

Long after the war, however, it was supposed that the Allies had narrowly escaped disaster. It is still widely believed that the Germans were far ahead of the Allies in developing jets and that only Hitler's blundering interference prevented them from getting jet fighters at an early date. But in fact the Germans enjoyed no lead in jet development. Their efforts were hampered mainly by factors beyond their control, but their difficulties were exacerbated by a series of mistakes even more amazing than those usually blamed on Hitler. German jet development was one fiasco in which he played a relatively small part.

The British, led by the genius of Sir Frank Whittle, were ahead of the Germans in the development of jets, while the Americans lagged far behind both. Britain and Germany produced operational jet fighters at about the same time in 1944. The British Meteor actually entered the combat a few days ahead of its German counterpart, the Messerschmitt 262. An impression to the contrary was fostered by the fact that the Meteor played a less prominent role in combat. British jets stayed at home to defend against the V-1s. Their activity over the Continent was limited to strafing, and they never shot down any manned aircraft.

Much publicity was later given to the fact that the Germans flew their first experimental jet, the Heinkel 178, as early as 1939, while the first British jet, the E28/39, did not fly until the spring of 1941. But the Heinkel 178's powerplant proved an engineering dead end, while Whittle went straight to a workable turbojet. By 1944 British jet engines were more powerful and reliable than their German counterparts. The Meteor was inferior to the Me-262, not because of its engines, but because of the latter's swept wings. In view of the many complaints later made by Germans about unnecessary delays in the development of *their* jet fighters, it is interesting to note that Whittle stoutly maintained that, with more backing, he could have had the Meteor, designed in 1940, in service by 1942.[15]

The Germans were ahead of the Allies in another aircraft development: the rocket fighter. But the Messerschmitt 163B rocket fighter, while a remarkable plane in many ways, was not a viable weapon. On May 10, 1941, it had reached the then-fantastic speed of 601 miles an hour. Udet, although curiously cool to turbojet development, was fascinated by the Me-163 and did his best to foster its development even in 1940–1941.

But for all its speed, it had many unenviable features. Its hydrogen peroxide fuel was costly, unstable, and difficult and dangerous to handle. Landing, on a skid rather than on conventional landing gear, was difficult. In a bad landing, unused fuel was liable to explode. The Me-163's worst limitation was its short endurance; it had an effective radius of just 50 miles. The pilot had time to fly straight to a target and make only one or two passes before gliding back to base. Bomber crews found the attacks of the rocket planes terrifying, but the Me-163s probably downed only eight Allied planes. Like the V-2, the Me-163 was a technological feat, but was not relevant to the Nazis' real needs. It represented the sort of "romantic" waste of resources to which the Nazis were prone. The rocket fighter proved to be a blind alley in aircraft development.[16]

The effort put into rocket planes would have been better expended on the less spectacular but more useful jets. The Nazis threw away some possibilities for early production of jet fighters. As early as 1940 two rival jet fighter projects had developed at the Heinkel and Messerschmitt firms, the Heinkel 280 and the Messerschmitt 262. The He-280 seems to have been somewhat further along than the Me-262.

The He-280 flew on admittedly inadequate jet engines in April 1941, shortly before the prototype Me-262 flew using piston engines; the Me-262 made a successful entirely jet-powered flight only in July 1942. Heinkel was sure that he had a lead time of a full year over the Me-262. Nevertheless, the He-280 was cancelled on September 15, 1942, and the Nazis laid all their bets on the Me-262; the reasons given were its longer endurance and heavier armament (four 30 mm. cannon instead of two.) Heinkel maintained that the real reason for the Air Ministry's action was political. Given Germany's desperate situation, whatever virtues the Me-262 had did not compensate for any delay. But shortages of critical materials, which would have hampered the production of any turbojet engine, made it doubtful that the He-280 could have entered combat in mid-1943, or even earlier, as has sometimes been suggested.[17]

The Me-262's development crawled along; official interest remained small. During 1942 it became apparent that its BMW jet engines were unsatisfactory; the Junkers Jumo 004 axial-compressor engine was substituted. In December 1942 it was decided to start limited production in January 1944, at a rate of just 20 a month. Milch and Messerschmitt were more interested in the Me-209, the cranky, propeller-driven successor to the Me-109.

But in May 1943 Galland flew a prototype Me-262 and was delighted with it. He urged that all-out production begin as soon as possible and that the Me-209 be stopped to free resources for it. Milch agreed to the first, but Messerschmitt managed to delay the cancellation of the Me-209 until November 1943. Hitler wholeheartedly favored jet development, and it secured a high priority.

On November 2, 1943, Messerschmitt mentioned to Goering that the Me-262 could haul 2,200 pounds of bombs. Hitler learned of this and decided that the Me-262 would make an ideal blitz bomber to deal with the coming invasion of France. His ideas were not totally unreasonable, but reflected overconfidence in the Luftwaffe's ability to defend Germany itself. And using the Me-262 to haul bombs threw away its unique feature—speed. The best use of the Me-262 was as an interceptor, to gain control of the air over Europe and cover attacks on the invasion fleet by conventional fighter-bombers. Astoundingly, despite his remarks, Messerschmitt had not designed bomb racks for the Me-262, although such racks were standard for propeller-driven fighters.

Production was delayed by attacks on the Messerschmitt plants. But the main problem was with the engines; work on them was slow. Nickel and chromium, used in the alloys desirable for turbine blades, were short. In a noteworthy achievement, the Germans dispensed with nickel and used little chromium in the Jumo 004B-1. But they paid a heavy price; its normal life was just 25 hours between major overhauls, compared with 125 hours for the Meteor's engine, and it had many faults. It was not really ready when the design was frozen for production, and deliveries were few and slow. As a result, only 16 Me-262s were delivered in April 1944, 7 in May; 28 in June; and 59 in July. Pilot training, begun in April 1944, was rushed and limited.

On May 23, 1944, Hitler learned that, against his orders, the ME-262 was being built solely as a fighter. He angrily ordered that it be produced only as a bomber, and insisted that all those already built be refitted as bombers. The modifications did not take long, but the bomber version of the Me-262 carried only two 550-pound bombs and only two 30 mm. guns. Inadequately armored against ground fire, with guns suited for attacking bombers rather than ground targets and a limited ammunition load, it was not much of a weapon. (By contrast, most Allied fighters could carry bombloads of up to a ton, and some much more.) In spite of Hitler's order, Me-262s nominally on test flights operated as fighters; during late July 1944 they began hunting Mosquitos and reconnaissance Spitfires over Germany. In the futile effort to stem the Allied advance, nine planes of Kampfgeschwader 51 were rushed to France. The unreadiness of the Me-262 units became clear; four planes were lost en route, and the attacks of the rest had little effect.

Speer managed to secretly give General Galland a few fighter-type Me-262s. Finally, in September, Hitler relented and allowed Me-262s to be built as fighters, because a light jet bomber, the Arado 234, was now coming off the assembly lines.

A fighter unit of thirty to forty Me-262s was formed. Named Kommando Nowotny, after its leader, Maj. Walter Nowotny, it entered combat in October, based at two fields near Osnabrück. But it rarely put up more than four planes a day. Jet operations were hampered by a shortage of spare parts, and the Luftwaffe's jet fuel was not very good. Despite the attack on the oil industry, enough of the fuel was produced, but its quality deteriorated. Nowotny's pilots were not well trained and achieved only modest successes against the vast Allied air fleets. The 30 mm. cannon were deadly when the jets got at the bombers, but they rarely did so, and the Me-262 was not especially dangerous to Mustangs.

American fighter pilots were eager to engage jets; the latter were not too maneuverable, and their engines seemed vulnerable to even a few hits. Basing Kommando Nowotny so far west was probably a mistake. The Allies knew that the jets were most vulnerable when taking off and landing, and the British Second Tactical Air Force, now based on the Continent, mounted standing patrols of Mustangs and Tempests over the jet bases.

The Germans countered by massing light flak guns to form protected flight lanes. A flight of conventional fighters covered each takeoff and landing, leading to full-scale battles. In a fight on November 8, Eighth Air Force fighters downed Nowotny and another pilot, while losing a P-51. Nowotny's unit had claimed only 22 Allied planes—probably an exaggeration—while losing 26 jet fighters. It was taken out of combat to become the nucleus for a bigger jet unit, Jagdgeschwader 7. The jet fighters did not return to action for some time, and then in numbers too small to make a real difference. The Allies did not fail to pay the forming jet units a visit. On November 18, a massive American fighter sweep of 402 planes went to the jet airfield at Lechfeld and destroyed 14 Me-262s on the ground.

USSTAF had not been passive as the jet threat arose. On July 19 the Eighth Air Force began to bomb some known jet airfields and the principal development centers at Lechfeld and Leipheim. The Fifteenth's attacks proved more effective. On July 18 and 20 it attacked jet plants at Friedrichshafen, the deer park of the strategic air war. These attacks were later estimated to have cost the Germans 950 jets. They were probably the most effective strikes of the anti-jet campaign; otherwise, production was too well dispersed and hidden to be vulnerable. (Attacks on foundries making the complicated special castings needed for jet engines would have crippled jet production, but this was not realized at the time.) In early September General Spaatz gave jet plants second priority after oil for two weeks, but the resulting attacks had little effect.

The jets were less of a threat than they seemed. Jet production had been too long delayed; the planes were too cranky; and above all, the Germans were too short of trained pilots to regain control of the air with a jet fighter force. Given the implacable shortage of nickel and chromium that had delayed engine development and left the resulting engines unreliable, Milch and Messerschmitt may have been right, if for the wrong reasons, in their disinterest in jets. The Luftwaffe might have been wiser to concentrate on getting the most advanced possible piston engine fighters (not necessarily the ones the Air Ministry preferred) at the earliest possible moment, for which the materials did exist. Had the Dornier 335 and Tank 152 been ready before the heavy losses of Big Week and the attacks on oil, they might have given the Allies far more trouble than many more jets could have a few months later.[18]

Decisive Offensives II: Transportation, September 1944–V-E Day

The Allied attacks on German oil production were depriving the German forces of more than fuel. The attacks were also crippling production of explosives, rubber, and artificial fertilizer, arguably spelling slow death for the whole German war effort. An attack on the German transportation system, begun gradually in the summer and fall, precipitated a quick collapse.

COMMAND ARRANGEMENTS, PRIORITIES, AND STRATEGY

Since April 1944 General Eisenhower had controlled the strategic bombers. The results could hardly have given even the most extreme air power advocate cause for complaint. Under Eisenhower's command, strategic bombing had finally achieved decisive results. But Portal disliked the arrangement.

Early in September, as the British delegation was en route to a conference between Roosevelt and Churchill at Quebec, Portal urged the other British chiefs of staff to seek a partial reversion to the earlier command arrangements. He and General Arnold should handle the air offensive for the Combined Chiefs of Staff. Portal argued that with the Allies firmly ashore, the situation had changed; there was now less need to use the bombers in direct support of the armies. He claimed that Eisenhower was not really concerned with the main aims of the strategic air offensive, and that the movement of Eisenhower's headquarters from England to France would impede coordination of the offensive. Keeping the bombers under Eisenhower might interfere with plans to use the strategic air forces to attack German morale directly. Portal, perhaps prudently, did not try to cite any instance where Eisenhower's control had actually been harmful.

The real flaw in the Allied command was not Eisenhower's control, but Portal's failure to control Sir Arthur Harris. This was already being shown by Harris's reversion to area attacks on German cities, at the expense of attacks on oil. But the British chiefs of staff pressed Portal's view at Quebec. It was not universally welcomed. Spaatz and Harris did not want a change; they were content to stay under Eisenhower, who naturally favored the existing arrangement.

Even Arnold at first opposed Portal's proposal, but the American chiefs were won over. Eisenhower was placated by assurances that he would still get any direct support he needed. It was agreed to put Arnold and Portal in control of the strategic air offensive, with Spaatz and Bottomley as their local representatives. The British favored having the Combined Chiefs of Staff set explicit objectives—oil, ball bearings, tank production, ordnance depots, and motor transport production, in that order of priority—in the directive establishing the command change, but this was not done.

The change in command did not directly affect American operations, but it probably hurt the strategic air offensive. Eisenhower, prompted by his deputy, Tedder, might have been less tolerant of Harris's independent line of action than Portal was. And, by reducing Tedder's influence, the change delayed and diluted a concentration of effort on what became the Allies' other main objective: German transportation. For although the influence of the Tedder-Zuckerman team had been unfortunate at an earlier stage, they now advocated a policy that would pay enormous dividends.

The apparatus for reviewing intelligence and recommending targets was reorganized. A Combined Strategic Targets Committee (CSTC) was formed, to oversee the inter-Allied bodies that assessed the campaigns against oil, aircraft production, ball bearings, tank and vehicle production, and V-weapons. The CSTC was composed of the heads of, or representatives of, the operations and intelligence departments of the Air Ministry, the USSTAF, the MEW (Ministry of Economic Warfare), the U.S. Embassy's Economic Objectives Unit, SHAEF (Supreme Headquarters Allied Expeditionary Forces), Bomber Command, and the Eighth Air Force. The CSTC itself took over the functions of the Joint Oil Targets Committee. It is astonishing that only now, for the first time, was there a solid inter-Allied advisory board combining economic and operational expertise to oversee the strategic air war. The CSTC did not always operate well or smoothly, but it was a far more useful innovation than the new command arrangement.[1]

On September 25 Spaatz and Bottomley issued their own directive spelling out targets for the bombers. The German oil industry, with special emphasis on gasoline, retained first priority. No less than three target systems shared second priority. Of these, the (1) "German rail and waterborne transportation systems" were mentioned first, followed by (2) tank plants, tank depots and ordnance depots and motor transport plants and depots. "Policing attacks" would be made on the Luftwaffe as the tactical situation required. When conditions were unsuitable for attacks on specific primary objectives, "important industrial areas" would be hit, using blind bombing when necessary.

The September 25 directive gave new importance to transportation, albeit diluted by a continuation of attacks on tank and truck plants and ordnance depots. A minor offensive against these targets had begun in August, but they were too many and too resistant to be easily smashed while oil had priority. The production of tank engines and transmissions, which had been concentrated and vulnerable, was now dispersed. The effort involved was too small to be decisive, but big enough to be a serious diversion.

The Germans responded with their last successful "special action" to preserve an industry under attack. Although 10,000 tons of bombs were dropped, they still ground out tanks, albeit perhaps a fifth less than they had planned. They did suffer a particular loss of heavy Tiger tanks; the plant at Kassel that built them was hit hard. Truck production fell to a little more than half of the German Army's minimum requirements, and many of the "new" trucks were really rebuilt damaged vehicles. But the drop in production was due more to transportation difficulties than to direct attacks. Even had more trucks been built, it is doubtful that there would have been fuel for them.[2]

THE GERMAN TRANSPORTATION SYSTEM

The Nazi economy and war effort depended on the efficient operation of a complex, dense, and well equipped transportation system. Little cargo went by road even before the attack on fuel production. Older means of transport—inland waterways and railroads—carried most of the freight. Rivers and canals were important, and carried a tenth of the freight load. Three-fourths of all freight went by the railroads. Lavishly equipped, they had been designed to keep the regular economy running while moving troops. There was excess capacity in lines, railroad yard space, and engine houses and plenty of preparation for air attack. Bunkers had been built in the larger yards.

The size of Germany's transportation system might have suggested that a crippling attack would be a gigantic task. But not all sectors were equally important; it was not necessary to wreck every bit of it to ruin Germany's economy. The main focal point for both rail and water transport was the Ruhr and neighboring areas along the Rhine. The British had overestimated the Ruhr's direct role in armaments production, and the vulnerability of its plants to direct attack. It was nevertheless crucial. Its mines supplied coal not just to its own industry but to much of the rest of Germany, including the railroads. To keep going, the Germans had to ship massive amounts of coal and other products from the Ruhr to points all over western Germany, and bring raw materials to the Ruhr plants. Germany's two other coal-based heavy industry areas, Upper Silesia and the Saar, were far less important than the Ruhr and were more immediately threatened by Allied armies. German war production might limp along without them, but it could not last long without the Ruhr.

As the Allies knew, the Ruhr particularly depended on inland waterways, especially the Dortmund-Ems and Mittelland canals. The Dortmund-Ems Canal connected the Rhine, the Ruhr, and the Ems river, while the Mittelland carried traffic from the Ruhr to the Elbe, and via the Rothensee ship lift, east to Berlin.

Allied analysts picked the spot where the Dortmund-Ems Canal crossed the Glane river near Ladbergen as a vulnerable point. They also singled out the points where the Mittelland Canal crossed the Aa river, at Gravenhorst, and the Weser river, near Minden, as good targets. At Minden an aqueduct carried the Mittelland over the Weser. At the other points the canals were raised above the surrounding countryside to let the Glane and the Aa flow under them through concrete tunnels. If the canal embankments were blown down, the water would spill out, halting navigation.

The Strategic Bombing Survey later concluded that these had not been the best possible targets. Relatively small attacks, dropping 500 tons or more of 2,000-pound (or larger) bombs on each of just four targets—the Münster locks in the Dortmund-Ems Canal, the Datteln locks in the Wesel-Datteln Canal, the Rothensee ship lift, and *any* bridge over the Rhine—would have paralyzed Germany's inland water transport system longer and more cheaply than the attacks that were made on the points the Allies chose. But the locks and the ship lift were never attacked.

Rail traffic out of the Ruhr depended on several critical marshalling yards, at Hamm (the biggest yard in Germany), Soest, Geisecke, Hagen-Vorhalle, Wedau, Hohenbudberg, and Münster. The movement of trains to and from the Ruhr depended on eighteen bridges and viaducts, of which two were most likely particularly critical: the Bielefeld Viaduct, on the line from Hamm to Hannover, and the Altenbecken Viaduct (near Paderborn), on the line from Soest to Hildesheim.[3]

Not all of the vulnerable points were quickly or consistently attacked, and the status of Germany's transportation network as a target system remained an open question for some time. This was strange, for it had been singled out as a good target system well before the war, and the Allies had periodically attacked it all along.

As part of the preinvasion campaign, the Allies had hit some of the bigger German marshalling yards. Such attacks had continued; 2,400 tons of bombs were dropped on German rail targets each month in July and August. As the Allied armies advanced, attacks on marshalling yards and interdiction efforts moved eastward. They had already hurt the Germans badly. The chaotic situation created by attacks on the railroads in France and Belgium was already spreading to Germany, especially to the Saar. The Germans stopped sending coal to the steel plants in Lorraine and Luxembourg that were still in their hands. German freight car loadings began to fall off, beginning in the week ending August 19, just as it became necessary to move the harvest. The Saar began to collapse, and German war production, using up stocks of finished components, peaked and began to drop.

The Allies, however, did not realize this. Tedder, the chief advocate of a concentration on German transportation, and especially of attacks on rail centers, met strong opposition. He had Eisenhower's full backing and was supported by elements in the Air Ministry, but Portal, Bufton, Arnold, USSTAF, the Eighth Air Force, and the Economic Objectives Unit all disliked the idea for one reason or another. The opponents dominated the newly-formed CSTC. The CSTC, and Spaatz, wanted an all-out concentration on oil and feared dilution of the oil effort. (Spaatz did not oppose attacking transportation, so long as oil's priority was absolutely clear.) After earlier disappointments, there was a general tendency to deprecate transportation as a target. Many doubted that the pre-invasion attacks on marshalling yards had been worthwhile, while some felt that transportation was a proper target for the tactical air forces, but not for the heavy bombers.

From the narrow standpoint of analysts interested solely in interrupting supplies and reinforcements to the German armies at the front, there might have been little to be said for bombing marshalling yards. Experience in France had already proven, although Tedder and Zuckerman continued to deny it, that such attacks were not too effective for that purpose. Only a fraction of the capacity of the dense rail network covering Western Europe and Germany was needed to move troops and supplies, not swiftly and efficiently, perhaps, but enough to maintain the minimal needs of a defending army. It was interdiction attacks that were responsible for the enemy's supply problems.

The critics of the Transportation Plan had been right. But those who assumed that a similar program directed against Germany must be futile overlooked the fact that the attacks on French rail centers had paralyzed the *French* economy, a point that Zuckerman had quickly established. That had been tolerable for the Germans, since their ultimate base lay in their homeland, not in France. But if *German* rail traffic fell by two-thirds, or even less, that base would cease to be effective. Troops might still be moved, but weapons, ammunition, and supplies would no longer be made.

Despite his numerous opponents, Tedder got his way. He cogently argued that enemy transportation was a "common denominator" on which the strategic and tactical air forces could cooperate, and that hitting transportation was complementary, not competitive, with hitting oil. It was a direct way to support the armies, and a better one than carpet bombing, which airmen disliked. Supporting Eisenhower's forces remained the paramount consideration. On September 12 Harris and Doolittle had already agreed to keep on hitting marshalling yards in the Ruhr. When clouds prevented visual attacks on oil plants, the Eighth would hit marshalling yards, using H2X. A massive program of attacks on rail centers, as well as line cutting by fighter-bombers, was launched to support the unsuccessful attempt to take a bridgehead over the Rhine.[4]

These attacks seemed to have little effect on German military operations. But on September 19 Harris agreed to attack the German canal system, and this had spectacular results.

RIVERS AND CANALS

On the night of September 23–24, 5 Group sent 136 Lancasters to the Dortmund-Ems Canal, near Ladbergen. Despite troublesome clouds, five Mosquitos marked the target and 617 Squadron dropped Tallboys, while the rest of the force dropped smaller bombs. The embankments were smashed, and the canal was drained. This was the beginning of a long campaign against the canals. The Germans mobilized masses of workers to repair the banks, but they were hampered by a lucky break: an attack on the Hamm marshalling yards destroyed 15 carloads of tools slated for the Dortmund-Ems job. One of the two passages of the Dortmund-Ems Canal was reopened on October 21, but another disaster for the Germans had taken place in the meantime.

Allied officers argued about whether to mount a major effort to cut off the German forces west of the Rhine by bombing the bridges over the river. Only *one* bridge had to be destroyed to block the river, however, and on October 14 a lucky accident destroyed the Cologne-Mulheimer Bridge. An attack on the Cologne marshalling yards accidentally set off demolition charges on the bridge. It fell, blocking navigation on the Rhine. After November 13, high water caused by autumn rains let barges with light loads pass over the wreckage for a few weeks; then damage to other bridges slowed traffic to a crawl. Finally, the destruction by the Ninth Air Force of another bridge, at Neuwied, on January 16 blocked the Rhine completely. Hours after the Cologne-Mulheimer Bridge fell, two very heavy British area attacks, each mounted by over 1,000 bombers, had wrecked Duisburg harbor, the main Rhine outlet of the Ruhr. This disrupted movement even of local traffic on the lower Rhine.

On October 26, 242 B-24s cut the Mittelland Canal at Minden. Repairs on both major canals were hurried, and by early November both had to be attacked again. On the night of November 4–5, 5 Group sent 176 bombers to the Dortmund-Ems Canal and again broke its banks. Only three planes were lost. The Germans again worked quickly.

Attacks by the Eighth Air Force and Bomber Command on November 6–7 misfired, but on November 21–22 the canal was broken again, by 128 planes; this time none was lost. The Germans now sealed off the narrower of the two channels and concentrated on repairing the other one. Also on November 21–22, 143 Lancasters smashed the Mittelland Canal at Gravenhorst, losing two bombers. Both canals were repaired once again. On January 1, 1945, 5 Group returned; 104 planes smashed the Dortmund-Ems, and 157 cut the Mittelland. Only two bombers were lost. Another attack on the Mittelland Canal, on February 21–22, shut it for the rest of the war; the Dortmund-Ems was reopened in February, but by then it made little difference. It was closed for the last time by an attack on the night of March 3–4.

For small losses the Allies had wrecked the German inland waterway system and thrown the burden of moving freight—above all, coal—onto the already overstrained railroads. Coal movement by water in Germany fell from 2,214,000 tons in August 1944 to 724,000 tons in October, then to 454,000 tons in November, rising slightly to 505,000 tons in December.[5]

THE ATTACK ON THE GERMAN RAILROADS

During October the attack on the German railroad system continued. The Fifteenth Air Force struck Vienna and Munich, as well as rail targets in the part of Southeastern Europe under Nazi control, while the Eighth Air Force and Bomber Command concentrated mostly on western Germany. The strategic air forces alone dropped 35,000 tons of bombs on rail targets. The weather in October was bad and was responsible for the degree of concentration against transportation. Nearly all the American attacks on marshalling yards were made on H2X.

Much of Bomber Command's contribution also fell through clouds; 3 Group, using the G-H formation technique, hit rail centers during the day, and there were night attacks as well. Bomber Command was far from concentrating all of its efforts on transportation, or oil, and many of its attacks were combined area and precision attacks. Often part of the force dispatched to a German city was directed at the center of the city, while part was directed at its marshalling yards.

The Allies remained poorly informed about the real effects of the attacks. Looking at the purely tactical and immediate aspects of the railroad campaign, many saw only that the Germans must be getting at least an essential minimum of supplies forward. Bad weather interfered with reconnaissance. The Allies had broken the German railroad administration code, but processing the enormous number of intercepted messages had a low priority. Nevertheless, remarks in other kinds of messages, which were processed, should have shown that transportation attacks were having a tremendous impact. In a message sent on October 20, and deciphered four days later, the Wehrmacht high command quoted Speer as reporting that 30–35 percent of armaments plants were at a standstill because of the destruction of traffic and lack of electric power—the latter due to the growing coal shortage.

There was much grumbling about the emphasis on transportation, especially in the CSTC, which was dominated by oil advocates. It favored attacks on the canals, but not bombing railroads. Until 1945 it remained skeptical of the effects of attacks on transportation, and Tedder had to force it to form a transportation subcommittee in October. He was the decisive force in keeping the campaign going. He concluded during October that it was too scattered and not adequately planned, and urged greater concentration against Ruhr and Rhine valley rail centers.

Tedder secured an agreement on an exclusive second priority for German transportation, after oil. On November 1 Spaatz and Bottomley issued a new directive. It dropped tank and vehicle production and ordnance depots as major targets and made "German lines of communication," with "particular emphasis on the Ruhr," the second priority for the strategic forces.[6] The term "German lines of communication" was designed to stress the concentration of effort in proximity to the front, and to placate the ground commanders for the loss of direct support that Tedder wished to arrange.

On November 8 the CSTC issued a plan for the attack, emphasizing short-run "tactical" considerations over the strategic disruption of the whole German economy, in which it had no great faith. But it realized the desirability of cutting off the Ruhr and the value of breaking the crucial Bielefeld and Altenbecken viaducts. The Reich was cut into nine transportation zones; British-based forces would handle the five western zones, concentrating their attacks between the Rhine and a line running through Hamburg, Hannover, Wurzburg, and Ulm, while the Fifteenth Air Force hit remoter zones in the south and east. While heavy bombers hit marshalling yards, fighter-bombers would attack the smaller targets left intact after the heavies went over.

As even more bombs fell on the marshalling yards, the Eighth Air Force's 2nd Bombardment Division took on the viaducts. On November 2, 172 B-24s damaged the Bielefeld Viaduct, and closed it for nine days. On November 26, 240 planes returned to the same viaduct, but the attack failed. Another visit, by 152 B-24s on November 29, shut it for eleven days. On the same day an attack by 144 B-24s shut the Altenbecken Viaduct until February 11, 1945. Targets of this sort, like the canals, would have been better dealt with by the RAF and its bigger bombs. But the Germans saw the handwriting on the wall and began building bypass lines around both viaducts. Allied fighter attacks, cold weather, and other difficulties prevented completion of these bypasses.

The transportation attack intensified, even though a new directive on December 5 gave direct attacks in support of the Allied armies second priority, ahead of transportation, for a time, and there was still widespread skepticism about the railroad campaign.

Even the unsystematic attack of September and October, with its inattention to interdiction, had been more effective than the Allies dreamed. Even troop movements were slower. In a report to Hitler on December 5, Speer had already warned of disaster looming in the Ruhr. The collapse of the German economy had started. Bombers alone were not responsible for the transportation disaster; fighter attacks were so common that the Germans normally did not run trains in daylight, west of a line running well east of the Rhine. Traffic in some areas was already severely restricted. On September 19 the left bank of the Rhine was closed to all freight except weapons, coal, and food.

The relentlessly falling bombs left marshalling yards unable to form trains and keep traffic moving. This was not an overnight process. As in the battle over oil, there was a struggle of repair efforts against growing, cumulative damage. The Strategic Bombing Survey later calculated that it took an average of six heavy attacks to more or less wreck a typical marshalling yard. On October 18 Hitler ordered that repairs to marshalling yards be given first call on labor. The Germans mobilized vast masses of workers; sometimes 8,000–12,000 men were needed to repair a yard after a big attack. But as in the repairs to canals and viaducts, the Germans found that pick-and-shovel laborers did not make up for their lack of the heavy earth-moving machinery Americans were used to. Bulldozers were better than slaves.

Traffic moved only in spurts. All coal movement by rail south from the Ruhr was stopped from October 14 to 18; after that, only a fifth of the usual hundred coal trains daily left the region.

Coal, the biggest item, piled up at the Ruhr mines, and iron ore failed to reach the steel plants of the region. Despite an emphasis on coal, car loadings of coal fell 39 percent in October. By November coal deliveries to factories in Bavaria had fallen by nearly 50 percent, and coal probably held up better than other commercial traffic. The Saar had already collapsed, and Upper Silesia could not make up for the losses from the Ruhr. Confusion spread from the Ruhr, and Silesia was already suffering from air attack. The average daily allocation of freight cars to coal movement in Germany as a whole fell steadily, from 127,000 in August 1944 (as compared to 134,000 in August 1943) to 115,000 in September, 105,000 in October, 99,000 in November, and 83,000 in December. Total monthly car loadings fell from 3,940,944 in August to 3,442,133 in September, 3,241,506 in October, 2,976,302 in November, and 2,570,707 in December. War production reeled toward collapse; in November and December stocks of coal and raw materials outside the Ruhr, and of finished parts everywhere, were used up, and much of what *was* made could not be moved. The production effort, assisted by a last partial recovery in oil production, had lasted long enough to equip and fuel the German forces for one last throw, but they could not be sustained for much longer.

Effective as the transportation campaign was, it might have achieved quicker results with more concentration and better use of the available resources. As Alfred Mierzejewski has noted, a concerted assault on just eight major marshalling yards controlling traffic from the Ruhr—Hamm, Hohenbudberg, Soest, Geisecke, Hagen, Vorhalle, Wedau, and Münster—and on the marshalling yards in the two Reichsbahn directorates of Halle and Oppeln, in central and eastern Germany, would have quickly wrecked the whole system. Even quicker results would have been attained had Bomber Command taken over the job of hitting the critical bridges and viaducts out of the Ruhr.[7]

THE FALL 1944 OIL BATTLE

The USSTAF's commitment to the land battle, and Sir Arthur Harris's disinterest in the oil campaign, sharply reduced the attacks on oil targets in late September. The Eighth Air Force nevertheless struck Merseburg-Leuna, two other central German oil plants, and the Bremen refineries, while the Fifteenth tackled Blechhammer, Odertal, and Auschwitz, and refineries at Budapest. German production and imports of oil fell to just 281,000 tons in September, including only 10,000 tons of aviation gasoline. The Germans ended all training for brand-new pilots, and fuel deliveries to the Luftwaffe were cut in half. The night fighter force rarely flew more than 50 sorties a night. Production of explosives fell steeply, as did that of glue and plastics. The Germans began diluting military explosives with fillers like rock salt; the manufacture of fertilizer and mining explosives was cut back in favor of immediate military needs.

Speer had foreseen immediate disaster if the air attacks went on at high intensity. Neglect and bad weather in October and November, and a reduction of fuel consumption at the relatively static front, helped him. The weather closed in earlier in 1944, and was even worse than it had been a year before. From October to December roughly 80 percent of the Eighth's bombing was on radar. Better guidance systems were now in use, at least over Western Germany. The Eighth now used G-H, and in November it introduced Micro-H. Pulses sent by forward ground stations were picked up by H2X receivers and steered planes with that apparatus to the target. But the Americans really had no substitute for seeing a target. Bomber Command was better equipped for bad weather, but Harris mounted only six small day, and no night, attacks on oil targets in October. Only 6 percent of Bomber Command's bombs were aimed at oil. The Eighth Air Force went after oil targets as hard as the weather allowed, but only four large oil missions were mounted, and the results were not especially good, even on visual attacks. The Fifteenth was more effective, hitting the oil plants at Odertal, Blechhammer, and Brux and the Austrian refineries. But it did not make up for the general lag.

In October German oil production recovered to a total of 316,000 tons, including 21,000 tons of aviation gasoline, and rose in November to 337,000 tons, including 39,000 tons of aviation gasoline. (Speer, whose reports sometimes show discrepancies with later Allied investigations, declared that 41,000 tons of aviation gasoline were made in November, and that automotive gasoline rose from 37,000 tons in October to 50,000 tons in November, while diesel and jet fuel rose from 66,000 tons to 73,000 tons.)

The Germans accumulated a reserve that they considered sufficient for an offensive, although it turned out that they had greatly underestimated their needs. In December the overall fuel shortage finally seriously hurt the mobility of the German army. It had already suffered serious shortages as early as the battle in Normandy, but that had been due mainly to attacks on supply routes and dumps close to the battle areas. The recovery in production was largely due to repairs to major synthetic plants. The output of the small benzol plants actually fell; they were only now being singled out for attack, and many that had not been spotted suffered in area attacks on the Ruhr.

As noted earlier, Allied reconnaissance was not keeping up with the offensive. There were too few reconnaissance planes, and their losses, small earlier, were rising as jets intercepted them. To supplement the specialized reconnaissance planes, cameras were installed in some ordinary fighters, but bad weather and smoke screens sometimes prevented any assessments.

On October 18 the CSTC resolved to do something Speer had feared for months: return to oil targets at short intervals without regard to reconnaissance or the lack of it. Weather and other things delayed this decision from being carried out; had it been implemented earlier, it would have denied the Germans the intervals between completion of repairs and Allied detection of recovery, during which they had produced much fuel.

During October the Allies realized that German fuel production was recovering. The USSTAF pressured the British to attack oil more. Portal was in the midst of a rather too gentle debate over oil with Harris, who still saw it as just another "panacea target." During November Harris, though still insisting that he was right, found it prudent to cave in to some extent. That month Bomber Command launched eleven day and five night attacks on oil targets, for the first time attacking refineries at Harburg; 24.6 percent of the tonnage of bombs dropped in November was aimed at oil targets, compared with 6 percent in October. During December, between bad weather and the "distraction" of the German attack in the Ardennes, Bomber Command actually took over much of the burden of the oil offensive, with two daylight and three night operations. For a time Harris had resisted attacking the bigger and more distant plants at Merseburg-Leuna and Poelitz, claiming that it would be too costly, but attacks on them in December showed that, as so often before, Harris had been wrong. Only 4 of the 497 bombers sent to Merseburg-Leuna, and 3 of the 207 attacking Poelitz, went down. Losses were no greater than those suffered in attacks on closer objectives. Apparently Harris was *still* unenthusiastic about the oil campaign, as suggested by Portal's complaint that he could have sent a force three times as big to Poelitz.

British losses were now low. Of 5,194 planes sent against oil plants in October–December 1944, only 57 were lost. Unfortunately, the RAF's growing efforts still did not make up for the weather difficulties afflicting the Americans. Although 37,096 tons of bombs were dropped on oil targets in November, more than in any other month of the war, this was not reflected in the damage done. The Eighth Air Force attacked oil targets on thirteen days in November, but visual bombing was possible on only four days.

GERMAN RESISTANCE IN THE AIR

The Luftwaffe sometimes opposed American attacks in central and eastern Germany, especially on oil targets. It occasionally inflicted awful losses. On September 27, during a mission to the Tiger tank plant at Kassel by the 2nd Bombardment Division, the 445th Group made a wrong turn and became separated from the rest of the force. A Sturmgruppe swarmed all over it, shooting down 25 of 37 B-24s in a few minutes, before Mustangs came to the rescue, downing 18 German fighters. This was the heaviest loss of any Eighth Air Force group on a single mission of the whole war. But the 445th Group nevertheless returned to Kassel with the rest of the 2nd Division the next day.

There were big battles with German conventional fighters on September 28 and October 6 and 7. Using high cloud as cover, Sturmgruppen jumped exposed squadrons and inflicted heavy losses, although at a high cost to themselves.

The Germans were far from through. After losing France, they had concentrated their fighters at home, leaving only minimal forces on the battlefronts. They planned a comeback, the Great Blow, a massed attack with conventional fighters to win a respite for the oil plants, and for conversion fully to jets.

The scheme was to field the biggest possible force, including flight instructors, with at least 2,000 single-engine fighters. Large formations built around Sturmgruppen were to be hurled against the bombers in the main attack, while smaller forces to the west engaged the Americans as they entered and left Germany. As many planes as possible of the main force would refuel and rearm for a second sortie. Night fighters would patrol the approaches to Switzerland and Sweden to catch bombers fleeing there. Galland hoped to down 400–500 bombers for the loss of 400 German fighters and 100–150 pilots.

Some of the Luftwaffe's operations during this period were practice for the Great Blow. On November 2, as 1,100 bombers and 873 escort fighters went to Merseburg-Leuna, some 300–400 fighters came up, the largest force to contest an Eighth Air Force operation since early June. Yet again, a German controller noted that two groups of the 1st Bombardment Division were away from the rest. A Sturmgruppe pounced on them, destroying 26 B-17s. The 3rd Division lost 12 planes, and 16 American fighters went down. But the Germans paid a terrific price; they lost perhaps 120 planes, with 70 pilots killed and 28 wounded—nearly a tenth of the available pilots. Hitler lost faith in the Great Blow. He decided to use the fighters in the Ardennes offensive, although a few large-scale intercepts did take place.

The German fighters did not engage again until November 21, when the Mustangs caught some enemy formations assembling. They again inflicted heavy losses on the Germans on November 26, although one whole bomber squadron went down. On November 27, as a comparatively modest force of 483 bombers, with 727 escorts, struck marshalling yards in western Germany, the Germans put up 750 sorties—their biggest effort of the whole war. But they mistook the escort force for the bombers and blundered right into it. Not one bomber was lost to any cause that day; the Americans claimed 98 German fighters for the loss of 12 P-51s and P-47s. The American claims were probably exaggerated, but 37 German pilots were killed and 14 wounded. The outcome of the November battle suggested that a comeback had never been a real possibility for the Luftwaffe. There were not enough trained pilots or, even with the partial recovery of fuel production, the fuel to permit the pilots they had to practice. Indeed, the very weather that hampered the Americans prevented a big operation or even the preparations for one.[8]

THE SECOND BATTLE OF THE RUHR

Bomber Command, because of its heavier bombs and greater accuracy, particularly in marginal weather, had a tremendous impact in the campaigns against oil and transportation—when Harris deigned to let it take part. He continued to concentrate on area attacks. In the last three months of 1944, 53 percent of Bomber Command's bombs went into area attacks and only 14 percent were used on oil targets, 15 percent on transportation, and 18 percent on military and naval targets.

Harris's ability to persist in the area offensive, despite inter-Allied directives, and the views of Portal and the Air Staff (not to mention reason and evidence) defies fully satisfactory explanation to this day. His close relationship with Churchill, whom he saw often, evidently deterred Portal from disciplining or replacing him. His dismissal, it was thought, would mean a scandal even if the Prime Minister did not intervene to stop it.

Churchill may not have had a burning interest in the strategic air war by this time, but he had never evinced any disapproval of the area offensive, or interest in alternative strategies. Nevertheless, it is unlikely that Churchill would have opposed a joint insistence by the British chiefs of staff that Bomber Command follow the priorities agreed on with the Americans. Fundamentally, Portal was unwilling to argue with the Prime Minister, or expose the fact that he was not fully in control of the RAF. He tried to "persuade" Harris, without effect.

On November 1 Harris rejected abandoning the area offensive as foolish; he insisted that it was near completion. It was only necessary to destroy Magdeburg, Halle, Leipzig, Dresden, Chemnitz, Breslau, Nuremburg, Munich, Koblenz, and Karlsruhe, and finish off Berlin and Hannover. (Later, on January 18, 1945, he declared that it would also be necessary to destroy Erfurt, Gotha, Weimar, Eisenach, and "Posen"—actually the Polish city of Poznan, off limits to area attack under the existing rules.) The "debate" lasted for months. Portal's arguments for the oil plan, and observation that Harris himself admitted that cities hit by area attacks were not totally destroyed, but recovered their industrial output in four or five months, simply bounced off. The area offensive continued to the end of the war; in fact, as we shall see, one infamous series of area attacks was backed by Portal himself.

The area attacks of the last part of the war were of unprecedented weight and ferocity. After penetrating to distant Stettin and Koenigsberg in August, Bomber Command switched to attacks, sometimes in the day, on nearer coastal cities such as Kiel, Bremerhaven, and Emden and scattered cities in the Rhineland and southwestern Germany.

A night attack on Darmstadt by 5 Group, on September 11, was especially destructive. It introduced a new technique designed to distribute the bombs so as to maximize destruction. The 218 Lancasters delivering the main attack converged on the target along different axes, bombing only after set delays after *passing* the markers. This insured that the bombs were not scattered too widely, nor some areas "overbombed." The efficient spread of the incendiaries in what the Germans called a "death fan" set off a firestorm like the ones at Hamburg and Kassel. Between 8,000 and 12,000 people were killed.

Bomber Command opened a second "Battle of the Ruhr" on October 6–7 with an attack on Dortmund. As in the first battle, the Ruhr was merely the main point of concentration. While blasting no less than 16 cities there, Bomber Command hit an equal number of cities in the rest of western Germany. The attacks on the Ruhr were truly gigantic; 9,000 tons of bombs fell on Duisburg within 24 hours. Essen was hit by 1,055 bombers on October 23–24 and another 771 on October 25. The Ruhr had been so devastated by fire in 1943 that there was little left to burn; 85 percent of the bombs dropped there now were high explosives. The destruction was not far short of what might be seen in a nuclear war. If not for excellent shelters, evacuation of many women and children, and the dispersal of many workers to villages, there would have been far more deaths. The Ruhr alone was hit by over 60,000 tons of bombs. In attacks on the generally less devastated German cities outside the Ruhr, Bomber Command used more firebombs, but there Harris usually sent far smaller forces. Not all of these were simply area attacks. In some cases a factory was the aiming point, as in the notable instance of the Krupps works in Essen, which was shut down permanently after a particularly heavy attack. The attack on Saarbrücken on the night of October 5–6 was launched at the request of Patton's Third Army in order to block the enemy's communications near the battle zone.

The effort expended against cities would have contributed more to victory—and have simplified postwar reconstruction—if it had instead been aimed at oil and transport targets. But such tremendous blows could not help but have a devastating impact, and even contribute directly to the oil and transportation campaigns. In the Ruhr, especially, area attacks smashed benzol plants the Allies had not located. Even though not aimed at railroad centers, the attacks on cities blocked transportation routes. British official historians later argued with some cogency that the final series of area attacks were mainly responsible for the collapse of industrial production in the Ruhr, although in the rest of Germany, it was the attack on transportation that caused industry to fail. The area attacks wrecked the Ruhr's internal transportation system and its gas and electric power grids. Coal was plentiful in the Ruhr, but it could not be moved to where it was needed. Even water was short.

The Germans tried frantically to keep the area going. Speer outlined the magnitude of the repair efforts to Hitler on November 11. He was sending 4,500 skilled workers to the Ruhr from the rest of Germany, and 50,000 slave laborers were being taken from digging defenses to repair transportation there, while 30,000 men would be taken from armaments production to help with this and to repair the Ruhr industries. Of the Ruhr miners, 10 percent would be transferred to such work. It had been found that the standard farm tractor could get along on naval fuel oil and coal tar oil, and 4,000, about a tenth of the tractors in Germany, would be sent to the Ruhr to haul food, along with a special allocation of 5,000 tons of fuel oil, and 8,300 coke and anthracite gas generators to power transport vehicles.[9] But all this was not enough.

At the other end of the tactical spectrum from the area bombing, Bomber Command launched many attacks in support of army and navy operations. In a series of difficult operations, 5 Group's 617 Squadron and 9 Squadron sank the battleship *Tirpitz* with Tallboys on November 12. This remarkable feat came too late to be of great value. Sinking the *Tirpitz* in 1942–1943 would have had great strategic significance, but the time was past when the release of the forces the battleship had tied down would have had great impact.[10] It is arguable that the two squadrons and their Tallboys might have been better used against the bridges and viaducts leading from the Ruhr.

THE BATTLE OF THE BULGE

The long-planned German offensive in the Ardennes began December 16. It was designed to cut off the northern Allied armies and retake Antwerp. Hitler hoped that this would cause the Western allies to make peace. The offensive and bad weather largely halted American strategic air operations from Britain for nearly a month, although the Fifteenth Air Force kept up the fight. The Eighth Air Force turned to helping the tactical air forces keep control of the air over the battle area and attacking supply routes in the enemy's immediate rear.

Bad weather prevented either side from flying much for several days. When the weather cleared on December 23, the gigantic Allied air concentration stopped German planes from attacking Allied troops. But when the Ninth Air Force's medium bombers flew to their targets that day despite the failure of their fighter escort to rendezvous, German fighters tore into them, downing 35 bombers. It was by far the Ninth's worst bomber loss of the war.

On December 24 the Eighth mounted its greatest mission of the whole war. Joined by 500 RAF bombers, it launched a maximum effort to insure control of the air. Even war-weary planes were sent up, as the Eighth dispatched 2,046 bombers, of which 1,884 reached their targets, escorted by 813 fighters. In one day the Eighth dropped 5,052 tons of bombs. Most fell on eleven airfields beyond the Rhine; the rest on transportation targets west of the river. More bombers were hitting a single German airfield than the Eighth had been able to send up on any one day before May 1943. There was tough opposition; 12 heavies and 10 fighters failed to return, and 23 bombers and 2 fighters were junked after the mission. The fighters alone claimed 74 German planes.

The Luftwaffe effort subsided for a time and was restricted, during the day, to the area behind the German lines. The Eighth reverted to attacking rail centers, shifting its emphasis to the targets in an "outer" line of interdiction partly beyond the Rhine, while the mediums operated nearer home. On the last day of 1944 the Eighth managed to mount a strategic mission; the 3rd Division sent 526 bombers to attack the oil refineries at Hamburg and Misburg.

On January 1 perhaps as many as 1,100 German fighters carried out a low-level attack on Allied forward air bases in Belgium and the Netherlands. The Germans achieved surprise, and destroyed about 300 planes, mostly on the ground. But their flying and shooting were bad, and Allied fighters took a heavy toll. The Germans lost about 300 planes themselves; 151 pilots were killed or wounded and 63 captured. Allied operations were not much affected, and the losses were quickly replaced. The "success" was just another nail in the Luftwaffe's coffin.

The results of the heavy bomber attacks on marshalling yards and bridges are hard to distinguish from those of attacks by the tactical air forces, but all air operations together had a terrific impact. Air power did not, of itself, defeat the Ardennes offensive. The German plans had been too optimistic, and went awry in the first 48 hours, at a time when both German and Allied planes were mostly grounded because of delays imposed by small American ground units. But aircraft wrecked the German supply arrangements and helped insure that the Germans were halted and driven back relatively quickly. Peter Elstob later concluded, "It was the almost complete disruption of communication which did most to halt the Ardennes offensive." The localized transportation attack caused the collapse of the German railroads just behind the battle front. This soon spread to the rest of the system.[11]

A NEW DIRECTIVE

As the Ardennes battle ended, there was intense gloom among the Western Allied leaders. It was seen not as a last-gasp effort but as evidence that the enemy was still strong. They feared that the enemy would succeed in putting large numbers of jets and new-type submarines into action.

Uncertainty seeped into the planning for the strategic air offensive. There was doubt about whether to persist with attacks on transportation (other than canals) or move to other objectives. On January 8 Eisenhower released the heavy bombers for a full-scale return to the oil offensive, which no one doubted was worthwhile, and the next day Spaatz gave attacks on jet plants equal priority with oil. In practice, however, the USSTAF did not get a chance to strike jet plants before a more relaxed view of the jet threat took hold. During January, three-quarters of the USSTAF effort went to tactical missions in support of the land armies.

On January 15 Bottomley and Spaatz issued a new general directive. Oil and transportation retained their priorities. Important industrial areas would be bombed when the weather was unsuitable for the other objectives. This sort of clause had usually been a device lending itself to British projects, but the Americans intended to use it to cover renewed attacks on tank plants. Jets had a high priority. This evaluation reflected American views; the British did not share the Americans' fears of a Luftwaffe resurgence. Marginal effort would be devoted to attacking certain U-boat objectives.

By the end of January the British had thought of a way to exploit the Soviet victories in Poland and eastern Germany. At a meeting on Malta January 31, Portal and Arnold's representative, General Laurence Kuter, agreed to revise the directive in terms of the immediate future. After oil, second priority went to "Berlin, Leipzig, Dresden and associated cities where heavy attack will cause great confusion in civilian evacuation from the east and hamper reinforcements," while as a third priority the strategic air force would attack transportation in the Ruhr-Cologne-Kassel area to prevent the Germans from transferring forces from their Western front to the east. The clause on Berlin, Leipzig, and Dresden is relevant to the background of one of the war's most controversial air attacks. Except for these alterations, designed to cover a temporary situation, the directive of January 15 governed the strategic air offensive for the rest of the war.[12]

DRESDEN AND OTHER AREA ATTACKS

Sir Arthur Harris continued the area offensive under the thin guise offered by directives allowing bombing of "industrial areas." Bomber Command attacked no less than 30 cities. This involved a smaller portion of its overall efforts than before—about 37 percent, compared to 26 percent on oil targets and 15 percent against transportation. But its power was now enormous; by January 1945 it had a daily average of 1,420 four-engine bombers and Mosquitos ready with crews. In the remaining months of the war it dropped 181,000 tons of bombs, a fifth of the total dropped in the whole war, against slight opposition. One of its attacks, on the city of Dresden, was one of the more devastating attacks on a civilian population of the war, and it became highly controversial. The origins of the Dresden attack were complex, and were interwoven with American operations more than most of Bomber Command's area attacks.

During 1944 the British had several times proposed combined attacks on major German objectives to smash morale, in which the British would aim at an area target. If the Americans refused to join in an area attack, they could hit precision targets in the same city. One plan, Thunderclap, had surfaced in July. It envisaged a series of attacks on Berlin, designed to shock, not German civilians, but the high command into seeing that Germany was finished. After much argument, Thunderclap was ordered on September 9. But it turned out that there were not enough fighters to cover it, and a reaction against the whole idea set in within Eisenhower's headquarters and the American Joint Chiefs of Staff. The plan was set aside.

As their willingness to consider Thunderclap suggests, the Americans did not always inflexibly oppose area attacks, or bombing aimed to undermine civilian morale, or even operations specifically aimed at killing civilians outright. The Eighth Air Force had explicitly aimed at killing civilians, albeit specialized sorts of workers, at Münster and (as a second choice) at Schweinfurt. Some operations, such as the first attack on Berlin, had been designed at least partly to strike at enemy morale. Some attacks on the Balkan satellite capitals, while aimed at marshalling yards in those cities, were also designed to frighten Romanians and Bulgarians and turn them against their rulers. The radar bombing of German targets that had begun in late 1943 often amounted to de facto area bombing. General Arnold, and some other officers, sometimes considered outright area bombing. In the B-29 campaign against Japan, the AAF turned to deliberate area attacks against cities after attempted precision bombing attacks failed to achieve results. While some American officers strongly disapproved of area attacks on ethical grounds, most of the air generals, like Spaatz, thought that the main reason for opposing them was that they were just not effective, although Eaker, at least, regarded them with distaste.

In the gloom and confusion of early 1945, the British reconsidered Thunderclap. Ironically, it was revived by Commodore Bufton and Air Marshal Bottomley, who were usually in favor of precision or selective attacks. The success of the Soviet offensive led Bufton to propose a heavy attack on Berlin as the Soviets drove west, supplemented by Fifteenth Air Force attacks on Breslau and Munich. The British Joint Intelligence Committee was skeptical of the morale effect of such attacks, but suggested that they might help the Soviet advance by hampering the movement of refugees from eastern Germany and inspiring flight from Berlin itself, disrupting German troop movements and the military and administrative machinery in the capital. Harris suggested supplementary operations against Chemnitz, Leipzig, and Dresden, all of which, of course, he had wanted to attack all along. Portal doubted that a Thunderclap-type operation against Berlin, expected to take four days and nights, would be decisive, but thought that big attacks on Berlin, Dresden, Leipzig, and Chemnitz, and perhaps other cities, were desirable to confuse evacuation and troop movements. Churchill liked the idea. In late January the British rejected a full-blown Thunderclap but decided to launch one big attack on Berlin and related attacks on Dresden, Leipzig, and Chemnitz—subject to overriding priorities, like attacks on oil. On January 31 Bottomley and Spaatz agreed to launch attacks on Berlin, Leipzig, and Dresden, and "associated cities where heavy attack will cause great confusion in civilian evacuation from the east and hamper movement of reinforcements from other fronts."[13] The phase of the moon and the weather delayed Bomber Command's execution of this plan.

On February 3, 937 Fortresses from the 1st and 3rd Air Divisions, as the Bombardment Divisions were now called, bombed Berlin, aiming at marshaling yards, major railroad stations, and the government district, while B-24s struck oil targets and marshalling yards around Magdeburg. Although it was winter, surprisingly most of the bombing was visual. But, as the American official historians admitted, civilian casualties were high, although the reports of 25,000 deaths seem to have been exaggerated. German records suggest that less than 1,000 people were killed. The strike was aimed at what had long been deemed military objectives, but the attack on stations, as well as the normally more important marshaling yards, was probably calculated to interfere with refugee as well as troop movements, and was bound to kill many civilians.

On February 4, as the dust settled in Berlin, the Combined Chiefs met their Soviet counterparts at Yalta. General Antonov, the Red Army's chief of staff, suggested that the Western air forces paralyze enemy communication centers like Berlin and Leipzig; he neither mentioned Dresden nor excluded it. On February 5, when proposing a bomb line, east of which Western bombing would be forbidden, he left Dresden open to Western air attack. Contrary to later claims, the Soviets never specifically asked for an attack on Dresden. The implication of their request was probably for more strikes on marshalling yards in eastern Germany, rather than area attacks. Antonov was probably thinking of attacks like the one on Berlin the previous day. Later Soviet propaganda exploitation of the bombing of Dresden tempted some Westerners to try to shift some or all of the blame for it onto the Soviets, but the record does not support this.[14]

On February 6 the Eighth Air Force, unable to hit oil targets, sent 1,310 bombers to the marshalling yards at Magdeburg and Chemnitz, although much of the force had to resort to attacks on small "targets of opportunity" in central Germany. On February 12 the Eighth decided to attack the Dresden marshalling yards on February 13; the RAF was planning to hit the city that night. Weather led the Eighth to postpone its attack until the 14th, after the RAF struck. As the experience of Hamburg should have shown, this was not a good idea.

On the night of February 13–14, 244 Lancasters of 5 Group set out for Dresden. A second wave of 529 Lancasters from other groups followed, while 320 Halifaxes of 4 Group hit the oil plant at Böhlen.

Harris ignored the emphasis of the January 31 directive on disrupting enemy transportation, or interpreted it with an odd twist of his own. He treated the Dresden operation as a conventional area attack on a residential and commercial area, albeit on a "virgin" target. Since Dresden had been bombed earlier only by small American forces aiming at the marshalling yards, there was plenty to burn. The force carried an unusually high proportion of incendiaries; three-fourths of the load consisted of firebombs. The British attacked the older part of the city, which did not contain any railroad stations and was far from the suburbs containing Dresden's not too important industries.

Precisely because it was not very important, Dresden had lost most of its anti-aircraft guns, and the German night fighters were even weaker and more confused than usual. There was no interception. The weather was fine, and 5 Group efficiently used its standard visual marking technique. The second wave carried out a Newhaven attack under the direction of a master bomber; by the time it arrived, fires were already raging. A gigantic firestorm spread over eight square miles, with the same hideous results as in Hamburg in 1943. The last fires did not go out for a week.

On February 14, while 294 Fortresses of the 3rd Division went to the Chemnitz marshalling yards and 340 B-24s struck those at Magdeburg, 311 B-17s of the 1st Division dropped 771 tons of bombs on Dresden. The Dresden force had intended to aim at marshalling yards too, but reports of clouds and smoke caused the force to use H2X and to alter the target to a railroad junction in the center of the city. The bombs missed it and hit residential areas instead. Some escort fighters strafed the banks of the Elbe, killing civilians. American bombs and bullets contributed little to the staggering catastrophe, but the Germans not unreasonably, if wrongly, concluded that the AAF was now fully joining in the British policy of area attack.

On February 15 weather prevented the Eighth's 1st and 3rd divisions from going to their primary targets at Böhlen and Ruhland. While most of the 3rd Division struck marshalling yards at Cottbus, 210 B-17s of the 1st Division bombed the Dresden marshalling yards through cloud, using H2X. The yards were not damaged much. In fact, neither the RAF's nor the Eighth's attacks had much effect on rail operations at Dresden; they returned to normal in three days. The RAF had also carried out an area attack on Chemnitz, on February 14–15, repeating the tactic of a double blow. Two waves of bombers, totalling

717 planes, struck the city, but the attack failed. The special series of attacks on eastern German cities came to an end, though the Eighth Air Force attacked the Dresden marshalling yards twice more before the war ended.

The number of victims at Dresden was never accurately known. The city's population had been swollen by refugees, and those who dealt with the disaster had more to worry about than an accurate tally of corpses. Wild stories of over 200,000 dead circulated; even in 1963, David Irving's well known book *The Destruction of Dresden* claimed that as many as 135,000 people had been killed, which would make Dresden by far the most destructive air attack in history. The true number of the dead was probably 35,000—still horrible and almost as many as those killed at Hamburg. But Dresden left a uniquely bad taste in many people's mouths. Hamburg had been a major industrial city and had been attacked in the middle of the war. The heavy loss of life, then and there, had been relatively acceptable. But Dresden was bombed late in the war, and it was widely realized even at the time that it was not of much significance to the enemy war effort.

The fact that something unusually bad had happened at Dresden became known at the time and evoked a new round of questioning of bombing policy in Britain, and to a lesser extent in the United States. With the war nearing its end, even those who had strongly favored area bombing now found it hard to swallow. The Dresden attack, and the increasing public distaste for the area attacks, prompted Churchill to start distancing himself from them and from Harris.

The Americans were also embarrassed. The fact that the RAF had bombed Dresden as a nominal part of a joint Anglo-American program was not yet widely known. But the fact that the RAF attack on Dresden was closely followed by two Eighth Air Force missions, which had, albeit unintentionally, hit residential areas there, and that these had succeeded an unusually destructive attack on Berlin, seemed to suggest that the Americans too were now resorting to a policy of terror bombing. The fact that even visual bombing was never quite so accurate as the AAF had liked to claim, and that radar bombing was even less accurate, was becoming understood by 1945. And this lent itself to the supposition that the Americans were deliberately carrying out area attacks. This was not really true. Although they had become more callous about casualties among enemy civilians, as the strafing attacks on February 14 showed, they were little closer to a policy of deliberate bombing of civilians than before. They might exploit a British operation with fighter attacks bound to kill civilians, but directing a major bomber operation for that purpose made no sense to them. Their basic presuppositions had changed no more than those of Harris.[15]

Indeed, the discussions and directives of January had not really caused the destruction of Dresden. It had after all, been on Harris's pet target list for months. He would undoubtedly have smashed it earlier, if not for the annoying insistence of his superiors that he attack other objectives, such as oil plants. Dresden was yet another victim of an area-bombing policy that was three years old and at least a year out of date. It was unusual only in that there was an effort to fit the attack on it into a pattern relevant to the larger picture of Allied military operations. Seen in the most immediate context (which, it should be said, is a misleading way to look at it), the bad reputation of the attack on Dresden is not entirely deserved. Horrible though it was, it made more sense than most area attacks in the latter part of the war. That, perhaps, is not saying very much.

THE RETURN TO OIL

During December the Fifteenth Air Force had maintained the strategic air offensive with help from the RAF; it had kept up strong blows against the Silesian synthetic oil plants and the Austrian refineries. Then it was grounded by weather until January 20. The Eighth Air Force, despite its "release" by Eisenhower on January 8, did not return to the oil campaign until January 14. Then, as the 1st Division attacked some Rhine bridges, the 2nd and 3rd Divisions struck synthetic plants at Magdeburg, a refinery at Hemmingstedt, and oil storage depots. For the first time in many weeks, and for the last time, a big force of conventional fighters tried to stop them. American and British fighter pilots ran wild. The Americans claimed to have shot down 155 German fighters while losing 11 fighters themselves; 5 more American fighters had to be scrapped. The British claimed 11 FW-190s, while losing 2 Spitfires. Only 7 bombers went down that day, although 5 more never flew again. The Germans actually lost 150 planes and 107 pilots killed or missing. It was the climactic air battle of the strategic air war. Although the Luftwaffe still had some tricks up its sleeve, it never again intercepted an Allied bomber force in strength. Many of the surviving conventional fighters were sent to face the Soviets. But the fuel situation was so bad that the Germans were towing planes from dispersal to runways with horses and oxen, on the rare occasions that the planes flew at all.

The Allies were taking on other targets in the last stages of the offensive. Tank plants, U-boat yards, jet plants, and airfields, and in the very last weeks, explosives plants, came under attack, often quite effectively. The Allied forces were now so strong, and the cumulative damage to oil and transportation so great, that attacks on other targets were not the dangerous diversions they had been earlier. But the very success of the oil and transportation campaigns arguably rendered them unnecessary.

The nature of the oil campaign changed somewhat. For the USSTAF it was very much a case of "doing business at the same old stand" over and over again, but the intensity and scope of the RAF operations were now greater. Bigger RAF forces were sent out, and they struck not only the Ruhr plants and those at Merseburg-Leuna and Poelitz, but the big Bergius plant at Brux; three of the central German synthetic plants, at Zeitz, Lutzkendorf, and Böhlen; and oil refineries at Hamburg, Harburg, and Misburg, as well as five large oil storage depots. Such depots, in which the fuel was in underground tanks, had not been considered vulnerable to bombs. But small attacks by Bomber Command, and somewhat larger ones by the Americans, wrecked the above-ground installations and denied the enemy fuel.

Weather, not German opposition, was the problem in January and much of February. Serious blows were delivered against oil targets only with great difficulty. On January 14–15, Bomber Command delivered a terrific blow against Merseburg-Leuna. A force of 561 bombers had to aim at sky markers; nevertheless, 2,000 tons of bombs were dropped accurately. On January 16 the Eighth hit the oil plants at Magdeburg and Ruhland, as well as tank plants; on January 17 it returned to the Hamburg-area refineries and also struck a U-boat yard there. During the rest of January, terrible weather let the Eighth mount only very small and difficult missions—only one employed more than 100 planes—against a few oil plants and tank plants. The Fifteenth Air Force hit an oil depot at Regensburg and Vienna-area refineries, on a modest scale, before being grounded entirely for nine days. On January 31 it managed a big attack on a large benzol plant at Vienna, before being shut out of Central Europe by weather for another four days.

On January 19 Speer had noted, in a report to Hitler, an intensification of the oil attack. Merseburg-Leuna, Poelitz, Brux, Blechhammer, and Zeitz were now out of operation for a considerable period. All the hydrogenation plants further west had been knocked out. Underground plants would not be in operation in the near future. He noted that the night attacks were much more effective than those during the day, "since heavier bombs are used and an extraordinary accuracy in attaining the target is reported." Complete and reliable figures for many aspects of German fuel production in 1945 are not available, but it seems that the total output of the hydrogenation plants fell from 56,000 tons in December to 37,000 tons in January. Benzol production appears to have declined, from 27,800 tons in December to 20,000 in January. Rubber production had already fallen to 15 percent of the level of early 1944, while nitrogen production fell to 25 percent of the level of October 1944.

When the weather lifted, the strategic picture had changed considerably. Upper Silesia, which had been the Germans' last relatively intact heavy industry area, and the Hungarian oilfields and refineries had fallen or were falling into Soviet hands. On February 8 Eisenhower launched the final offensive in the West. Much of the British and American heavy bombers' effort went either to support the battle for the Rhineland or to make the special series of attacks designed to support the Soviet advance in the east. During much of February the weather was poor. Most American attacks were delivered on radar, many against the marshalling yards, which made relatively good targets. With the bombers flying whenever the weather was not utterly impossible, and dropping greater tonnages of bombs, the last two months of the strategic air war were the most furious of all.

The Soviet advance shortened the Fifteenth Air Force's target list, and it concentrated its blows on the marshalling yards and oil refineries around Vienna, on benzol plants there and at Linz, on the oil storage depots at Regensburg, on the tank plant at St. Valentin, and on jet plants at Regensburg and Neuberg, sharing the last target with the Eighth. By February 21 several big missions to Vienna had left the oil and railroad targets there largely wrecked. Three more missions, on March 12, 15, and 19, finished off Vienna's oil production before the Soviets arrived on April 10. During March, the Fifteenth "poached" on the Eighth's usual targets, hitting the Ruhland oil plant on March 15, 22, and 23 and attacking a tank-engine plant at Berlin on March 24. It delivered two especially effective attacks on jet production at Regensburg on February 16 and at Neuberg on March 21 and 24, claiming the destruction of nearly 50 finished jet fighters on the factory airfields. On March 25 the Fifteenth made a last strategic attack on tank plants and air bases around Prague; after that, it operated in direct support of the Allied armies.

The strategic air war lasted a bit longer for the forces based in Britain. Bomber Command did most of the work necessary against German oil production in the Ruhr, as well as extending its efforts elsewhere, but the weather, which left only western Germany open to bombing, caused the Eighth to hit benzol plants and the sole oil refinery in the Ruhr. Otherwise it stuck to pounding away at the central German oil plants and the refineries in the Hamburg and Hannover areas. Three missions on February 24, March 5, and March 11, the last combined with an attack on the U-boat yards, left the great crude-oil refineries at Hamburg in no need of further attention. The largest remaining Bergius plants, at Merseburg-Leuna and Brux, were handled by Bomber Command; the Eighth planned one last mission to Merseburg on March 31, but it was aborted by weather and it was decided that it was not necessary to reschedule it.

The Bergius and Fischer-Tropsch plants made 13,000 tons of fuel in February and 12,000 tons in March. Perhaps only 500 tons of aviation gasoline were produced in February. Between the efforts of the two Allied air forces, most of the larger synthetic plants were shut by the end of February and the rest in March; only some benzol plants and coal-tar distillation units were still working as the Allied troops arrived. The Eighth Air Force hit its last oil production center on March 31, attacking a few storage depots thereafter. Bomber Command made one last attack on Lutzkendorf on April 8–9.[16]

Direct attacks on weapons production, although perhaps unnecessary, proved more effective than before. Small Eighth Air Force attacks on the main German explosives plants proved very effective. There was a concurrent attack on tank production, which was already disintegrating thanks to the transportation snarl. After an attack on the Tiger plant at Kassel on March 9, production there stopped, as did Panther tank production at Hannover after a mission there on March 14.

Bomber Command and the Eighth Air Force attacked U-boat yards and submarine bases to stop the new-type German submarines. The British found that Tallboys penetrated the bunkers protecting the U-boats, while Mosquitos dropped 4,000-pound bombs on construction slips. The main constraint on building new U-boats, however, was probably the transportation problem. The Germans had prefabricated their new U-boats at inland sites; only the final assembly took place in the traditional shipyards. This was a good counter to the sort of campaign against submarine yards that had been waged in 1943, but the attacks on the canals made it hard to get the various sections to the ports. In all, bombing is estimated to have cost the Germans the production of 30 of the large Type 21 submarines and 14 of the shorter-range Type 23s, while Allied bombers sank 15 finished Type 21s and one Type 23, as well as 18 older U-boats.[17]

THE LAST STRUGGLE OF THE LUFTWAFFE

Despite some successful attacks on plants, the Germans continued making jet fighters. Late in 1944 they even embarked on a wild project to produce a cheap, small "people's fighter," the Heinkel 162, to be flown by boys from the Hitler Youth. It was aerodynamically unsound and at best could only have been handled by a very experienced pilot, and the hundred or so built were never used operationally. Possibly the Luftwaffe command had the sense to see that this particular scheme was useless.

The fighter versions of the Me-262, operated by Jagdgeschwader 7 and Kampfgeschwader (J) 54 (the latter a fighter-bomber unit) were more dangerous. After rarely appearing for some weeks, they attacked bombers heading for Lutzkendorf on February 9, shooting down one. JG 7 did not become fully operational until March, and it never reached full strength, but it had better trained pilots than Kommando Nowotny. Another, smaller jet fighter unit, Jagdverbande 44, was formed in February. Galland, ousted as inspector of fighters for insufficient pandering to the fantasies of the Nazi leaders, had been allowed to form this squadron-sized unit, which had 25 Me-262s and 50 pilots, including many of Germany's top aces. But JV 44 did not get into action until late March.

The Germans had devised new formations and tactics for the jets, and they developed a new type of 55 mm. air-to-air rockets, the R4M. It was far superior to the big, clumsy tube-launched rockets the Luftwaffe had used in 1943. An Me-262 could carry 24 R4Ms in underwing racks, and a single hit could destroy a bomber. Fortunately, they rarely had a chance to use it. Had three or four full-strength Me-262 geschwader existed a year earlier, equipped with R4Ms, the bombing of Germany would have been stopped dead.

On March 3 the jets and Me-163s engaged bombers and fighters en route to central German oil and rail targets. They destroyed three bombers and six P-51s. The Americans resumed "capping" the jet bases with fighter patrols to catch the Me-262s taking off and landing. There was a lull in jet operations for two weeks. Then, on March 18, a mission against tank plants and railroad stations in Berlin led to the biggest battle with the jets of the war. JG 7, using R4Ms for the first time, shot down most of the 13 American bombers and 6 fighters that were lost (15 bombers and 1 fighter were junked.) The escort fighters downed two Me-262s. Jets continued to pick off a few bombers on each mission. The Eighth estimated that it lost 30 bombers to the jets in March.

On April 7 the Germans uncorked an unpleasant surprise. Propeller-driven fighters reappeared, in an operation more typical of the Japanese than the Germans. The latter had long considered suicidal devices, including a piloted version of the V-1, and FW-190s carrying special heavy bombs, to crash-drive enemy ships. The pilots, in each case, were supposed to bail out in the final dive, although they were not likely to succeed. But for one reason or another these projects had fallen through. In March 1945 the Nazis formed a special "volunteer" unit, Sonderkommando Elbe, of 150 pilots. They were to ram American bombers, aiming at the fuselage in front of the tail, and if possible bail out. On April 7, covered by jets from JG 7 and some conventional fighters, 120–130 planes of Sonderkommando Elbe attacked, accompanied by propaganda exhortations over the radio. A nightmarish and furious air battle resulted. Up to 8 of the 17 bombers lost that day were rammed; astoundingly, 2 bombers were rammed but survived. The escort fighters claimed to have downed 64 planes, the bomber gunners 40. For once these were understatements—the Germans may have lost 133 planes. Sonderkommando Elbe did not reappear. The air force that had once ruled the sky from the English Channel to Russia had sunk to relying on kamikazes.

The Germans launched a last-ditch operation against Bomber Command. On March 3, having scraped up a last reserve of fuel, they sent 100 night fighters to England on the first major intruder mission since 1941. Taking the British by surprise, they downed 22 bombers returning from Germany, losing only 6 planes themselves. On subsequent nights, smaller forces bombed and strafed Eight Air Force bases, but they achieved nothing.

Jet operations continued for a few more weeks. In practice, despite their potential, the jets did not cause all that much trouble. As many as 1,433 Me-262s may have been built, although possibly not all were complete; but no more than 200 were ever operational. They had destroyed only about 150 Allied planes, while 100 of the German jets were lost in air combat.[18]

THE FINAL CAMPAIGN AGAINST GERMAN TRANSPORTATION

The final collapse of the Germans' ability to sustain their war effort was caused by the concentrated Allied attack on transportation. In the last stages of the transportation campaign, the efforts of the strategic and tactical air forces converged. The latter's attacks on supply lines near the front merged with the heavy bombers' attacks on the transportation system as a whole.

The Allies did not realize how effective their attacks had been, and that the German economy was already collapsing. By January German rail traffic had fallen to 40 percent of the level before the transportation campaign had begun. What was left of the marshalling yards and sidings were so jammed with cars that could no longer be formed into trains that on December 9 the Germans began derailing vast numbers of cars to free space. Coal traffic had sunk so low that all factory workers were furloughed from December 24 to January 1 to conserve fuel. Coal stocks outside the Ruhr dwindled to a few days' supply, and most of the stocks of parts that had allowed the continuation of arms production were used up during December. Weapons production fell steeply in January 1945, declining 30 percent from its peak in July 1944. Coal and coke piled up in the Ruhr; mining was cut back. Elsewhere, locomotives lacked coal, while weapons and ammunition that could not be moved jammed factory yards and warehouses. Within the Ruhr, steel production fell to a third of the normal level. The steady, although insufficiently systematic, attack on the marshalling yards had largely isolated the Ruhr by early 1945; Speer's ministry described the region as an "island" on January 18. On January 30 Speer reported to Hitler that the war was lost. "After the loss of Upper Silesia, the German armaments industry will no longer be able even approximately to cover the requirements of the front for armaments, ordnance and tanks." The Soviet conquest of Silesia, which had been providing 60 percent of Germany's coal, thus started the final slide to ruin, by rendering Germany wholly dependent on the tottering western industrial areas. But the Allies were slow to devise a sound plan to hasten and complete that collapse.[19]

Bad weather continued to interfere with assessing the results of attacks, and many influential figures still opposed a general strategic attack on transportation. The British Ministry of Economic Warfare, having completed a bizarre swing from its wild overoptimism in the earlier years of the war, now insisted that no fall in German armaments production could be expected in the near future—a conclusion that might have afforded Hitler and Speer some wry amusement. On January 17 the CSTC recommended that direct attacks on weapons production receive second priority after oil, and that attacks on transportation be limited to the area just behind the front.

But Tedder, with Eisenhower's backing, opposed this and again had his way. He was assisted by the Soviet advance in Silesia, which converted Derek Wood, the head of the working committee that surveyed transportation for the CSTC, to the view that halting coal shipments from the Ruhr would now have immediate results. (An alternative interpretation is that the Soviet advance gave Wood and others a face-saving excuse to change.) Tedder's victory was secured during February by a revision of the intelligence picture. After the Battle of the Bulge, Bottomley had ordered a review of the handling of "ultra" information related to the attack on transportation. It showed that vast numbers of messages on the German economy had been intercepted but ignored, and that, at least as early as October, German war production had been in steep decline. On February 10 Eisenhower's headquarters and the CSTC agreed to isolate the Ruhr, to paralyze both commercial traffic and troop movements. This was part of the preparation for Eisenhower's planned double envelopment of the area, after the main crossing of the Rhine was made in the north.

The Ruhr isolation plan was actually formulated by the Ninth Air Force. Both heavy and medium bombers would hit marshalling yards, but there was a new emphasis on interdiction—breaking down the eighteen bridges and viaducts that connected the Ruhr with the rest of Germany. Some of the targets were far from the Ruhr proper; they ranged from the Arnsbergen Bridge over the Weser, near Bremen, to Neuwied, on the Rhine well above the Ruhr. The plan really involved the isolation of all of northwest Germany. Six of the eighteen targets were allotted to the strategic air forces, the rest to the tactical air forces.[20]

Although not formally approved until March 1, the plan was put into operation on February 21. The Ruhr and the neighboring interdiction targets took a fearful pounding. Allied heavy and medium bombers dropped 31,635 tons of bombs on transport targets within the Ruhr in the first three weeks of March, while from February 21 to March 21, 5,657 tons of bombs were dropped on the critical bridges and viaducts.

The finishing touch to the six targets given to the strategic air forces was supplied by the huge British bombs. The Bielefeld Viaduct was smashed with Tallboys on February 22 but once again was repaired. The British now introduced the Grand Slam, the full-scale "earthquake bomb" Wallis had envisaged years earlier. On March 13 the Grand Slam was successfully tested, and the very next afternoon 617 Squadron sent 14 Lancasters with Tallboys and one with a Grand Slam to the Bielefeld Viaduct. They made such a mess of the viaduct that it was never rebuilt; after the war the Germans built a bypass. Tallboys and Grand Slams also swiftly smashed the Altenbecken Viaduct and the Arnsberg, Arburgen, Nienburg, and Bremen bridges. By March 24 the Ruhr had been practically isolated for all purposes. Ten of the eighteen exits were destroyed; three were damaged and impassable; two were closed by Allied artillery fire; one was partly passable; and two were usable. The practical effects of the interdiction plan were perhaps limited, but it showed what might have been accomplished had interdiction of the Ruhr started earlier. On March 23 the Allies crossed the Rhine north of the Ruhr. As usual, much of the strategic air forces' work was in support of the attack on the ground; the Eighth Air Force bombed no less than 34 airfields to prevent interference by the Luftwaffe. On April 1 the U.S. Ninth Army, flanking the Ruhr from the north, met the First Army, which had broken out of the Remagen bridgehead to the south, and trapped German Army Group B, with 325,000 men, in the great industrial region.

The Allies were attacking transportation far beyond the Ruhr, and not only in the special attacks designed to aid the Soviets. The Eighth Air Force alone had attacked marshalling yards on 17 days in January; in February and March, respectively, it flew against railroad targets on 15 and 18 days, hitting at least 90 different marshalling yards, as well as railroad bridges. If anything, it dispersed its efforts too widely.

On February 22–23 the Eighth and the other Allied forces carried out a special operation, Clarion, combining the attack on transportation with one on enemy morale. British and American planes ranged all over Germany, attacking marshalling yards, bridges, and stations located in small towns. Both heavy and medium bombers bombed from much lower than usual. Many had not liked this plan. Eaker felt that it would cause excessive civilian casualties, and others criticized it as a dispersion of effort. Spaatz and SHAEF, however, considered it worth trying. They proved wrong; Clarion did little harm to the enemy.

The blows hitting the enemy transportation system were so staggering that this made little difference. By the end of March car loadings were 11 percent of normal; only 7,000 of the 23,000 locomotives were working. Steel output fell to a quarter of normal; during that month even flak began to die off. Speer turned from trying to keep the economy going against Allied assault, to sabotaging Hitler's "scorched-earth" plan, announced on March 19, to destroy everything of economic importance in Germany as the Allies advanced. Most of Germany's mines and factories, even now, were more or less intact. Postwar surveys showed that even in the Ruhr, the most heavily bombed area, only 30 percent of the machinery had been smashed, and 20 percent damaged. It was the links between the mines and industries, and the vital oil industry, which produced the lifeblood of so many of the others, that had been destroyed.

By the end of March the strategic air offensive was largely finished. Only a few missions against oil targets and explosives plants remained. Bomber Command and the USSTAF focused largely on destroying German equipment and supplies already in being. On April 7 the RAF finally ended area bombing. Missions of decreasing size were sent against those marshalling yards still behind the German lines, as well as U-boat bases, airfields, and supply and oil storage depots. On April 14–15 the Eighth flew two big missions to support a foolish French attack on German forces that were holding out on the Bay of Biscay. The escort fighters now rarely saw the enemy in the air, and they rampaged over the jammed airfields still in German hands, destroying fantastic numbers of planes on the ground.

On April 16 Spaatz and Bottomley declared the strategic air war over. A few missions, mostly against the Germans' last marshalling yards, followed. On April 25, 554 planes flew the last heavy bomber mission of the war, against the Skoda works at Pilsen, which still seemed capable of supplying armored vehicles to the relatively intact German forces in western Czechoslovakia, and against Pilsen airfield and several marshalling yards. The bombers then stayed on the ground until May 2, when they took up a very different sort of work, dropping food to the starving Dutch behind the German lines and flying liberated Allied prisoners from a ruined Germany to Britain.[21]

Conclusions

The air offensive against Germany was costly in economic resources and in manpower. At their peak strength, the Royal Air Force and the Army Air Force in Europe deployed 1,335,000 men and 28,000 combat planes. Together they lost just under 160,000 men, and 40,000 planes were destroyed or damaged. While the strategic air campaign was responsible for only part of the losses in the air, Bomber Command alone, which bore the brunt of the loss of life, had 55,000 dead or missing, 9,838 taken prisoner, and 8,403 wounded on planes that returned. The Eighth Air Force lost 43,742 killed or missing. The efforts of the tactical and strategic air forces cannot be neatly separated. Up to D-Day the tactical forces played an important role in gaining air superiority, and in the final phase of the transportation campaign their efforts fused with those of USSTAF and Bomber Command. The heavy bombers and their escorts expended much of their efforts in support of the invasion and advance of the land armies. It has been calculated that, counting the antisubmarine and V-weapons campaigns, no less than 46 percent of the Eighth's sorties went to supporting or defensive operations, rather than to the strategic air offensive proper.[1]

The terrible losses of Bomber Command, in particular, cast a grim light on prewar hopes that strategic bombing would be a "cheap" way to wage a war, or at least far less costly in lives than the deadly land battles of World War I. While it was true that the numbers of men were but a fraction of the numbers that had been committed at the Somme and Ypres, and the total number killed was far smaller than the number of men killed on the ground in the earlier struggle, the death rate in Bomber Command was proportionately higher than that on the Western Front, and formed a substantial part of British losses in World War II. The economic costs of the offensive to the Western powers are a matter of dispute. The British official history estimated that Bomber Command consumed 7 percent of Britain's military and industrial manpower (the most important factor in a labor-starved economy), but others have claimed that it consumed up to one-third of Britain's industrial effort. The AAF itself estimated that the American air offensive cost $27.5 billion, about 11 percent of the total cost of the war.

Disregarding for the moment its effects on the German war effort, the bomber offensive killed many enemy civilians. Approximately 593,000 Germans died from air attacks, mostly the British area attacks. Although outside of Britain and Germany this toll seems to have attracted less obloquy than the far smaller number of Japanese civilians killed by American atomic bombs, it accounts for much of the distaste with which the strategic bombing campaign was recalled after the war.

The story of that campaign is a bit different in some ways from that generally accepted, and this is particularly true of the British side of things. The RAF's shift to area bombing was more gradual, and more reluctant, than is generally supposed. The adoption of area attack, or more exactly, the recognition that it was all that Bomber Command was really capable of, took place in 1941. But it did not become an inflexible commitment until later. The directives under which Bomber Command operated in 1942 and 1943 assumed, at least implicitly, that precision bombing would be a better bet, that the RAF should switch over to it when possible, and that "selective area attacks" designed to undermine particular industries should be undertaken. Originally, Sir Arthur Harris was not a fanatical advocate of area attack. His attempts to use heavy bombers in daylight operations, and the numerous mixed precision and area attacks tried in 1942, suggest that it was only late in that year that he became obsessed with the notion, which he never really gave up, that general area attack was the only way to win the war.

The problem of area bombing, indeed night bombing in general, is easily misunderstood. The difference between precision and area bombing was not a sharp distinction, but one between varying shades in a spectrum. Up to 1942, neither was possible. As capabilities improved during that year, successful area bombing became possible, but it was still not a regular or dependable result. At the same time, attacks on some specific factories—for example, the Renault plant—became possible, but only in unusual conditions of weather and moonlight, and against light defenses. After the introduction of Oboe and other aids in 1943, area bombing attacks were usually successful, at least within Oboe range, while precision attacks on very large factories also became possible, even in difficult and heavily defended areas like the Ruhr. Real precision bombing at night, against most important targets, became possible in the latter half of 1943, probably by the late summer, even though the capability for it was not exploited until well into 1944.

Yet another misunderstood watershed for Bomber Command was its recovery of the ability to penetrate deep into Germany in the summer of 1944. It appears that this was due primarily to the belated development of countermeasures to the Germans' radar and homing devices, and not, as is usually said, to the crippling of the German defenses by the loss of territory and gasoline.

The Army Air Force's actions have also sometimes been misunderstood. Its leaders, or at least those on the spot in Europe, were disillusioned with the self-defending bomber formation long before the disastrous losses of the summer and fall of 1943. The deep-penetration attacks were a gamble, to keep the offensive against aircraft and ball bearings going until fighter escort became available. The failure of these attacks was not due just to the fact that unescorted attacks were too horribly costly even as an occasional venture. The selection of ball bearings as an objective proved a fundamental mistake. It was not the vulnerable spot that it seemed, although the Germans themselves shared this illusion. On the other hand, the Germans never had a chance of recovering air superiority with jets, as is commonly supposed.

CRITIQUES OF STRATEGIC BOMBING

For a variety of reasons, the historical reputation of the strategic air offensive against Germany has not been high, particularly in the last 25 years. The most recent general histories of World War II, by Martin Gilbert, John Keegan, and Robert Leckie, give short shrift to the bombing of Germany or are actively critical of the campaign. The low repute of the strategic air offensive is partly due to a tendency to identify the whole offensive with the British area attacks. Horror at the slaughter of civilians, and the knowledge that those attacks broke neither German morale nor the German economy, led to revulsion against the area offensive, which, with considerable although not complete justification, was regarded as a costly failure.

There was disillusion with the claims of some of the more extreme air power advocates, and disappointment with the air offensive's results. The hopes nursed by many people (but not the Allied leaders) during the war that bombing would avert an invasion of France and bloody land battles were disappointed, and there was a widespread, if unjustified, assumption that such a result had been expected. The revelation that German war production rose until September 1944, and the fact that the dramatic impact of the attack on oil and transportation came late in the war, tended to suggest that the offensive had not been worthwhile. Indeed, the rise in German production was often cited out of context, with no mention of what happened after that, and the achievements of the oil and transportation offensives were often ignored.

Hostile critics, both in Britain and America, sometimes distorted the facts to serve the interests of the Army and Navy in interservice rivalries; others did so from more ideological motives. Although in the 1940s liberals and the Left had been air power advocates, the political Left became retrospectively hostile to strategic bombing. Although the bombing of North Vietnam during the second Indochina war had little in common in either means or purpose with the bombing of Germany, critics of that war belittled the earlier campaign in the belief that this would somehow support their views. A picture was painted of armadas of bombers, manufactured at disastrous expense to the rest of the war effort, dropping enormous tonnages of bombs either on cities or centers of armaments production with magically little effect, failing in their supposed task of defeating Germany without an invasion.[2]

But this is not a true characterization even of the results of the British area attacks in 1942–1944, although these attacks certainly did not accomplish what they were supposed to. The bombers were never expected to win the war alone or avert an invasion, and they received a far lower priority than would have been the case had this been planned. The numbers of bombers remained quite small until 1943, and in the British case they usually did not attack German industry. Bomber Command's operational strength was usually below 500 planes until 1943; the Eighth Air Force rarely put more than 100 planes into the air until the middle of that year. The buildup of the bomber force did not precede, but coincided with, the buildup for the D-Day invasion. Most of the bombs dropped on Germany—72 percent, in the case of the Eighth Air Force—fell *after* D-Day. And once large bomber forces were available, able to fly anywhere in Germany with fighter escort, decisive results were gained in a few months, despite serious mistakes in the choice of targets and the obtuseness of Sir Arthur Harris.

It should be noted, however, that although they stress the achievements of the strategic air offensive in other respects, even some able historians of the air war have given credence to a lesser criticism. Max Hastings wrote that by the winter of 1944, when Bomber Command had the means to destroy German cities, "the purpose had gone, for the Allied armies were evidently on the verge of complete victory on the ground, and it was only a combination of their own shortcomings and the Wehrmacht's genius that delayed the end so long."[3] In a similar comment on the Allied air forces generally, R. J. Overy wrote, "All the great expectations of air power as a war-winning weapon that had been kept alive, despite the failure in 1940, by the single-mindedness of the bomber school, were confounded by the fact that even the winning of the war in the air could not measurably reduce the time that it took to defeat the German armies in Europe."[4] The fallacy here is the odd assumption that the land battles in 1944–1945 proceeded independently of the air war and were unaffected by the shortage of fuel and disruption of transportation. But accounts of German operations tell a different story. By the fall of 1944, despite the partial recovery of fuel production, "fuel was sufficient to maintain operations, even during the static period, only by resorting to horse-drawn transport from railheads to tactical supply dumps, 40 to 50 percent reduction in the use of vehicles, a harsh system of rationing available supplies, and use of charcoal-burning transport."[5] And, although the Germans gathered reserves permitting an offensive, they proved insufficient. General Hasso von Manteuffel, who commanded the Fifth Panzer Army in the Ardennes, noted the enormous difficulties created for his forces by the transportation campaign.[6] As F. W. von Mellenthin later observed, "during the last months of the war communications were entirely disrupted, so that it was impossible for any replacement to reach its destination. . . . Even though the necessary equipment was available in Germany, it could not always reach the front line—at least in sufficient quantities." It took longer to transfer troops from one end of Germany to the other than it had once taken to send them from France to Russia.[7]

ACHIEVEMENTS AND FAILURES OF THE STRATEGIC AIR OFFENSIVE

At the risk of repetition, let us sum up the achievements and failures of the offensive against Germany. Until the spring of 1944, a watershed period, it fell short of expectations. But it let the Western powers strike at Germany when there was no other way to do so, and it helped sustain British morale in 1940–1941, when that nation was virtually alone.

By 1943–1944 it was tying down an enormous and increasing German force in a defensive effort, including up to 1.5 million soldiers and civilians and enormous numbers of planes, guns, and other equipment, most or all of which could have been devoted instead to German operations in Russia and the Mediterranean and to preparations for the defense of France. On at least two occasions the bombing directly hindered work on coastal defenses by causing the Germans to withdraw laborers from them.

Although merely diverting efforts from other fronts and operations may seem a minor result—and it was not one much desired by the airmen or one they pointed to with pride—this was not so. It is worth noting that the Italian campaign was nothing more than a diversionary operation, to tie down German forces and keep them away from the decisive fronts in Russia and France when the Western powers could not have attacked the enemy elsewhere. The defensive effort forced on the Germans would have justified strategic bombing even if it never accomplished a more positive aim. It is hard to see how any other use of Allied resources could have similarly affected the enemy in the same time period.

This was not the only effect on the Germans of the bombing. In 1943 and early 1944 the Allies could not seriously interrupt the production of existing German weapons, but they did delay new ones, notably the V-weapons and new types of aircraft. And although German armaments production grew, the bombings diminished that growth somewhat, possibly depressing it in 1943 by 9 percent and in 1944 by 17 percent below the level it would otherwise have reached. Finally, in the winter and spring of 1944 the air offensive won control of the air over Europe and paved the way for the Normandy invasion. It should be noted that all these achievements, except for the last, were chiefly due to RAF rather than to American efforts.

During this period, however, the strategic air forces did not accomplish their explicit assigned aims, as set out in the Casablanca and combined bomber offensive directives. They made no important contribution to the winning of the Battle of the Atlantic and did not seriously impair German morale, reduce overall German war production, or stop the manufacture of any critical items. The ball bearings campaign, and to a lesser extent the attack on aircraft plants, failed. The Allies were foiled by the fact that German morale, and the German economy, were quite different from what they, and particularly the proponents of the area offensive, imagined; by the RAF's related failure to use its growing capability for precision attack; by poor target selection on the part of the Americans; and by the Eighth Air Force's lack of long-range escort. Nevertheless, even in 1943 the Allies came close to doing decisive damage in at least one instance, which was the attack on the Ruhr dams. As we shall see later in this chapter, they may have narrowly missed other opportunities to do crippling damage to Germany in that year, but it was lack of knowledge, rather than the inherent limitations of the available air power, that was responsible.

From the spring of 1944, however, things were drastically different. The attack on oil crippled the Luftwaffe, and then the mobility of the German army, and it sharply reduced production of explosives, rubber, and other items dependent on the oil industry. If not for Harris's reluctance to commit his forces, the oil shortage would have taken effect even faster. The transportation attack then wrecked the whole economy, while slowing and disrupting troop movements. The fighting from the fall of 1944 onward would have been very different without the oil and transportation offensives. The Strategic Bombing Survey later concluded that even had the Allied armies never crossed the Rhine or the Oder, armaments production would have come to a "virtual standstill by May (1945); the German armies, completely bereft of ammunition and motive power, would almost certainly have had to cease fighting by June or July."[8]

It should be noted that even in these offensives the effect of strategic bombing cannot be isolated from other operations. By capturing Ploesti, and later the Hungarian oilfields and the easternmost German synthetic oil plants, the Soviets enabled the Fifteenth Air Force to concentrate its efforts on a smaller number of targets in the last part of the war, while the capture of Upper Silesia precipitated the final collapse of the German economy. There seems to be little reason, however, to assume that the Western air forces would not have finished off the oil industry and isolated Silesia, as they did the Ruhr, even had the Red Army never reached those areas. The Soviet advance affected the duration rather than the outcome of the oil and transportation campaigns.

But the Allied air forces made bad mistakes and missed major opportunities to harm the Nazis, even during the successful final offensives. Had the RAF used its capability of attacking precise objectives, it might have begun dealing with the oil industry in late 1943. As the AAF's historians later admitted, and the Combined Chiefs suggested at the time, the USSTAF should have attacked the synthetic oil plants during Big Week, instead of pursuing the campaigns against aircraft and ball bearing production. Had the attack on oil started earlier, it would have taken effect more quickly, since the Germans would not have had the chance to accumulate reserves of fuel. The battle for air superiority could have been won just as well over the oil plants as over the aircraft and ball bearings plants—indeed, more easily, since the oil plants in central Germany were less distant than Berlin was.

Above all, the oil offensive was hurt by the RAF's inadequate participation. Even before it regained the ability to fly deep into Germany in July 1944, it could have hit the northwestern oil refineries. Harris's obsession with area attack let oil production recover in the fall and probably prolonged the war into 1945. Alan Milward later wrote that "by the narrowest of margins, the strategic air offensive failed to smash Germany's economy by this one method of attack."[9]

The transportation offensive, too, was less effective than it might have been. Germany's inland waterways could have been paralyzed more easily and effectively. The early railroad attacks were unsystematic. The Allies failed to concentrate on the most critical marshalling yards and did not interdict the crucial bridges and viaducts around the Ruhr until late in the day.

But some Allied mistakes went much further back.

BOMBER COMMAND: MISTAKES AND OPPORTUNITIES

A mistake that the prewar RAF shared with the American Army Air Force, was the belief in the self-defending daylight bomber formation. As far as the RAF was concerned, this illusion was promptly, and literally, shot down in 1939. But its reaction to this discovery was about as flawed as was the Americans' clinging to the idea until 1943. Although it has rarely been attacked even by Bomber Command's most vehement critics, the decision to shift to night bombing was a bad mistake. It was based on three mistaken assumptions:

1. Long-range fighter escort to targets in Germany would never be possible.
2. Night bombing would not be much less accurate than bombing during the day, or at least, a capability for accurate night attack would be easily attained.
3. The German defenses at night would never be much more formidable than they were in 1940.

The first and last assumptions were disproven by events, and it took years for the British to gain the ability to carry out accurate attacks at night. The whole unsatisfactory practice of area attack was a result of the change to night operations.

Had the RAF banked on developing long-range fighters instead, it would have had to forego attacking Germany for a long time. But it is likely that, by early 1943 at the latest, it would have had a plane like the Mustang (if not the Mustang itself) and would have been able to bomb accurately anywhere in Germany in daylight. With American help, it could have started decisive offensives against oil and transportation in 1943. World War II would have taken a radically different course.

Given the switch to night bombing, which could not be accurate for a long time, it would have been wise to slow the buildup of Bomber Command in favor of Coastal Command's antisubmarine activities, as was done to some extent. This would have led to earlier victory in the Battle of the Atlantic and would have been a more effective employment of bomber-type aircraft than were the attacks on Germany in the early years of the war. A smaller Bomber Command could have continued to bomb Germany, pinning down German resources in defense and gaining operational experience for the day when effective attacks could take place.

Through much of 1943 there was little alternative to area bombing. But had the British leaders regarded general area attack as a last resort, instead of embracing it, they might have handled things differently even in 1942 and early 1943, better exploiting what limited capability for attacking specific targets they had. They could have placed more emphasis on developing new techniques for precision attack at night, and tailoring the target list to suit Bomber Command's limitations, they could have concentrated against industry more than they did. Even in 1942 precision attack was possible against a few targets, as the attack on the Renault plant showed. Some RAF officers, like Oxland, believed that similar targets could have been found. The introduction of Oboe in 1943 made possible attacks on still other very large industrial plants inside its range.

The British could also have directed area attacks, wherever possible, against cities where industrial installations were relatively concentrated, as the Americans did on their radar bombing mission in 1943–1944. The plants and industrial areas suited for such attacks were few and would have offered only a limited alternative to conventional area attacks on primarily nonindustrial areas. The additional damage to the German war effort would probably still have been marginal, but especially if coupled with a policy of selective area attack against towns associated with a particular industry, even when the industrial plants themselves could not be hit, the maximum possible concentration against industry would probably have hurt the Nazis worse in 1942 and 1943 than the policy of nearly "pure" general area attack that was followed.

Bomber Command's great mistake was the failure to switch to precision bombing when that finally became possible against most targets in the latter part of 1943, and Harris's insistence on continuing the area attacks, whenever he could get away with them, right up to the war's end. The failure to pursue the oil offensive properly in the summer and fall of 1944, and the destruction of Dresden, were only the last and most obvious consequences of his fanaticism. But the British had missed important opportunities earlier. Most notable of these was the failure to start the oil offensive sooner and the delay in attacking the critical and extremely vulnerable bottleneck in tank engine and transmission production at Friedrichshafen. That vital target could have been struck in 1943. The failure to send the main strength of Bomber Command against Friedrichshafen, long before Harris reluctantly attacked it in April 1944, was one of the worst, if little noted, blunders of the war.

Moreover, while much of the capability for night precision bombing rested on devices that only became available during 1943, one precision bombing method might have been developed much earlier than it was, namely 5 Group visual. Low-level marking could conceivably have been introduced as soon as Gee, a concentrated bomber stream, and marker bombs came into regular use, making precision attack in good weather possible against all but the most heavily defended targets in Germany as early as 1942.

As a result of the fixation on area attack, Bomber Command's contribution to victory, although great, was far less than it could have been. But it should be remembered, especially by Americans, that the RAF did most of what damage was done to Germany through 1943, forcing the Nazis to build vast and costly air defenses. Dangerous as it was to serve in the Eighth Air Force, especially in 1943, the men of Bomber Command were even worse off for most of the war. And much of the Eighth Air Force's success rested on a base of British support and expertise.

ARMY AIR FORCE MISTAKES

The AAF's biggest blunder in relation to strategic bombing was its failure to get long-range fighters as early as possible. They were desirable not only for escorting the bombers, but for other purposes. The length of amphibious jumps behind the enemy front in the South Pacific and the Mediterranean was determined by the maximum range at which land-based fighters could cover a landing.

The failure to obtain long-range fighters can be broken down into a number of lesser mistakes. First, and best known, was the AAF's disinterest in the P-51 Mustang, which could have been in action six months or more earlier. But two less well known blunders contributed to the predicament of the Eighth Air Force in 1943. First was the failure to modify the P-38 so it would be better suited to high-altitude combat in Europe, and second, and more important, was the Air Material Command's sluggishness in developing drop-tanks.

The AAF's other major blunder was its poor target selection during 1943 and its obsession with the intermediate objective of beating the German air force by directly attacking aircraft production. The aircraft and ball bearings industries were just not vulnerable to attack. But there were several small target systems, manufacturing vital items, that would have been better choices for attack, and the Eighth Air Force's small bomber force could have smashed them, at least if it had fighter escort to penetrate deep into Germany.

Synthetic rubber was made in just four plants, one small, and there were stocks of rubber for only a few months. As the attack on Huls in 1943 showed, these plants were vulnerable. Of Germany's explosives and ammunition, 70 percent was made in just seven plants, which proved very vulnerable when hit late in the war. Rebuilding an explosives plant would have taken six to nine months even in the best conditions. Nitrogen production, vital for explosives and fertilizers, was concentrated in a few plants; the two biggest plants produced nearly half of Germany's nitrogen, and ten plants made 80 percent of the country's requirements. A reduction of 70–80 percent in nitrogen production would have led to critical shortages of ammunition within nine months to a year. Aluminum production was concentrated in fourteen plants; as the 1943 attack on the plant at Heroya showed, they too were vulnerable. The constituents of ethyl fluid (ethylene dibromide and tetraethyl lead), a vital additive for aviation gasoline, were made in just three plants in Germany and one in France, and attacks on these plants, if successful, would have crippled the Luftwaffe in a short time.

Some of these target were known at the time, although others were only fully disclosed by the Strategic Bombing Survey after the war. Rubber and light metals were recommended targets at the time, and were only eclipsed by what was wrongly thought to be the better target of ball bearings. American analysts knew that nitrogen was important but nevertheless underrated it and believed the Germans' productive capacity greater than it was. Explosives and ammunition plants were overlooked for a long time, although it should have been obvious that their very nature made them wonderful targets. Some experts suggested attacking the production of ethyl fluid as early as 1942, but unfortunately the location of the biggest German tetraethyl lead plant was unknown until 1944. In the other cases noted above, it was not vital data that was missing but correct interpretation of information that was available.[10]

Most of the target systems discussed above were scattered throughout Germany and could not have been smashed without the fighter escort that should have been available, but was not. Synthetic rubber production was a partial exception; it was located largely in western Germany, although one major plant was far to the east at Schkopau.

But two target systems were near England and might have been identified at the time. The three lubricating-oil refineries at Hamburg could have been struck no later than the AAF attack on that city in July 1943. Had the Allies correctly understood the inland waterway system, they could have blocked traffic on the Rhine and the northwest German canals with a few attacks as early as late 1943, overburdening the rail system and slowing freight movement. It was want of correct analyses, not lack of information, that prevented the Allies from recognizing these targets. Had the AAF leaders recognized the impractical nature of deep penetrations and tailored their operations to the limits of the available fighter cover, a review of targets in the accessible area of Germany might have disclosed what was already in their grasp.

There was nothing secret about the inland waterway system, and the crude-oil refineries were well known to foreigners. Many were owned by Western companies and had depended on overseas imports before the war. The Allies cannot be blamed for not knowing, for instance, the extent of German ball bearings stocks (of which the Germans themselves were ignorant), but their failure to understand other aspects of the German economy is hard to understand. Prewar Nazi Germany was not sealed off from the rest of the world by anything resembling the Iron Curtain, and it traded heavily with the Western democracies. Even during the war it was open to Swedish, Swiss, and other neutrals. The allied feats in intelligence during World War II have been well publicized, but the success in code breaking was not paralleled in economic intelligence.

The mistaken selection of targets in 1943 was important. Had the Allies chosen more wisely, successful American attacks on one or more of the small target systems mentioned above (and RAF attacks on tank components production at Friedrichshafen) would not have caused the instant collapse of Germany. The Germans were more formidable than that. They probably would have rebuilt rubber plants underground, or built dispersed lubricating-oil refineries in eastern Europe, or in some other way have recovered from these attacks, eventually—as they could not get around the destruction of the whole oil industry or transportation system. But in 1943 almost anything that seriously hurt war production or halted a vital item for months would have made it practically impossible for the Germans to replace the equipment and supplies lost in the defeats of the summer of 1944. The war could not have been prolonged into 1945.

The last price exacted by the mistakes of the combined bomber offensive plan was simply the persistence in it through the early months of 1944. Spaatz and Portal did not realize that the Luftwaffe could be defeated by shifting the attack from aircraft plants to oil production, as the Combined Chiefs of Staff suggested at the time. That, too, helped prolong the war.

NAZI MISTAKES

The Nazis made military mistakes, too, which contributed to the Allied victory. Their blunders in air matters fell into three categories: technical development, production and training, and tactics. The grossest and perhaps most avoidable blunders committed by the Germans lay in their lapse in technical development after the introduction of the Me-109 and their standard bombers. This lapse may already have begun in the late 1930s, and not just after the fall of France, when Hitler, assuming that the war was already won, ruled against long-range development programs and Germany failed to produce sound follow-ons to the planes it had in 1939. While the Allies produced many new types of planes, some of which, like the Mustang, were designed after the war began, Germany introduced only one new type of plane on a large scale, the Focke-Wulf 190. It also lagged behind in developing high-octane aviation gasoline. Much of its resources were wasted on the rocket fighter and the Army's V-2 program, but contrary to a widespread myth, Germany was not ahead in jet development, and while its jet fighter development was mismanaged, it is doubtful that even an all-out effort to get the Heinkel 280 into action would have had much effect.

Given its lack of alloy materials, instead of developing jet fighters and rocket-powered ballistic missiles that could not be accurately aimed, the Germans might have been wiser to concentrate on getting the most advanced possible piston-engine successor to the Me-109 and FW-190, and antiaircraft missiles. Instead of the V-1 and V-2, the Germans could have tried to develop a turbojet-powered cruise missile with some type of command guidance system, capable of attacking precision targets like factories and ships. A weapon with a warhead comparable to that on the V-1, but steerable to a small target, would have been a dangerous threat to the Allies. Had even the pulse-jet-powered V-1 been a little faster, it would have been extremely hard for Allied fighters to catch. A faster, turbojet-powered missile might have been nearly immune to the Allied propeller-driven interceptors, while the short life and unreliability of the German jet engines would have mattered less in a missile than in a manned aircraft. Eventually the Allies would probably have jammed any radio-guidance systems the Germans could have developed for either antiaircraft or offensive missiles, but a combination of fast fighters like the Do-335 and missiles might have enabled the Germans to regain air superiority and even do serious damage to Allied bases for a time.

The Germans' failure to fully mobilize for war until 1942 left the Luftwaffe far smaller than it need have been. Their failure to build more fighters was exacerbated by their reluctance to stop bomber production in favor of fighters until 1944. The Germans also blundered in handling their training program. Initially it was just not big enough; later they fell for the temptation to turn out as many pilots as they could as soon as possible, even though they were less well trained. This proved foolish, as the inadequately trained pilots proved easy prey for Allied pilots. The Strategic Bombing Survey later concluded that "the deterioration of quality of German pilots appears to be the most important single cause of the defeat of the German Air Force."[11]

The Germans made other, tactical mistakes. In night defense their one major mistake was to end the night intruder operations over Britain in 1941. In day fighting their mistakes were more numerous. During 1943 they usually avoided engaging American escort fighters, either striking after the escorts had left the bombers or evading them to hit the bombers in preference. The concentration on shooting down bombers was understandable up to a point, but it let American fighter units grow in experience and fly deeper and deeper into Germany. The Luftwaffe's mistaken, or at least overlong, reliance on the clumsy twin-engine fighters stemmed from and accentuated the concentration on fighting bombers. So did its addiction to assembling large formations before engaging the enemy. Given the vast superiority of the Allies in numbers and quality, however, the Luftwaffe's tactical errors probably merely speeded up the Allied victory in the air.

COULD STRATEGIC BOMBING HAVE WON THE WAR ON ITS OWN?

Strategic bombing was always viewed as a prelude and accompaniment to a land invasion. It is unlikely that the Western powers would ever have willingly staked victory on bombing alone. But in certain circumstances they might have been forced to do so. We now know that Stalin was willing to make peace on at least one occasion, although Hitler seems to have flatly opposed anything of the sort. Had Hitler either come to an accord with Stalin or defeated the

Soviets in 1942, the Western powers could probably never have invaded the European mainland, and they would have had to rely on air power alone to defeat Germany.

Had the invasion of France in 1944 failed, the Western Allies might have been forced to rely on bombing as their main contribution in finishing off Germany. This was not beyond the realm of possibility. Had Hitler allowed a saner strategic policy, of withdrawal from outlying positions and retreats to shorter fronts in the east, the German forces in France could have been greatly reinforced before D-Day. Had the invasion been defeated on the Normandy beaches, the Allied offensives against German oil and transportation might well have gone on much as they did. The war would have lasted longer, but the Nazis would have been defeated, although the position of the Western powers, vis-à-vis the Soviets, would have been considerably worse.

To return to the earlier case, had the Nazis defeated the Soviets or made peace with them in 1942, the course of the strategic air offensive would have been considerably different. The Germans would have been able to put much greater resources into air defense. Even in the short run, it is likely that the fighters released from the Eastern front would have sufficed to stop penetration by American bombers beyond escort range in the spring of 1943. In a somewhat longer length of time, the Germans would have been able to reinforce their night defenses to the point where British bomber losses would have been unacceptable. Bomber Command, facing a considerably stronger German night defense, might never have regained the ability to attack well inside Germany at night. The whole burden of the strategic air offensive would have then fallen on the Eighth Air Force, at least for a time. (The British might eventually have shifted back to day bombing themselves.)

The Americans would have been stymied for a time by their lack of long-range fighters, but would undoubtedly have gotten them after a while—perhaps, because the necessity would have been obvious, even faster than they did in the actual circumstances of 1943. Peace in the east would have let the Germans devote more of their resources to aircraft production, but the Western powers could also have committed more resources to the air war; the Allies would have outproduced the Germans in the end, much as they did. The Western powers would have gained air superiority, albeit after a longer and costlier struggle than the one that took place, and would have been able to strike decisive target systems.

The target systems might have had to be different from the ones the Allies actually hit, for German access, by conquest or trade, to Soviet resources, and by the Trans-Siberian railroad to East Asia, would have drastically changed the economic picture. Access to Japanese supplies of rubber would have rendered synthetic rubber unimportant as a target, while the Baku oilfields alone produced two and a half times as much oil as all of Axis Europe, so the oil plants might have become a much less important target. (The responsible German officials, however, had serious doubts about whether they could transport much oil from the Caucasus to Germany.)[12]

Had the Germans had access to large oil supplies in the east, the Allies might have successfully switched their attention to the German electric power system. Prewar planners had singled this out as a good target system, but it was neglected during the war. Postwar examination, however, confirmed that it would have been vulnerable to bombing. Although the number of targets in the electric power system was larger, and the targets themselves smaller than those involved in oil production, there would have been no way for the Germans to get around their destruction; they later estimated that a loss of 60 percent of their electric power would have produced a collapse of production.[13] Campaigns against electric power and transportation would eventually have reduced Germany to helplessness, and it is hard to see how the Nazi regime could have survived. But it seems doubtful whether conventional bombing would have taken full effect before atomic weapons became available.

Notes

CHAPTER 1

1. B. H. Liddell-Hart, *The Real War 1914–1918* (Boston: Little, Brown, 1964), pp. 313, 316–318, 398, 408, 446–447; C. R. M. F. Cruttwell, *History of the Great War* (London: Granada, 1982), pp. 176, 260–261, 440, 463, 475, 513; J. E. Johnson, *The Story of Air Fighting* (New York: Bantam, 1986), pp. 1–83; Arthur Hezlet, *Aircraft and Seapower* (New York: Stein and Day, 1970), pp. 24–103. See, however, David Divine, *The Broken Wing* (London: Hutchinson, 1966), p. 137.

2. Raymond Fredette, *The Sky on Fire: The First Battle of Britain, 1917–1918* (New York: Holt, Rinehart and Winston, 1966), pp. 5, 7, 30–33; Douglas Robinson, *The Zeppelin in Combat* (London: G. T. Foulis, 1962); Douglas Robinson, *Giants in the Sky*, rev. ed. (Seattle: University of Washington Press, 1979), pp. 84–142.

3. Fredette, *Sky on Fire*, pp. 37–218, 231–237, 261; Robinson, *Zeppelin in Combat*, p. 348; Charles Webster and Noble Frankland, *The Strategic Air Offensive against Germany*, (London: Her Majesty's Stationery Office, 1961), vol. 1, pp. 43–47; Cruttwell, *History of the Great War*, pp. 497–498; Barry D. Powers, *Strategy without Slide Rule* (London: Croom Helm, 1976), pp. 52–74, 107–109. But see Divine, *Broken Wing*, pp. 136–137, and Basil Collier, *A History of Air Power* (New York: Macmillan, 1974), p. 74, for arguments that the airplane attacks were not profitable for the Germans.

4. Powers, *Strategy Without Slide Rule*, p. 90.

5. Fredette, *Sky on Fire*, pp. 199–200, 221–227; Webster and Frankland, *Strategic Air Offensive*, vol. 1, pp. 40–41, 44–47; Powers, *Strategy without Slide Rule*, pp. 80, 90–103; Lee Kennett, *A History of Strategic Bombing* (New York: Scribner's, 1982), pp. 27–33.

6. Malcolm Smith, *British Air Strategy between the Wars* (Oxford: Clarendon Press, 1984), pp. 14, 28–31, 58–71, 74; Powers, *Strategy without Slide Rule*, pp. 122–134, 148–149, 155–157, 171–173, 188–189; Kennett, *History of Strategic Bombing*, pp. 45–76; Fredette, *Sky on Fire*, pp. 231–234, 240–243; Webster and Frankland, *Strategic Air Offensive*, vol. 1, pp. 47–48, 60–64; Divine, *Broken Wing*, pp. 156–179, 185.

7. Smith, *British Air Strategy*, pp. 77, 82, 109–110, 114–115, 137, 144, 153–154, 160–161, 164–165, 169–174, 179–195, 214–218, 229–230, 253–257; Webster and Frankland, *Strategic Air Offensive*, vol. 1, pp. 75–88.

8. Webster and Frankland, *Strategic Air Offensive*, vol. 1, pp. 92–107, 115–116, 122–125; Smith, *British Air Strategy*, pp. 236–243, 247, 253–266, 269–274, 279–303; Max Hastings, *Bomber Command* (New York: Dial, 1979), pp. 41–45, 53–57, 60; Divine, *Broken Wing*, pp. 191, 195, 200, 206, 210–212, 216–217, 231.

9. Webster and Frankland, *Strategic Air Offensive*, vol. 1, pp. 81, 125–129; Divine, *Broken Wing*, pp. 195–212; Smith, *British Air Strategy*, pp. 253–262; Hastings, *Bomber Command*, pp. 56–58, 82–83; Peter C. Smith, *A History of Dive Bombing* (Annapolis, Md.: Nautical and Aviation Publishing Company of America, 1981), pp. 34–36; Derek Dempster and Derek Wood, *The Narrow Margin*, rev. ed. (New York: Paperback Library, 1969), pp. 84, 172.

10. Thomas Fabyanic, *Strategic Air Attack in the United States Air Force: A Case Study* (Manhattan, Kans.: Kansas State University/Aerospace Historian, 1976), pp. 2–38; Wesley F. Craven and James Lea Cate, *The Army Air Forces in World War II* (Chicago: University of Chicago Press, 1948–1958), vol. 1, pp. 17–21, 25–29, 35–43, 46–65; DeWitt Copp, *A Few Great Captains* (New York: Doubleday, 1980), especially pp. 20, 105–106, 300–302, 318–322; Thomas Coffey, *Hap* (New York: Viking, 1982), pp. 168–169, 198–199; Edgar S. Gorrell, "An American Proposal for Strategic Bombing in World War I," *Airpower Historian*, April 1958, pp. 102–117.

11. Coffey, *Hap*, pp. 173–176, 181, 225; Martin Caidin, *Flying Forts* (New York: Ballantine, 1969), pp. 4–5, 48–117; Copp, *A Few Great Captains*, pp. 257, 300–302, 324–331, 379, 389–392; Martin Caidin, *The Fork-Tailed Devil* (New York: Ballantine, 1971), pp. 19–55; Craven and Cate, *Army Air Forces*, vol. 1, pp. 66–70, 104–111; Robert Schlaifer, *The Development of Aircraft Engines* (New York: Pergamon, 1970; originally published by Harvard University, 1950), pp. 3–31, 37–38, 44, 50–56, 78–83, 257–259, 264, 276–279, 303, 307–313.

12. Dempster and Wood, *The Narrow Margin*, p. 185.

13. Kennett, *History of Strategic Bombing*, pp. 79–84.

14. R. J. Overy, *The Air War* (New York: Stein and Day, 1980), pp. 45, 132–133; Matthew Cooper, *The German Air Force* (New York: Janes, 1981), pp. 1–2, 7, 12–13, 27, 64, 68–72; Air Ministry, *The Rise and Fall of the German Air Force* (New York: St. Martin's 1983), pp. 48–49; Williamson Murray, *Strategy for Defeat* (Maxwell Air Force Base, Ala.: Airpower Research Institute, 1983), pp. 9–16; Edward L. Homze, "The Luftwaffe's Failure to Develop a Heavy Bomber before World War II," *Aerospace Historian*, Spring/March 1977, pp. 20–26; Dempster and Wood, *Narrow Margin*, pp. 37, 47.

15. Overy, *Air War*, pp. 26, 42–43; Cajus Bekker (Hans Dieter Berenbrok), *The Luftwaffe War Diaries* (Garden City, N.Y.: Doubleday, 1966), pp. 137–141, 182–183, 256, 258; Air Ministry, *Rise and Fall of the German Air Force*, pp. 21, 27–33, 44, 81–82, 86, 107, 402; Murray, *Strategy for Defeat*, pp. 6, 14–16, 44–46, 48–50, 132; Cooper, *German Air Force*, pp. 48, 52, 55, 71–72, 83, 92–94, 261–268, 276, 280–282; Schlaifer, *Development of Aircraft Engines*, pp. 221–222; Dempster and Wood, *Narrow Margin*, pp. 37, 43, 47.

16. Webster and Frankland, *Strategic Air Offensive*, vol. 1, pp. 271–283, 287, 292–294; Alan Milward, *The German Economy at War* (London: University of London Press, 1965), pp. 1–65; Berenice Carroll, *Design for Total War* (the Hague: Mouton, 1968), pp. 93, 99–103, 181–190; United States Strategic Bombing Survey, *The Effects of Strategic Bombing on the German War Economy* (Washington: Government Printing Office, 1945), pp. 68–78, 81–82, 87, 103, 109, 126; Alfred Mierzejewski, *The Collapse of the German War Economy, 1944–1945* (Chapel Hill: University of North Carolina Press, 1987), pp. xiii, 4–6, 54, 61, 76–77; Murray, *Strategy for Defeat*, pp. 27–30; Overy, *Air War*, pp. 28–29; Hastings, *Bomber Command*, pp. 109, 251–253.

CHAPTER 2

1. Webster and Frankland, *Strategic Air Offensive*, vol. 1, pp. 134–143, 191–201; Hastings, *Bomber Command*, pp. 17–34, Michael Bowyer, *2 Group RAF* (London: Faber and Faber, 1974), pp. 58–61; Cajus Bekker (Hans Dieter Berenbrok), *Hitler's Naval War* (New York: Zebra, 1978), pp. 33–38.

2. Webster and Frankland, *Strategic Air Offensive*, vol. 1, pp. 112, 139–141, 201–212, 215–232, 244–246; Hastings, *Bomber Command*, pp. 80–84.

3. Webster and Frankland, *Strategic Air Offensive*, vol. 1, pp. 143–154, 305, and vol. 4, pp. 115–126; Bowyer, *2 Group RAF*, pp. 75–109, 114–124; Hastings, *Bomber Command*, pp. 59–64, 84–87; Arthur Harris, *Bomber Offensive* (London: Collins, 1947), p. 93; W. J. Lawrence, *No. 5 Bomber Group RAF* (London: Faber and Faber, 1951), pp. 31–44; Dempster and Wood, *Narrow Margin*, pp. 270, 286, 291–293, 318–320, 344, 374; Roger Parkinson, *Summer 1940* (New York: David McKay, 1977), pp. 20, 47, 111, 148, 155–156, 158–159, 216–220; Telford Taylor, *The Breaking Wave* (New York: Simon and Schuster, 1967), pp. 150–151. For a different view of the Battle of Britain, see J. E. Johnson, *Story of Air Fighting*, pp. 166–169; Cooper, *German Air Force*, pp. 128–162.

4. Constantine FitzGibbon, *The Winter of the Bombs* (New York: Norton, 1958); Richard Collier, *The City That Would Not Die* (New York: Dutton, 1961); Alfred Price, *Instruments of Darkness* (London: Kimber, 1967), pp. 20–49; Brian Johnson, *The Secret War* (New York: Methuen, 1978), pp. 11–61; R. V. Jones, *The Wizard War* (New York: Coward, McCann and Geoghegan, 1978), pp. 129, 135, 172–179.

5. Webster and Frankland, *Strategic Air Offensive*, vol. 1, pp. 153–165, 215–232, and vol. 4, pp. 128–133; Hastings, *Bomber Command*, pp. 93–103, 108.

6. Webster and Frankland, *Strategic Air Offensive*, vol. 1, pp. 164–235, 247, 303–306; John Terraine, *The U-Boat Wars* (New York: Putnam's 1989), p. 346; S. W. Roskill, *The War at Sea* (London: Her Majesty's Stationery Office, 1954–1961), vol. 1, p. 459; Karl Doenitz, *Ten Years and Twenty Days* (Cleveland, Ohio: World, 1959), p. 409; Ralph Barker, *The Ship-Busters* (London: Chatto and Windus, 1957), pp. 61–67.

7. Webster and Frankland, *Strategic Air Offensive*, vol. 1, pp. 169–185, 249–254, and vol. 4, pp. 5, 98, 213; Harris, *Bomber Offensive*, pp. 73–79, 94–95; Hastings, *Bomber Command*, pp. 106–109, 117–122; Jack McElroy, "Incendiary Warfare on Germany," pp. 71–76, Horatio Bond, "The Fire Attacks on German Cities," pp. 76–79, and Horatio Bond, "Some Observations and Conclusions," pp. 244–245, in *Fire and the Air War*, edited by Horatio Bond (Boston: National Fire Protection Association, 1946); William Noyes, ed., *Chemistry* (Boston: Little, Brown, 1948), p. 398.

8. Webster and Frankland, *Strategic Air Offensive*, vol. 1, pp. 185–187, 254–257, and vol. 4, p. 142; Price, *Instruments of Darkness*, pp. 60–64; Werner Held and Holger Nauroth, *The Defense of the Reich* (New York: Arco, 1982), pp. 7–8, 71, 89; Brian Johnson, *Secret War*, pp. 103–110; Cooper, *German Air Force*, pp. 182–184; Murray, *Strategy for Defeat*, p. 132.

CHAPTER 3

1. Webster and Frankland, *Strategic Air Offensive*, vol. 1, pp. 320–325, 344–351, 461–463, and vol. 4, pp. 143–151, 152.

2. Webster and Frankland, *Strategic Air Offensive*, vol. 1, pp. 200–201, 217, 220, 340–343, 345–347, and vol. 4, pp. 239–243; Hastings, *Bomber Command*, pp. 34–35, 132–139; Harris, *Bomber Offensive*, pp. 73, 76–77.

3. Webster and Frankland, *Strategic Air Offensive*, vol. 1, pp. 266, 290–291, 346–350, 461–467, and vol. 4, pp. 228–230, 244, 249.

4. Hastings, *Bomber Command*, p. 111.

5. Webster and Frankland, *Strategic Air Offensive*, vol. 1, pp. 257, 310, 318, 325–336, 341–344, 416, 447, 452; Hastings, *Bomber Command*, pp. 110–118.

6. Webster and Frankland, *Strategic Air Offensive*, vol. 4, pp. 4–6; Price, *Instruments of Darkness*, pp. 98–105; Jones, *Wizard War*, p. 215; Brian Johnson, *Secret War*, pp. 83–89; Harris, *Bomber Offensive*, pp. 76, 94–95, 124; Dudley Saward, *The Bomber's Eye* (London: Cassell, 1959), pp. 39, 62–63, 100–103, 146, 165.

7. Webster and Frankland, *Strategic Air Offensive*, vol. 4, pp. 7–11; Gordon Musgrove, *Pathfinder Force* (London: MacDonald's and Janes, 1976), pp. 220–231, Jones, *Wizard War*, pp. 274–276; Saward, *Bomber's Eye*, p. 109; Brian Johnson, *Secret War*, pp. 89–91, Price, *Instruments of Darkness*, pp. 123, 133, 138, 190–191.

8. Webster and Frankland, *Strategic Air Offensive*, vol. 4, pp. 11–15; Musgrove, *Pathfinder Force*, pp. 35, 232–239; Price, *Instruments of Darkness*, pp. 134–135, 185–186, 213–215, 225; Brian Johnson, *Secret War*, pp. 91–100, 119, Saward, *Bomber's Eye*, pp. 138–139, 144, 175, 217, 228, 241–249.

9. Webster and Frankland, *Strategic Air Offensive*, vol. 1, pp. 310, 382–386, and vol. 4, pp. 37–38; D. C. T. Bennett, *Pathfinder* (London: Muller, 1958), pp. 175–176; Hastings, *Bomber Command*, pp. 142–170; Harris, *Bomber Offensive*, pp. 97–102; Lawrence, *No. 5 Bomber Group RAF*, pp. 69, 79.

10. Webster and Frankland, *Strategic Air Offensive*, vol. 1, pp. 387–389, 489, Bennett, *Pathfinder*, p. 131; United States Strategic Bombing Survey, *Renault Motor Vehicles Plant, Billancourt, Paris* (Washington: Government Printing Office, 1947), pp. 1–12.

11. Webster and Frankland, *Strategic Air Offensive*, vol. 1, pp. 293–294, 339, 389–402, Ralph Barker, *The Thousand Plan* (London: Chatto and Windus, 1965), pp. 33–39.

12. Webster and Frankland, *Strategic Air Offensive*, vol. 1, pp. 402–417; Barker, *Thousand Plan*, pp. 39ff; Harris, *Bomber Offensive*, pp. 108–122; Lawrence, *No. 5 Bomber Group RAF*, pp. 71–75.

13. Webster and Frankland, *Strategic Air Offensive*, vol. 1, pp. 441–446, 451–454; Hastings, *Bomber Command*, pp. 182–183.

14. Webster and Frankland, *Strategic Air Offensive*, vol. 1, pp. 342–343, 419–435; Harris, *Bomber Offensive*, pp. 128–131; Musgrove, *Pathfinder Force*, pp. 5–13, 247; Bennett, *Pathfinder*, p. 162.

15. Webster and Frankland, *Strategic Air Offensive*, vol. 1, pp. 482–490; Alfred Price, *Blitz on Britain* (London: Ian Allan, 1977), pp. 132–142, Jones, *Wizard War*, pp. 250–253; Cooper, *German Air Force*, pp. 190–191, Air Ministry, *The Rise and Fall of the German Air Force*, pp. 192–196; David Irving, *The Mare's Nest* (Boston: Little, Brown, 1965), pp. 18–22, 304.

CHAPTER 4

1. Webster and Frankland, *Strategic Air Offensive*, vol. 2, pp. 99–105, 115 (note 1), 134, III, 122; Musgrove, *Pathfinder Force*, pp. 249–250.

2. Webster and Frankland, *Strategic Air Offensive*, vol. 4, pp. 18–20, 138–140; Price, *Instruments of Darkness*, pp. 81–88, 94, 106–111, 128–130; Jones, *Wizard War*, pp. 236–249, 270; Brian Johnson, *Secret War*, pp. 106–109, 112–113; F. H. Hinsley et al., *British Intelligence in the Second World War* (Cambridge: Cambridge University Press, 1979–1988), vol. 2, pp. 246–257.

3. Webster and Frankland, *Strategic Air Offensive*, vol. 1, pp. 244, 257–258; United States Strategic Bombing Survey, *Gustahlfabrik Friedrich Krupp* (Washington: Government Printing Office, 1947); United States Department of Commerce, *The Ruhr* (Washington: Government Printing Office, 1949), pp. 32–34; Norman J. G. Pounds, *The Ruhr* (Bloomington: Indiana University Press, 1952), pp. 197, 223–224, 241–247.

4. Webster and Frankland, *Strategic Air Offensive*, vol. 2, pp. 96–98; Lawrence, *No. 5 Bomber Group RAF*, pp. 107–108; Harris, *Bomber Offensive*, 137.

5. Webster and Frankland, *Strategic Air Offensive*, vol. 2, p. 135.

6. Webster and Frankland, *Strategic Air Offensive*, vol. 2, pp. 102–137, 248–260, Musgrove, *Pathfinder Force*, pp. 40–42; Lawrence, *No. 5 Bomber Group RAF*, pp. 109–111.

7. John Sweetman, *Operation Chastise* (London: Janes, 1982), pp. 1–83, 96; Webster and Frankland, *Strategic Air Offensive*, vol. 2, pp. 168–175, 288–290; Kenneth Macksey, *Commando* (New York: Stein and Day, 1986), p. 158.

8. Sweetman, *Operation Chastise*, pp. 89–187; Albert Speer, *Inside the Third Reich* (New York: Avon, 1972), pp. 365–368. As Sweetman shows, the official history, Webster and Frankland, *Strategic Air Offensive*, in vol. 2, pp. 178–179, 290–292, unduly minimizes the effects of the dams attack. Later writers, e.g. Anthony Verrier, *The Bomber Offensive* (New York: Macmillan, 1968), pp. 19, 220–225, are even more extreme.

9. Jones, *Wizard War*, p. 304.

10. Webster and Frankland, *Strategic Air Offensive*, vol. 2, pp. 187–188; Lawrence, *No. 5 Bomber Group RAF*, pp. 139–144; Martin Middlebrook, *The Peenemunde Raid* (Indianapolis, Ind.: Bobbs-Merrill, 1982), pp. 23, 50–52; Harris, *Bomber Offensive*, pp. 165, 182; Musgrove, *Pathfinder Force*, pp. 54–55.

11. Martin Middlebrook, *The Battle of Hamburg* (New York: Scribner's 1981), pp. 33–34, 75–98; Webster and Frankland, *Strategic Air Offensive*, vol. 2, pp. 147–148; Gordon Musgrove, *Operation Gomorrah* (London: Janes, 1981), pp. v–vii, 3; United States Strategic Bombing Survey, *Oil Division, Final Report* (Washington: Government Printing Office, 1947), p. 75.

12. Webster and Frankland, *Strategic Air Offensive*, vol. 2, pp. 140–145; Middlebrook, *Battle of Hamburg*, pp. 68–70, 112, 125–128; Price, *Instruments of Darkness*, pp. 113–120, 141, 145, 163–164; Jones, *Wizard War*, pp. 287–290.

13. Webster and Frankland, *Strategic Air Offensive*, vol. 2, pp. 149–153; Middlebrook, *Battle of Hamburg*, pp. 98–234; Musgrove, *Operation Gomorrah*, pp. 4–63.

14. Middlebrook, *Battle of Hamburg*, pp. 234–276; Musgrove, *Operation Gomorrah*, pp. 65–116; Webster and Frankland, *Strategic Air Offensive*, vol. 2, pp. 153, 238.

15. Middlebrook, *Battle of Hamburg*, pp. 282–320; Musgrove, *Operation Gomorrah*, pp. 127–161; Webster and Frankland, *Strategic Air Offensive*, vol. 2, pp. 154–155.

16. Middlebrook, *Battle of Hamburg*, pp. 276–280, 322–336; Musgrove, *Operation Gomorrah*, pp. 162–168; Webster and Frankland, *Strategic Air Offensive*, vol. 2, pp. 155, 260–263; Speer, *Inside the Third Reich*, pp. 369–370; United States Strategic Bombing Survey, *A Detailed Study of the Effects of Area Bombing on Hamburg* (Washington: Government Printing Office, 1947).

17. Middlebrook, *Peenemunde Raid*, passim; Irving, *Mare's Nest*, pp. 28, 69–71, 83, 112–120, 307–309; Musgrove, *Pathfinder Force*, p. 250; Basil Collier, *The Battle of the*

V-Weapons (New York: Morrow, 1965), pp. 138–139, 143–144; Walter Dornberger, *V-2* (New York: Bantam, 1979), p. 180.

18. Martin Middlebrook, *The Berlin Raids* (New York: Viking, 1988), pp. 7–9, 21–103; Webster and Frankland, *Strategic Air Offensive*, vol. 2, pp. 34–36, 60–67, 146–149, 160–167.

19. Webster and Frankland, *Strategic Air Offensive*, vol. 2, pp. 164–165, 201–203; Price, *Instruments of Darkness*, pp. 135, 172–176, 179, 181, 220–221; Murray, *Strategy for Defeat*, pp. 179, 214; Brian Johnson, *Secret War*, pp. 112–114, 118–119; Middlebrook, *Berlin Raids*, pp. 15–18, 179, 221–224; Martin Middlebrook, *The Nuremberg Raid* (New York: Morrow 1974), pp. 58–64, 68–73.

20. Webster and Frankland, *Strategic Air Offensive*, vol. 2, pp. 57, 145–146, 149, 166, 189, 202–203, IV, pp. 15–16; Musgrove, *Pathfinder Force*, pp. 187–188, 228–229; Middlebrook, *The Nuremberg Raid*, pp. 32–33; Middlebrook, *Berlin Raids*, pp. 95, 100, 180; Saward, *Bomber's Eye*, pp. 169–172.

21. Webster and Frankland, *Strategic Air Offensive*, vol. 2, p. 190.

22. Webster and Frankland, *Strategic Air Offensive*, vol. 2, pp. 47–48, 54–61, 245–246.

23. Middlebrook, *Berlin Raids*, pp. 104–304, 381–386; Murray, *Strategy for Defeat*, pp. 214–217; Webster and Frankland, *Strategic Air Offensive*, vol. 2, pp. 190–207, and vol. 4, pp. 162–163, 165–167; Bennett, *Pathfinder*, pp. 211–212.

24. Webster and Frankland, *Strategic Air Offensive*, vol. 2, pp. 207–211; Middlebrook, *Nuremberg Raid*, pp. 78–301; Murray, *Strategy for Defeat*, pp. 217–221.

CHAPTER FIVE

1. Roger A. Freeman, *B-17 Fortress at War* (New York: Scribner's, 1979), pp. 12, 25; Caidin, *Flying Forts*, pp. 125–142; Coffey, *Hap*, p. 239.

2. Freeman, *B-17 Fortress at War*, pp. 26–33, 38; Caidin, *Flying Forts*, pp. 121–122, 143–159; Walter D. Edmonds, *They Fought with What They Had* (Boston: Little, Brown, 1951), pp. 298, 329, 332–333.

3. Craven and Cate, *Army Air Forces*, vol. 1, pp. 120, 131–133, 145–148; Fabyanic, *Strategic Air Attack*, pp. 46–51; DeWitt Copp, *Forged in Fire* (Garden City, N.Y.: Doubleday, 1982), pp. 154–157, 175–176.

4. Craven and Cate, *Army Air Forces*, vol. 1, pp. 559–664; Winston Churchill, *The Grand Alliance* (New York: Bantam 1962), pp. 527, 577–593.

5. Roger A. Freeman, *The Mighty Eighth* (Garden City, N.Y.: Doubleday, 1970), pp. 4–10; Craven and Cate, *Army Air Forces*, vol. 1, pp. 617–642; Thomas Coffey, *Decision over Schweinfurt* (New York: Doubleday, 1977), pp. 100–121.

6. Craven and Cate, *Army Air Forces*, vol. 1, pp. 575, 590; and vol. 2, pp. 209, 231–233, 235, 237–238, 243–254, 260, 268, 308–309, 311; Freeman, *Mighty Eighth*, pp. 13–15, 24–25, 33–41.

7. Craven and Cate, *Army Air Forces*, vol. 1, pp. 594, 597–598, 600–602, II, pp. 297–299; Coffey, *Decision over Schweinfurt*, pp. 136–142, 152–155; Webster and Frankland, *Strategic Air Offensive*, vol. 1, pp. 354–358, 375–376, 451–454; Hastings, *Bomber Command*, pp. 182–184.

8. Webster and Frankland, *Strategic Air Offensive*, vol. 4, pp. 153–154.

9. Craven and Cate, *Army Air Forces*, vol. 2, pp. 213–216, 277–281, 288–295, 301–307; Fabyanic, *Strategic Air Attack*, pp. 53–77; Webster and Frankland, *Strategic Air Offensive*, vol. 2, pp. 10–15, and vol. 4, pp. 153–154.

10. Martin Middlebrook, *Convoy* (New York: Morrow, 1976), pp. 308–314; John M. Waters, *Bloody Winter*, rev. ed. (New York: Jove, 1986), pp. 254–262.

11. J. E. Johnson, *The Story of Air Fighting*, p. 219.

12. Freeman, *Mighty Eighth*, pp. 11–16; John Vader, *Spitfire* (New York: Ballantine, 1969), pp. 133–135. Interestingly, many works on the Spitfire barely mention the Mark 8 model; some do not mention it at all.

13. Freeman, *Mighty Eighth*, pp. 10–11; Coffey, *Decision over Schweinfurt*, pp. 122–123, 129, 134; Wilbur Morrison, *The Incredible 305th* (New York: Belmont, 1977), p. 19; Craven and Cate, *Army Air Forces*, vol. 1, p. 657.

14. Craven and Cate, *Army Air Forces*, vol. 2, pp. 219–225; Caidin, *Flying Forts*, pp. 244–253; Freeman, *Mighty Eighth*, p. 18.

15. Craven and Cate, *Army Air Forces*, vol. 2, pp. 232–236, 242–272; Freeman, *Mighty Eighth*, pp. 18–25, 31; Alfred Price, *Battle over the Reich* (New York: Scribner's 1973), pp. 32–38, 61; Coffey, *Decision over Schweinfurt*, pp. 174–182, 186; *Impact 5* (New York: James Porson, 1980) September 1943, pp. 30–33.

16. Craven and Cate, *Army Air Forces*, vol. 2, pp. 311–333, 337–345; Freeman, *Mighty Eighth*, pp. 25–32; Webster and Frankland, *Strategic Air Offensive*, vol. 2, pp. 287–288; Copp, *Forged in Fire*, p. 388; United States Strategic Bombing Survey, *Focke-Wulf Aircraft Plant, Bremen* (Washington: Government Printing Office, 1945), pp. 1, 7.

17. Murray, *Strategy for Defeat*, pp. 137–138, 149, 163, 224, 228–229, 254, 312–314; Air Ministry, *Rise and Fall of the German Air Force*, pp. 201, 220–221, 234, 289; Webster and Frankland, *Strategic Air Offensive*, vol. 2, p. 46 (note); Cooper, *German Air Force*, pp. 260–261, 303–304, 322. For different figures see Craven and Cate, *Army Air Forces*, vol. 2, pp. 333–334.

18. Craven and Cate, *Army Air Forces*, vol. 2, pp. 334–337; Freeman, *Mighty Eighth*, pp. 40–44; Coffey, *Decision over Schweinfurt*, pp. 169, 187, 195–201, 211; Robert Johnson with Martin Caidin, *Thunderbolt* (New York: Ballantine, 1959), pp. 74–111; Hubert Zemke and Roger A. Freeman, *Zemke's Wolfpack* (New York: Orion, 1988), pp. 47, 51, 62–63, 68, 73, 84, 93–96.

19. Webster and Frankland, *Strategic Air Offensive*, vol. 2, pp. 15–21.

20. Webster and Frankland, *Strategic Air Offensive*, vol. 2, pp. 15–30, 269–272, and vol. 4, pp. 155–158; Craven and Cate, *Army Air Forces*, vol. 2, pp. 349–376; Fabyanic, *Strategic Air Attack*, pp. 78–88; United States Strategic Bombing Survey, *The German Anti-Friction Bearings Industry* (Washington: Government Printing Office, 1947), pp. 1–2, 4–6; Martin Caidin, *Black Thursday* (New York: Bantam, 1987), pp. 17–22; Speer, *Inside the Third Reich*, p. 365.

CHAPTER 6

1. Craven and Cate, *Army Air Forces*, vol, 2, pp. 609, 611, 613–615, 635–640, 665–673; Freeman, *Mighty Eighth*, pp. 46–54, Strategic Bombing Survey, *Effects of Strategic Bombing on the German War Economy*, pp. 84–85; Coffey, *Decision over Schweinfurt*, pp. 188–194.

2. Craven and Cate, *Army Air Forces*, vol. 2, pp. 654–655, 679–681, 683, Freeman, *Mighty Eighth*, pp. 80–82; Copp, *Forged in Fire*, pp. 398–404; Coffey, *Decision over Schweinfurt*, pp. 187–188, 202; Zemke and Freeman, *Zemke's Wolfpack*, pp. 67–68, 102, 108–109, 117, 134.

3. Craven and Cate, *Army Air Forces*, vol. 2, pp. 673–681; Freeman, *Mighty Eighth*, pp. 63–67, 80–81; Caidin, *Flying Forts*, pp. 392–398; Middlebrook, *Battle of Hamburg*, pp. 199–232; Coffey, *Decision over Schweinfurt*, pp. 218–220; Price, *Battle over the Reich*, pp. 63–65, 83–84,

95–96; B. J. Peaslee, "The Devastation Bombing of Heroya, 24 July 1943," *Aerospace Historian* (Winter/December 1982), pp. 260–264.

4. Craven and Cate, *Army Air Forces*, vol. 2, pp. 9–10, 13–40; John Sweetman, *Ploesti* (New York: Ballantine, 1974), pp. 50–65; James Dugan and Carroll Stewart, *Ploesti* (New York: Ballantine, 1973), pp. 3–15.

5. Craven and Cate, *Army Air Forces*, vol. 2, pp. 358, 366, 477–481; Sweetman, *Ploesti*, pp. 78–113; Dugan and Stewart, *Ploesti*, pp. 35–79.

6. Craven and Cate, *Army Air Forces*, vol. 2, pp. 481–483; Sweetman, *Ploesti*, pp. 112–159; Dugan and Stewart, *Ploesti*, pp. 82–234; Kenneth C. Rust, *The Ninth Air Force in World War II*, 2d ed. (Fallbrook: Aero Publishers, 1970), pp. 39–42.

7. Martin Middlebrook, *The Schweinfurt-Regensburg Mission* (New York: Penguin, 1985); Coffey, *Decision over Schweinfurt*, pp. 3–80, 234–237; Craven and Cate, *Army Air Forces*, vol. 2, pp. 483–484, 682–687; Webster and Frankland, *Strategic Air Offensive*, vol. 2, p. 272; Freeman, *Mighty Eighth*, pp. 67–69, Morrison, *Incredible 305th*, p. 73; Elmer Bendiner, *The Fall of the Fortresses* (New York: Putnam's, 1980), pp. 159–174; Brian D. O'Neill, *Half a Wing, Three Engines and a Prayer* (Blue Ridge Summit: Tab 1989), pp. 29–37; Rust, *Ninth Air Force*, p. 43; Speer, *Inside the Third Reich*, pp. 371–372; Walter Boyne, *Messerschmitt 262: Arrow to the Future* (Washington: Smithsonian Institute Press, 1980), p. 180.

8. Craven and Cate, *Army Air Forces*, vol. 2, pp. 687–688; Freeman, *Mighty Eighth*, pp. 70–71; Bendiner, *Fall of the Fortresses*, pp. 187–188; O'Neill, *Half a Wing*, pp. 52–70; John Comer, *Combat Crew* (New York: Morrow, 1987), pp. 94–107; Irving, *Mare's Nest*, pp. 123–124.

9. Craven and Cate, *Army Air Forces*, vol. 2, pp. 689–694, and vol. 3, pp. 13–15; Freeman, *Mighty Eighth*, pp. 73–75, 83–84, 92.

10. Craven and Cate, *Army Air Forces*, vol. 2, pp. 695–699; Freeman, *Mighty Eighth*, pp. 75–77; O'Neill, *Half a Wing*, pp. 87–92.

11. Caidin, *Black Thursday*, passim; Craven and Cate, *Army Air Forces*, vol. 2, pp. 701–705; Coffey, *Decision over Schweinfurt*, pp. 241, 254–296; Freeman, *Mighty Eighth*, pp. 78–79; Bendiner, *Fall of the Fortresses*, pp. 214–224; O'Neill, *Half a Wing*, pp. 94–120; Comer, *Combat Crew*, p. 185.

12. Craven and Cate, *Army Air Forces*, vol. 2, pp. 701–705; Webster and Frankland, *Strategic Air Offensive*, vol. 2, pp. 273–277; Coffey, *Decision over Schweinfurt*, pp. 296–298, 306–309; Strategic Bombing Survey, *German Anti-Friction Bearings Industry*, pp. 2, 29–30, 37–54; Caidin, *Black Thursday*, pp. 215–216; Speer, *Inside the Third Reich*, pp. 371–373.

CHAPTER 7

1. Craven and Cate, *Army Air Forces*, vol. 2, pp. 563–573, 716–717, 723–726, and vol. 3, pp. 7–8, 11, 18, 25; Freeman, *Mighty Eighth*, pp. 98–99; Rust, *Ninth Air Force*, p. 52.

2. Murray, *Strategy for Defeat*, pp. 149, 183–184, 188, 224–226, 237.

3. Craven and Cate, *Army Air Forces*, vol. 2, pp. 705–706, vol. 3, pp. 13–22; Webster and Frankland, *Strategic Air Offensive*, vol. 2, p. 292; Bowyer, *2 Group RAF*, p. 292; Freeman, *Mighty Eighth*, pp. 99–104; O'Neill, *Half a Wing*, pp. 145–149; David Irving, *The German Atomic Bomb* (New York: Da Capo, n.d., originally published New York: Simon and Schuster, 1967), pp. 193–195; Speer, *Inside the Third Reich*, p. 684, note 16.

4. Craven and Cate, *Army Air Forces*, vol. 3, pp. 9–12; Caidin, *Fork-Tailed Devil*, especially pp. 112–113, 117–121, 131–136, 161–172, 176–179; Freeman, *Mighty Eighth*, pp. 92–95; Joe Christy and Jeffrey Ethell, *P-38 Lightning at War* (New York: Scribner's, 1979), pp. 27, 37–39, 88, 100–103, 116.

5. Craven and Cate, *Army Air Forces*, vol. 3, pp. 11–12, and vol. 5, pp. 320, 336; Mark Bradley "The P-51 over Berlin," *Aerospace Historian*, Fall 1974, pp. 125–128; William Hess, *P-51 Mustang* (New York: Ballantine, 1971); Copp, *Forged in Fire*, pp. 412–414, 420–421; H. H. Arnold, *Global Mission* (New York: Harper, 1949), p. 376; Coffey, *Hap*, p. 308; Jeffrey Ethell and Alfred Price, *Target Berlin* (London: Janes, 1981), pp. 12–13; Freeman, *Mighty Eighth*, pp. 95–97, 119, 122–124.

6. Webster and Frankland, *Strategic Air Offensive*, vol. 2, pp. 224–243, Speer, *Inside the Third Reich*, pp. 251–282, 291–292; Carroll, *Design for Total War*, pp. 221, 227–229, 245–247.

7. Craven and Cate, *Army Air Forces*, vol. 2, pp. 708–710, 712–714; Webster and Frankland, *Strategic Air Offensive*, vol. 2, pp. 224–234, 248, 252–255, 268, 279–288; Strategic Bombing Survey, *Effects of Strategic Bombing on the German War Economy*, pp. 10–12, 90, 148, 157; Speer, *Inside the Third Reich*, p. 363. See Dudley Saward, *Bomber Harris* (Garden City, N.Y.: Doubleday, 1985), p. 308.

8. Webster and Frankland, *Strategic Air Offensive*, vol. 2, pp. 295–296; Speer, *Inside The Third Reich*, p. 363; Murray, *Strategy for Defeat*, pp. 183, 190, 226, 250–251; Hastings, *Bomber Command*, pp. 230, 241; Cooper, *German Air Force*, pp. 332–333, 340–341; Air Ministry, *The Rise and Fall of the German Air Force*, pp. 289, 298, 321–322; Price, *Blitz on Britain*, pp. 155–170.

9. Webster and Frankland, *Strategic Air Offensive*, vol. 4, pp. 164–165.

10. Ibid.

11. Webster and Frankland, *Strategic Air Offensive*, vol. 2, pp. 69, 82–84, and vol. 4, pp. 160–167; Craven and Cate, *Army Air Forces*, vol. 2, pp. 738–739, 749–750, 754; and vol. 3, pp. 5–8, 27–29; Coffey, *Hap*, pp. 328–333.

12. Freeman, *Mighty Eighth*, p. 119; United States Strategic Bombing Survey, *The Defeat of the German Air Force* (Washington: Government Printing Office, 1947), p. 7–12; William Emerson, *Operation Pointblank* (Colorado Springs, Colo.: USAF Academy, 1962); Copp, *Forged in Fire*, pp. 450–457.

13. Craven and Cate, *Army Air Forces*, vol. 3, pp. 12–26, 30–31, 350–352; Strategic Bombing Survey, *Defeat of the German Air Force*, pp. 7–11, Price, *Battle over the Reich*, pp. 117–121; Freeman, *Mighty Eighth*, pp. 92–107, 119–121; Rust, *Ninth Air Force*, p. 53.

14. Craven and Cate, *Army Air Forces*, vol. 3, pp. 30–45; Freeman, *Mighty Eighth*, pp. 107–113, 122; Price, *Battle over the Reich*, pp. 122–124; Robert Johnson, *Thunderbolt*, pp. 180–182; Murray, *Strategy for Defeat*, pp. 237–243, 275; Bekker, *Luftwaffe War Diaries*, pp. 345–351.

15. Craven and Cate, *Army Air Forces*, vol. 3, pp. 46–47; Price, *Battle over the Reich*, pp. 123, 126; Murray, *Strategy for Defeat*, pp. 240, 243; Kenneth C. Rust and William N. Hess, "The German Jets and the U.S. Army Air Force" *American Aviation Historical Society Journal*, Fall, 1963, p. 156; United States Strategic Bombing Survey, Aircraft Division *Industry Report* (Washington: Government Printing Office, 1947), pp. 68–69.

16. Craven and Cate, *Army Air Forces*, vol. 3, pp. 48–53; Freeman, *Mighty Eighth*, pp. 114–115, 123–126; Ethell and Price, *Target Berlin*, passim; Bekker, *Luftwaffe War Diaries*, pp. 351–352.

17. Craven and Cate, *Army Air Forces*, vol. 3, pp. 54–56; Ethell and Price, *Target Berlin*,

p. 153; Murray, *Strategy for Defeat*, p. 240; Freeman, *Mighty Eighth*, pp. 116–117, 136–140; Adolf Galland, *The First and the Last* (New York: Bantam 1978), pp. 200–201, 209–210, 214–216.

18. Craven and Cate, *Army Air Forces*, vol. 3, pp. 59–64; Murray, *Strategy for Defeat*, pp. 240, 243–245, 251–255; Price, *Battle over the Reich*, pp. 132–133; Chester Wilmot, *The Struggle for Europe* (London: Fontana, 1980), pp. 178, 505; Strategic Bombing Survey, *Effects of Strategic Bombing on the German War Economy*, pp. 156, 159, 161–162; United States Strategic Bombing Survey, *Over-All Report (European War)* (Washington: Government Printing Office, 1945), pp. 16–17, 22; Strategic Bombing Survey, Aircraft Division, *Industry Report*, pp. 6–8, 17–18, 24, 30, 67–69, 82–84; United States Strategic Bombing Survey, *Dornier Works, Friedrichshafen* (Washington: Government Printing Office, 1947).

19. Robert Leckie, *The Wars of America* (New York: Bantam 1969), vol. 1, p. 512.

CHAPTER 8

1. Webster and Frankland, *Strategic Air Offensive*, vol. 4, pp. 167–170.

2. Webster and Frankland, *Strategic Air Offensive*, vol. 3, pp. 13–25; Craven and Cate, *Army Air Forces*, vol. 3, pp. 56–57, 79–83, 142, 149, 164.

3. Walt Rostow, *Pre-Invasion Bombing Strategy* (Austin: University of Texas 1981), p. 44.

4. Rostow, *Pre-Invasion Bombing Strategy*, p. 4.

5. Craven and Cate, *The Army Air Forces*, vol. 3, p. 78.

6. Craven and Cate, *Army Air Forces*, vol. 3, pp. 72–79, 149–150; Webster and Frankland, *Strategic Air Offensive*, vol. 3, pp. 21–39; Rostow, *Pre-Invasion Bombing Strategy*, pp. 3–14, 31–60; Hinsley et al., *British Intelligence*, vol. 3, part 2, pp. 498–499. Hinsley is probably in error in suggesting that Spaatz seized on the oil plan only as an alternative to the transportation plan. While a valuable source, Rostow's suggestion that Eisenhower was presented with "false alternatives: marshalling yards versus oil. The true alternatives were oil, plus a systematic attack on bridges and dumps versus marshalling yards" (p. 43) is unreasonable. Eisenhower must have been aware of the interdiction possibility all along, since it antedated the Transportation Plan in earlier plans for air support for the invasion.

7. Webster and Frankland, *Strategic Air Offensive*, vol. 2, pp. 179–186, 292–295, and vol. 3, pp. 123–158; Musgrove, *Pathfinder Force*, pp. 120–124; Lawrence, *No. 5 Bomber Group RAF*, pp. 155–186; Harris, *Bomber Offensive*, pp. 199–202; United States Strategic Bombing Survey, *Maybach Motor Works, Friedrichshafen* (Washington: Government Printing Office, 1947), pp. 1–11.

8. Craven and Cate, *Army Air Forces*, vol. 3, pp. 50–162, 219–227; Rust, *Ninth Air Force*, pp. 70–73; Freeman, *Mighty Eighth*, pp. 140, 143, 151; Russell Weigley, *Eisenhower's Lieutenants* (Bloomington: Indiana University Press, 1981), pp. 59–68; Rostow, *Pre-Invasion Bombing Strategy*, pp. 57–75; Wilmot, *Struggle for Europe*, pp. 233–238.

9. Craven and Cate, *Army Air Forces*, vol. 3, pp. 162–172; Webster and Frankland, *Strategic Air Offensive*, vol. 3, pp. 141–143; Freeman, *Mighty Eighth*, pp. 141, 143; Lawrence, *No. 5 Bomber Group RAF*, p. 188; Musgrove, *Pathfinder Force*, pp. 126–130.

10. Craven and Cate, *Army Air Forces*, vol. 3, pp. 89–106, 525–546; Freeman, *Mighty Eighth*, pp. 173–174; Irving, *Mare's Nest*, pp. 72, 121, 160–162, 179, 187–189, 194–196, 199, 212–225, 241–253, 292–295, 302–312; Peter Cooksley, *Flying Bomb* (New York: Scribner's, 1979); Collier, *Battle of the V-Weapons* especially pp. 34–35, 37, 47–49, 60–61,

77–78, 84–95, 112–121, 127–133, 138–149; Webster and Frankland, *Strategic Air Offensive*, vol. 3, p. 181; Hinsley, *British Intelligence*, vol. 3, part 2, pp. 537–540.

11. Craven and Cate, *Army Air Forces*, vol. 3, pp. 190–192, 207–209, 212–214, 216, 219–227, 229–235, 273, 277, 502–505, 561, 602, 627, 631–632; Webster and Frankland, *Strategic Air Offensive*, vol. 3, pp. 165, 181; Freeman, *Mighty Eighth*, pp. 140–143, 153–154, 157–158, 165–168, 174–176, 181, 185, 188–189; Musgrove, *Pathfinder Force*, pp. 125–126, 132–136; R. W. Thompson, *Battle of the Rhineland* (New York: Ballantine, 1959), pp. 140, 154, 172; Galland, *The First and the Last*, pp. 227–236, 240, 242–243, 247; Murray, *Strategy for Defeat*, pp. 279–283, 288.

CHAPTER 9

1. This point is often misunderstood, as in Hastings, *Bomber Command*, pp. 272, 278. Hastings exaggerates the Allied leaders' dissatisfaction with the "bomber barons," wrongly assuming that they expected more from the strategic air offensive than they did and that they fully realized how little had been accomplished. See Hinsley, *British Intelligence*, vol. 3, part 1, pp. 53, 6–64, 549–550.

2. Hinsley, *British Intelligence*, vol. 3, part 2, p. 513 (note); Webster and Frankland, *Strategic Air Offensive*, vol. 3, pp. 226–229, 235–236; United States Strategic Bombing Survey, Oil Division, *Final Report*, pp. 1–4, 28, 56; United States Strategic Bombing Survey, *The German Oil Industry, Ministerial Report* (Washington, Government Printing Office, 1947), p. 3; Strategic Bombing Survey, *Effects of Strategic Bombing on the German War Economy*, pp. 10–12, 71–78; Murray, *Strategy for Defeat*, pp. 272–273.

3. Craven and Cate, *Army Air Forces*, vol. 3, pp. 175–179; Freeman, *Mighty Eighth*, pp. 141–144; Zemke and Freeman, *Zemke's Wolfpack*, pp. 169–171; Hinsley, *British Intelligence*, vol. 3, part 2, pp. 499–502; Murray, *Strategy for Defeat*, pp. 272–273.

4. Webster and Frankland, *Strategic Air Offensive*, vol. 3, pp. 157–162; Lawrence, *No. 5 Bomber Group RAF*, p. 195.

5. Webster and Frankland, *Strategic Air Offensive*, vol. 3, pp. 163–170; Price, *Battle over the Reich*, p. 141.

6. Price, *Instruments of Darkness*, pp. 145–146, 213–215, 219–220, Jones, *Wizard War*, pp. 392–396; Brian Johnson, *Secret War*, pp. 119–121.

7. Webster and Frankland, *Strategic Air Offensive*, vol. 3, pp. 173–180, and vol. 4, p. 24; Price, *Battle over the Reich*, p. 141; Hinsley, *British Intelligence*, vol. 3, part 2, pp. 506, 509–515.

8. Craven and Cate, *Army Air Forces*, vol. 3, pp. 280, 284–286; Freeman, *Mighty Eighth*, pp. 156–157.

9. Webster and Frankland, *Strategic Air Offensive*, vol. 4, pp. 321–325.

10. Strategic Bombing Survey, Oil Division, *Final Report*, pp. 28–33, 84, 91, 121–122, 128–129; Price, *Battle over the Reich*, pp. 142–143; Strategic Bombing Survey, *Effects of Strategic Bombing on the German War Economy*, pp. 12, 81–82, 87; Strategic Bombing Survey, *German Oil Industry*, pp. 51, 53–59; Speer, *Inside the Third Reich*, pp. 445, 449–451.

11. Hinsley, *British Intelligence*, vol. 3, part 2, pp. 502, 505–508, 510–513.

12. Craven and Cate, *Army Air Forces*, vol. 3, pp. 279–301; Freeman, *Mighty Eighth*, pp. 160, 163, 165, 174–177.

13. Craven and Cate, *Army Air Forces*, vol. 3, pp. 177, 281–283, 290–292, 296–299; Dugan and Stewart, *Ploesti*, pp. 252–264; Leroy Newby, *Target Ploesti* (Novato, Calif.:

Presidio Press, 1983), pp. 27, 80, 102–103, 119, 139, 160, 187, 210–211; Albert Seaton, *The Russo-German War* (New York: Praeger, 1972), pp. 472–485; Hinsley, *British Intelligence*, vol. 3, part 2, pp. 505, 509; Webster and Frankland, *Strategic Air Offensive*, vol. 3, pp. 229–230; Murray, *Strategy for Defeat*, p. 286; Strategic Bombing Survey, *Effects of Strategic Bombing on the German War Economy*, p. 78; Steve Birdsall, *Log of the Liberators* (New York: Doubleday, 1973), p. 229; *Impact 5*, December 1944, pp. 36–53.

14. Glenn Infield, *The Poltava Affair* (New York: Macmillan, 1973); Craven and Cate, *Army Air Forces*, vol. 3, pp. 308–319; John R. Deane, *The Strange Alliance* (Bloomington: Indiana University Press, 1973), pp. 107–125; Freeman, *Mighty Eighth*, p. 158.

15. Schlaifer, *Development of Aircraft Engines*, pp. 321–377, 429; Edward Constant, *The Origins of the Turbojet Revolution* (Baltimore: Johns Hopkins University Press, 1980), pp. 194, 235; John Golley, *Whittle, The True Story* (Washington: Smithsonian Institution Press, 1987), especially pp. 80, 122, 167–169, 222; Frank Whittle, *Jet* (London: Müller, 1953), especially pp. 242, 290.

16. Craven and Cate, *Army Air Forces*, vol. 3, pp. 295, 300, 659; Jeffrey Ethell and Alfred Price, *The German Jets in Combat* (London: Janes, 1979), pp. 113ff; Brian Johnson, *The Secret War*, pp. 276–283; Price, *Battle over the Reich*, pp. 145–148; Galland, *The First and the Last*, pp. 267–271; Freeman, *Mighty Eighth*, pp. 177–178, 184, 193.

17. Ernst Heinkel, *He1000* (London: Hutchinson 1956), pp. 252–266; Rust and Hess, "German Jets," pp. 155–156; Brian Johnson, *Secret War*, p. 275; Boyne, *Messerschmitt 262*, pp. 14, 16–17, 21, 23, 28, 144, Schlaifer, *Development of Aircraft Engines*, pp. 377–410.

18. Boyne, *Messerschmitt 262*, pp. 21ff; Freeman, *Mighty Eighth*, pp. 161, 163, 190, 193–194; Craven and Cate, *Army Air Forces*, vol. 3, pp. 291–292, 295, 657, 659–660; Strategic Bombing Survey, Oil Division, *Final Report*, pp. 8, 70, 92; Rust and Hess, "German Jets," pp. 156–184; Ethell and Price, *German Jets in Combat*, pp. 12, 43, 58, 64; Galland, *The First and the Last*; pp. 271–288, Schlaifer, *Development of Aircraft Engines*, pp. 412–435.

CHAPTER 10

1. Webster and Frankland, *Strategic Air Offensive*, vol. 3, pp. 57–63, 67–68, 212–216, and vol. 4, pp. 170–172; Craven and Cate, *Army Air Forces*, vol. 3, pp. 319–322; Mierzejewski, *Collapse of the German War Economy*, pp. 102, 122.

2. Webster and Frankland, *Strategic Air Offensive*, vol. 3, pp. 63–64, 266–269, and vol. 4, pp. 172–174; Craven and Cate, *Army Air Forces*, vol. 3, pp. 646–649; Milward, *German Economy at War*, pp. 123–125; Strategic Bombing Survey, *Effects of Strategic Bombing on the German War Economy*, p. 170.

3. United States Strategic Bombing Survey, *The Effect of Strategic Bombing on German Transportation* (Washington: Government Printing Office, 1947), pp. 1–2, 5, 9, 17–18, 50–53, 81; Webster and Frankland, *Strategic Air Offensive*, vol. 3, pp. 188, 246–248; Mierzejewski, *Collapse of the German War Economy*, pp. 22–59, 97–102.

4. Mierzejewski, *Collapse of the German War Economy*, pp. 78–92, 98–102; Strategic Bombing Survey, *Over-all Report*, p. 63; Craven and Cate, *Army Air Forces*, vol. 3, pp. 650–653; Webster and Frankland, *Strategic Air Offensive*, vol. 3, pp. 63–65.

5. Webster and Frankland, *Strategic Air Offensive*, vol. 3, pp. 181–182, 185–186, 188–189; Strategic Bombing Survey, *Effect of Strategic Bombing on German Transportation*, pp. 17–18, 22–25, 83; Mierzejewski, *Collapse of the German War Economy*, pp. 104–106, 128–130.

6. Webster and Frankland, *Strategic Air Offensive*, vol. 4, pp. 177–179.

7. Webster and Frankland, *Strategic Air Offensive*, vol. 3, pp. 68–71, 190–191, 245–250, and vol. 4, pp. 335, 350–358, 520–523; Craven and Cate, *Army Air Forces*, vol. 3, pp. 652–656; Strategic Bombing Survey, *Effect of Strategic Bombing on German Transportation*, pp. 3, 50–61, 78–80; Mierzejewski, *Collapse of the German War Economy*, pp. 103–160; United States Strategic Bombing Survey, *Effects of Bombing on Railroad Installations in Regensburg, Nuremberg, and Munich Divisions* (Washington: Government Printing Office, 1947); Hinsley, *British Intelligence*, vol. 3, part 2, pp. 526–527.

8. Craven and Cate, *Army Air Forces*, vol. 3, pp. 640–646, 657–664; Hinsley, *British Intelligence*, vol. 3, part 2, pp. 527–530; Webster and Frankland, *Strategic Air Offensive*, vol. 3, pp. 76–89, 184–187, 233–238, 241–242, and vol. 4, pp. 298–300; Strategic Bombing Survey, Oil Division, *Final Report*, pp. 2, 5, 87; Price, *Battle over the Reich*, pp. 171–173, Werner Girbig, *Six Months to Oblivion* (New York: Hippocrene, 1975), pp. 18–38; Galland, *The First and the Last*, pp. 249, 256–260; Johnson, *Wing Leader*, pp. 263–264.

9. Webster and Frankland, *Strategic Air Offensive*, vol. 3, pp. 76–93, 179–180, 184–186, 190, 252, 262–265, and vol. 4, pp. 349–356; Hastings, *Bomber Command*, pp. 302–336; Musgrove, *Pathfinder Force*, pp. 154–167.

10. B. B. Schofield, *The Russian Convoys* (New York: Ballantine 1967), pp. 43, 202–211; David Woodward, *The Tirpitz and the Battle for the North Atlantic* (New York: Berkley 1965); Webster and Frankland, *Strategic Air Offensive*, vol. 3, pp. 191–196.

11. Craven and Cate, *Army Air Forces*, vol. 3, pp. 670, 686–705; Girbig, *Six Months to Oblivion*, pp. 40–118; Hugh M. Cole, *The Ardennes* (Washington: Office of the Chief of Military History, 1965), pp. 660–663; Peter Elstob, *Hitler's Last Offensive* (New York: Macmillan, 1971), pp. 320–321, 358–359; Freeman, *Mighty Eighth*, pp. 201–205; J. E. Johnson, *Wing Leader* (New York: Ballantine, 1957), pp. 269–273; Hasso von Manteuffel, "The Ardennes," in *The Fatal Decisions*, edited by Seymour Freidin and William Richardson (New York: Berkley, 1973), pp. 249–250, 272, 276. Quoted from Elstob, *Hitler's Last Offensive*, p. 321.

12. Webster and Frankland, *Strategic Air Offensive*, vol. 3, pp. 95–104, and vol. 4, pp. 181–183; Craven and Cate, *Army Air Forces*, vol. 3, pp. 663, 715–722. Quoted from *Strategic Air Offensive*, vol. 3, p. 104.

13. Craven and Cate, *The Army Air Forces*, vol. 3, p. 725.

14. Mark A. Clodfelter, "Culmination Dresden: 1945" *Aerospace Historian* (Fall/September 1979), pp. 143–144; Craven and Cate, *Army Air Forces*, vol. 3, pp. 638–640, 724–727; Webster and Frankland, *Strategic Air Offensive*, vol. 3, pp. 52–56, 72–73, 98–99, 113, 198–199; Ronald Schaeffer, *Wings of Judgment* (New York: Oxford University Press, 1985), pp. 37, 54–58, 61–63, 67, 70, 75, 83; United States Department of State, *Foreign Relations of the United States: Conferences at Malta and Yalta* (Washington: Government Printing Office, 1955), pp. 576, 583, 599, 605.

15. Clodfelter, "Culmination Dresden: 1945," pp. 135–136, 144–145; Craven and Cate, *Army Air Forces*, vol. 3, pp. 727–728, 730–733; David Irving, *The Destruction of Dresden* (New York: Holt, Rinehart and Winston, 1964); Webster and Frankland, *Strategic Air Offensive*, vol. 3, pp. 109–110.

For a different interpretation, claiming that there was little or no difference between the British and American policies and that the AAF was simply carrying out British-style area bombing when it attacked on radar, see Hastings, *Bomber Command*, pp. 339–344. In my own view, this argument cannot stand examination. The Eighth Air Force's attacks on radar were different from Bomber Command's area attacks and those by the

B-29s on Japanese cities, not only in intention but in results. The H2X-directed attacks, and some made visually, like the February 3 attack on Berlin, could cause tremendous harm to civilians. However, with the aiming points and the weapons used—largely high-explosive bombs—loss of life was usually far smaller than from the British area attacks, which were normally made with largely incendiary loads.

It should be stressed that my intention here is merely to lay out what happened as accurately as possible, not to argue that the Americans and the AAF were morally better than the British and the RAF. Whatever moral obloquy attaches to the British for area bombing in Europe attaches equally to the Americans for their fire attacks on Japanese cities. In Europe, however, there was, a real difference between their bombing policies. It should also be noted that originally the Americans followed the same policy against Japan that they followed in Europe: daylight precision bombing. They changed over to night area bombing from lower levels only after they failed to hit anything because of winds at high altitudes. The best description of the strategic air offensive against Japan is still in Craven and Cate, *Army Air Forces*, vol. 5.

16. Craven and Cate, *Army Air Forces*, vol. 3, pp. 728–747; Webster and Frankland, *Strategic Air Offensive*, vol. 3, pp. 199–202, 234–236, and vol. 4, pp. 337–340; Strategic Bombing Survey, *The German Oil Industry*, p. 77; Strategic Bombing Survey, Oil Division, *Final Report*, pp. 2, 20, 43, 87; Musgrove, *Pathfinder Force*, pp. 165–167; Freeman, *Mighty Eighth*, pp. 206–222; Girbig, *Six Months to Oblivion*, pp. 119–124; Air Ministry, *Rise and Fall of the German Air Force*, p. 385.

17. Webster and Frankland, *Strategic Air Offensive*, vol. 3, pp. 266–267, 274–277, and vol. 4, pp. 524–525; Craven and Cate, *Army Air Forces*, vol. 3, pp. 740–741, 743; Strategic Bombing Survey, Oil Division, *Final Report*, pp. 61–68.

18. Craven and Cate, *Army Air Forces*, vol. 3, pp. 729, 740, 744–745, 752; Freeman, *Mighty Eighth*, pp. 214, 218–221, 224–226; Girbig, *Six Months to Oblivion*, pp. 129–139; Price, *Battle over the Reich*, pp. 164, 169, 173–188; Price and Ethell, *German Jets in Combat*, pp. 41–62; Boyne, *Messerschmitt 262*, p. 48; Galland, *The First and the Last*, pp. 287–290, 293–302.

19. Mierzejewski, *Collapse of the German War Economy*, pp. 131–132, 138, 141–146, 148, 154–160; Strategic Bombing Survey, *Effect of Strategic Bombing on German Transportation*, pp. 2–3, 14–15, 80, 83–85.

20. Mierzejewski, *Collapse of the German War Economy*, pp. 155–171; Webster and Frankland, *Strategic Air Offensive*, vol. 3, pp. 110–111, 253–255; Craven and Cate, *Army Air Forces*, vol. 3, pp. 732–734, 771–772; Milward, *German Economy at War*, pp. 172–186.

21. Webster and Franklin, *Strategic Air Offensive*, vol. 3, pp. 111–117, 202–203, 255–256; Craven and Cate, *Army Air Forces*, vol. 3, pp. 728–754, 772–782, 784; Freeman, *Mighty Eighth*, pp. 210–214, 222–232; Mierzejewski, *Collapse of the German War Economy*, pp. 171–180.

CHAPTER 11

1. Strategic Bombing Survey, *Over-all Report*, pp. 1–2; Webster and Frankland, *Strategic Air Offensive*, vol. 3, p. 287; Craven and Cate, *Army Air Forces*, vol. 3, pp. 794–797.

2. Carroll Quigley, *Tragedy and Hope* (New York: Macmillan, 1966), pp. 798–804, and Robert Leckie, *Delivered from Evil* (New York: Harper and Row, 1987), pp. 641–647, are examples of the tendency, even of otherwise knowledgeable and intelligent writers,

to belittle strategic bombing. David Halberstam's ignorant remarks in his best-selling book on Vietnam, *The Best and Brightest* (Greenwich, Conn.: Fawcett, 1973), pp. 161–162, 475, are a good example of the interaction of this tendency, at a lower level, with anti-Indochina war propaganda in the 1960s and 1970s. For comments on the distortion of the Strategic Bombing Survey for later political purposes, see Guenter Lewey, *America in Vietnam* (New York: Oxford University Press, 1978), p. 395.

The well-known economist, John Kenneth Galbraith, a director of the Strategic Bombing Survey, sniped at strategic bombing in many of his influential popular writings. An interesting summary of his views is provided in his interview with Studs Turkel in the latter's best-seller, *The Good War* (New York: Pantheon, 1984), pp. 208–209. In the interview, Galbraith mixes some truths with many half-truths and downright falsehoods, difficult to relate to the actual evidence compiled by the survey or to other sources. Galbraith makes much of the failure of the British area attacks (although even here his remarks are not entirely accurate) and the failure of the ball bearings campaign. Less defensibly he dismisses the attacks on aircraft plants as a "total failure" and barely mentions the success against German oil production, and that in a misleading way. The attack on German transportation is not mentioned at all, enabling Galbraith to conclude that "strategic bombing was designed to destroy the industrial base of the enemy and the morale of its people. It did neither."

3. Hastings, *Bomber Command*, p. 351.

4. Overy, *Air War*, p. 100.

5. Robert Merriam, *The Battle of the Bulge* (New York: Ballantine, 1965), p. 169.

6. Manteuffel, "Ardennes," pp. 249–250.

7. F. W. von Mellenthin, *Panzer Battles* (New York: Ballantine, 1971), pp. 433–434.

8. Strategic Bombing Survey, *Effects of Strategic Bombing on the German War Economy*, pp. 13–14.

9. Milward, *German Economy at War*, pp. 168–170.

10. Webster and Frankland, *Strategic Air Offensive*, vol. 3, pp. 237; Strategic Bombing Survey, Oil Division, *Final Report*, pp. 2, 49–50, 75; Strategic Bombing Survey, *German Oil Industry*, p. 68; Strategic Bombing Survey, *Effects of Strategic Bombing on the German War Economy*, pp. 83–90; Strategic Bombing Survey, *Over-all Report*, pp. 45–58, 66–68; United States Strategic Bombing Survey, *The Light Metals Industry of Germany* (Washington: Government Printing Office, 1947). The Strategic Bombing Survey noted in *Maybach Motor Works, Friedrichshafen*, p. 11, that "the predominant importance of Maybach as being the bottleneck up to early 1944 for heavy tank engines was never fully realized despite the fact that it was well known that all tank and half track motors were of Maybach manufacture or design."

11. Strategic Bombing Survey, *Over-all Report*, p. 22.

12. Barry Leach, *German Strategy against Russia* (New York: Oxford University Press, 1972), p. 146.

13. Strategic Bombing Survey, *Effects of Strategic Bombing on the German War Economy*, pp. 121–127.

Bibliography

BOOKS

Air Ministry. *The Rise and Fall of the German Air Force*. New York: St. Martin's, 1983.
Arnold, H. H. *Global Mission*. New York: Harper, 1949.
Barker, Ralph. *The Ship-Busters*. London: Chatto and Windus, 1957.
—— . *The Thousand Plan*. London: Chatto and Windus, 1965.
Bekker, Cajus. (Hans Dieter Berenbrok.) *Hitler's Naval War*. New York: Zebra, 1978.
—— . *The Luftwaffe War Diaries*. Garden City, N.Y.: Doubleday, 1966.
Bendiner, Elmer. *The Fall of the Fortresses*. New York: Putnam's, 1980.
Bennett, D. C. T. *Pathfinder*. London: Muller, 1958.
Birdsall, Steve. *Log of the Liberators*. New York: Doubleday, 1973.
Bowyer, Michael. *2 Group RAF*. London: Faber and Faber, 1974.
Boyne, Walter. *Messerschmitt 262: Arrow to the Future*. Washington: Smithsonian Institute Press, 1980.
Caidin, Martin. *Black Thursday*. New York: Bantam, 1987.
—— . *Flying Forts*. New York: Ballantine, 1969.
—— . *The Fork-Tailed Devil*. New York: Ballantine, 1971.
Carroll, Berenice. *Design for Total War*. The Hague: Mouton, 1968.
Christy, Joe, and Ethell, Jeffrey. *P-38 Lightning at War*. New York: Scribner's, 1979.
Churchill, Winston. *The Grand Alliance*. New York: Bantam, 1962.
Coffey, Thomas. *Decision over Schweinfurt*. New York: Doubleday, 1977.
—— . *Hap*. New York: Viking Press, 1982.
Cole, Hugh M. *The Ardennes*. Washington: Office of the Chief of Military History, 1965.
Collier, Basil. *The Battle of the V-Weapons*. New York: Morrow, 1965.
—— . *A History of Air Power*. New York: Macmillan, 1974.
Collier, Richard. *The City That Would Not Die*. New York: Dutton, 1961.
Comer, John. *Combat Crew*. New York: Morrow, 1987.
Constant, Edward. *Origins of the Turbojet Revolution*. Baltimore: Johns Hopkins University Press, 1980.
Cooksley, Peter. *Flying Bomb*. New York: Scribner's, 1979.
Cooper, Matthew. *The German Air Force*. New York: Janes, 1981.

Copp, DeWitt. *A Few Great Captains*. New York: Doubleday, 1980.

——— . *Forged in Fire*. Garden City, N.Y.: Doubleday, 1982.

Craven, Wesley, F., and Cate, James Lea. *The Army Air Forces in World War II*. 8 vols. Chicago: University of Chicago Press, 1948–1958.

Cruttwell, C. R. M. F. *History of the Great War*. London: Granada, 1982.

Deane, John R. *The Strange Alliance*. Bloomington: Indiana University Press, 1973.

Dempster, Derek, and Wood, Derek. *The Narrow Margin*. Rev. ed. New York: Paperback Library, 1969.

Divine, David. *The Broken Wing*. London: Hutchinson, 1966.

Doenitz, Karl. *Ten Years and Twenty Days*. Cleveland, Ohio: World, 1959.

Dornberger, Walter. *V-2*. New York: Bantam, 1979. Dugan, James, and Stewart, Carroll. *Ploesti*. New York: Ballantine, 1973.

Edmonds, Walter D. *They Fought with What They Had*. Boston: Little, Brown, 1951.

Elstob, Peter. *Hitler's Last Offensive*. New York: Macmillan, 1971.

Emerson, William. *Operation Pointblank*. Colorado Springs, Colo.: USAF Academy, 1962.

Ethell, Jeffrey, and Price, Alfred. *The German Jets in Combat*. London: Janes, 1979.

——— . *Target Berlin*. London: Janes, 1981.

Fabyanic, Thomas. *Strategic Air Attack in the United States Air Force: A Case Study*. Manhattan, Kans.: Kansas State University/Aerospace Historian, 1976.

FitzGibbon, Constantine. *The Winter of the Bombs*. New York: Norton, 1958.

Fredette, Raymond. *The Sky on Fire: The First Battle of Britain, 1917–1918*. New York: Holt, Rinehart and Winston, 1966.

Freeman, Roger A. *B-17 Fortress at War*. New York: Scribner's, 1979.

——— . *The Mighty Eighth*. Garden City, N.Y.: Doubleday, 1970.

——— . *The Mighty Eighth War Diary*. New York: Janes, 1981.

Galland, Adolf. *The First and the Last*. New York: Bantam, 1978.

Gilbert, Martin. *The Second World War: A Complete History*. New York: Henry Holt, 1989.

Girbig, Werner. *Six Months to Oblivion*. New York: Hippocrene, 1975.

Golley, John. *Whittle, The True Story*. Washington: Smithsonian Institution Press, 1987.

Halberstam, David. *The Best and Brightest*. Greenwich, Conn.: Fawcett, 1973.

Harris, Arthur. *Bomber Offensive*. London: Collins, 1947.

Hart, Liddell B. H. *The Real War, 1914–1918*. Boston: Little, Brown, 1964.

Hastings, Max. *Bomber Command*. New York: Dial, 1979.

Heinkel, Ernst. *He1000*. London: Hutchinson, 1956.

Held, Werner, and Nauroth, Holger. *The Defense of the Reich*. New York: Arco, 1982.

Hess, William N. *P-51 Mustang*. New York: Ballantine, 1971.

Hezlet, Arthur. *Aircraft and Seapower*. New York: Stein and Day, 1970.

Hinsley, F. H., E. E. Thomas, C. F. G. Ransom, R. C. Knight, and C. A. G. Simkins. *British Intelligence in the Second World War*. 3 vols. Cambridge, London: Cambridge University Press, 1979–1988.

Infield, Glenn. *The Poltava Affair*. New York: Macmillan, 1973.

Impact reprint New York: James Parton 1980. 8 vols.

Irving, David. *The Destruction of Dresden*. New York: Holt, Rinehart and Winston, 1964.

——— . *The German Atomic Bomb*. New York: Da Capo, n.d. (originally published New York: Simon and Schuster, 1967).

——— . *The Mare's Nest*. Boston: Little, Brown, 1965.

Johnson, Brian. *The Secret War*. New York: Methuen, 1978.

Johnson, J. E. *The Story of Air Fighting*. New York: Bantam, 1986.

——— . *Wing Leader.* New York: Ballantine, 1957.

Johnson, Robert, with Caidin, Martin. *Thunderbolt.* New York: Ballantine, 1959.

Jones, R. V. *The Wizard War.* New York: Coward, McCann and Geoghegan, 1978.

Keegan, John. *The Second World War.* New York: Viking, 1990.

Kennett, Lee. *A History of Strategic Bombing.* New York: Scribner's, 1982.

Lawrence, W. J. *No. 5 Bomber Group RAF.* London: Faber and Faber, 1951.

Leach, Barry. *German Strategy against Russia.* New York: Oxford University Press, 1972.

Leckie, Robert. *Delivered from Evil.* New York: Harper and Row, 1987.

Lewey, Guenter. *America in Vietnam.* New York: Oxford University Press, 1978.

Macksey, Kenneth. *Commando.* New York: Stein and Day, 1986.

von Mellenthin, F. W. *Panzer Battles.* New York: Ballantine, 1971.

Merriam, Robert. *The Battle of the Bulge.* New York: Ballantine, 1965.

Middlebrook, Martin. *The Battle of Hamburg.* New York: Scribner's, 1981.

——— . *The Berlin Raids.* New York: Viking, 1988.

——— . *Convoy.* New York: Morrow, 1976.

——— . *The Nuremberg Raid.* New York: Morrow, 1974.

——— . *The Peenemunde Raid.* Indianapolis, Ind.: Bobbs-Merrill, 1982.

——— . *The Schweinfurt-Regensburg Mission.* New York: Penguin, 1985.

Middlebrook, Martin, and Everitt, Chris. *The Bomber Command War Diaries.* London: Penguin, 1990.

Mierzejewski, Alfred. *The Collapse of the German War Economy, 1944–1945.* Chapel Hill: University of North Carolina Press, 1987.

Milward, Alan. *The German Economy at War.* London: University of London Press, 1965.
    Morrison, Wilbur. *The Incredible 305th.* New York: Belmont, 1977.

Murray, Williamson. *Strategy for Defeat.* Maxwell Air Force Base, Ala.: Airpower Research Institute, 1983.

Musgrove, Gordon. *Operation Gomorrah.* London: Janes, 1981.

——— . *Pathfinder Force* (London: MacDonald's and Janes, 1976).

Newby, Leroy. *Target Ploesti.* Novato, Calif.: Presidio Press, 1983.

Noyes, William, ed. *Chemistry.* Boston: Little, Brown, 1948.

O'Neill, Brian D. *Half a Wing, Three Engines and a Prayer.* Blue Ridge Summit, Pa.: Tab, 1989.

Overy, R. J. *The Air War.* New York: Stein and Day, 1980.

Parkinson, Roger. *Summer 1940.* New York: David McKay, 1977.

Pounds, Norman J. G. *The Ruhr.* Bloomington: Indiana University Press, 1952.

Powers, Barry D. *Strategy without Slide Rule.* London: Croom Helm, 1976.

Price, Alfred. *Battle over the Reich.* New York: Scribner's, 1973.

——— . *Blitz on Britain.* London: Ian Allan, 1977.

——— . *Instruments of Darkness.* London: Kimber, 1967.

Quigley, Carroll. *Tragedy and Hope.* New York: Macmillan, 1966.

Robinson, Douglas. *Giants in the Sky.* Rev. ed. Seattle: University of Washington Press, 1979.

——— . *The Zeppelin in Combat.* London: G. T. Foulis, 1962.

Roskill, S. W. *The War at Sea.* 3 vols. London: Her Majesty's Stationery Office, 1954–1961.

Rostow, Walt. *Pre-Invasion Bombing Strategy.* Austin: University of Texas, 1981.

Rust, Kenneth C. *The Ninth Air Force in World War II.* 2d ed. Fallbrook, CA: Aero Publishers, 1970.

Saward, Dudley. *Bomber Harris.* Garden City, N.Y.: Doubleday, 1985.

——. *The Bomber's Eye*. London: Cassel, 1959.

Schaffer, Ronald. *Wings of Judgment*. New York: Oxford University Press, 1985.

Schlaifer, Robert. *The Development of Aircraft Engines*. New York: Pergamon, 1970 (originally published by Harvard University Graduate School of Business Administration, 1950).

Schofield, B. B. *The Russian Convoys*. New York: Ballantine, 1967.

Seaton, Albert. *The Russo-German War*. New York: Praeger, 1972.

Smith, Malcom. *British Air Strategy between the Wars*. Oxford: Clarendon Press, 1984.

Smith, Peter C. *A History of Dive Bombing*. Annapolis, Md.: Nautical and Aviation Publishing Company of America, 1981.

Speer, Albert. *Inside the Third Reich*. New York: Avon, 1972.

Sweetman, John. *Operation Chastise*. London: Janes, 1982.

——. *Ploesti*. New York: Ballantine, 1974.

Taylor, Telford. *The Breaking Wave*. New York: Simon and Schuster, 1967.

Terraine, John. *The U-Boat Wars*. New York: Putnam's, 1989.

Thompson, R. W. *Battle of the Rhineland*. New York: Ballantine, 1959.

Turkel, Studs. *The Good War*. New York: Pantheon, 1984.

United States Army Air Forces. *Impact, 1943–1945*. Reprinted in 8 vols. New York: James Parton, 1980.

United States Department of Commerce. *The Ruhr*. Washington: Government Printing Office, 1949.

United States Department of State. *Foreign Relations of the United States: Conferences at Malta and Yalta*. Washington: Government Printing Office, 1955.

United States Strategic Bombing Survey. *The Defeat of the German Air Force*. Washington: Government Printing Office, 1947.

——. *A Detailed Study of the Effects of Area Bombing on Hamburg*. Washington: Government Printing Office, 1947.

——. *Dornier Works, Friedrichshafen*. Washington: Government Printing Office, 1945.

——. *The Effects of Bombing on Railroad Installations in Regensburg, Nuremberg, and Munich Divisions*. Washington: Government Printing Office, 1947.

——. *The Effects of Strategic Bombing on German Transportation*. Washington: Government Printing Office, 1947.

——. *The Effects of Strategic Bombing on the German War Economy*. Washington: Government Printing Office, 1945.

——. *Focke-Wulf Aircraft Plant, Bremen*. Washington: Government Printing Office, 1945.

——. *The German Anti-Friction Bearings Industry*. Washington: Government Printing Office, 1947.

——. *The German Oil Industry, Ministerial Report*. Washington: Government Printing Office, 1947.

——. *Gustahlfabrik Friedrich Krupp*. Washington: Government Printing Office, 1947.

——. *The Light Metals Industry of Germany*. Washington: Government Printing Office, 1947.

——. *Maybach Motor Works, Friedrichshafen*. Washington: Government Printing Office, 1947.

——. *Over-All Report (European War)*. Washington: Government Printing Office, 1945.

——. *Renault Motor Vehicles Plant, Billancourt, Paris*. Washington: Government Printing Office, 1947.

United States Strategic Bombing Survey, Aircraft Division, *Industry Report*. Washington: Government Printing Office, 1947.

United States Strategic Bombing Survey, Oil Division, *Final Report*. Washington: Government Printing Office, 1947.

Vader, John. *Spitfire*. New York: Ballantine, 1969.

Verrier, Anthony. *The Bomber Offensive*. New York: Macmillan, 1968.

Waters, John M. *Bloody Winter*. Rev. ed. New York: Jove, 1986.

Webster, Charles, and Frankland, Noble. *The Strategic Air Offensive against Germany*. 4 vols. London: Her Majesty's Stationery Office, 1961.

Weigley, Russell. *Eisenhower's Lieutenants*. Bloomington: Indiana University Press, 1981.

Whittle, Frank. *Jet*. London: Muller, 1953.

Wilmot, Chester. *The Struggle for Europe*. London: Fontana, 1980.

Woodward, David. *The Tirpitz and the Battle for the North Atlantic*. New York: Berkley, 1965.

Zemke, Hubert, and Freeman, Roger A. *Zemke's Wolfpack*. New York: Orion, 1988.

ARTICLES

Bond, Horatio. "The Fire Attacks on German Cities," pp. 76–79. In *Fire and the Air War*, edited by Horatio Bond. Boston: National Fire Protection Association, 1946.

—— ."Some Observations and Conclusions," pp. 244–245. In *Fire and the Air War*, edited by Horatio Bond. Boston: National Fire Protection Association, 1946.

Bradley, Mark. "The P-51 over Berlin." *Aerospace Historian*, Fall 1974, pp. 125–128.

Clodfelter, Mark A. "Culmination Dresden: 1945." *Aerospace Historian*, Fall/September 1979, pp. 134–147.

Gorrell, Edgar S. "An American Proposal for Strategic Bombing in World War I." *Airpower Historian*, April 1958, pp. 102–117.

Homze, Edward L. "The Luftwaffe's Failure to Develop a Heavy Bomber before World War II." *Aerospace Historian*, Spring/March 1977, pp. 20–26.

von Manteuffel, Hasso. "The Ardennes," pp. 237–277. In *The Fatal Decisions*, ed. by Seymour Freidin and William Richardson. New York: Berkley, 1973.

Jack McElroy, "Incendiary Warfare on Germany," pp. 71–76. In *Fire and the Air War*, edited by Horatio Bond. Boston: National Fire Protection Association, 1946.

Peaslee, B. J. "The Devastation Bombing of Heroya, 24 July 1943." *Aerospace Historian*, Winter/December 1982, pp. 260–264.

Rust, Kenneth C., and Hess, William N. "The German Jets and the U.S. Army Air Force." *American Aviation Historical Society Journal*," Fall 1963, pp. 155–184.

Index

ABOUT THE AUTHOR

ALAN J. LEVINE is a historian specializing in Russian history, international relations, and World War II. Born and raised in New York City, he received a Ph.D. from New York University. Mr. Levine has worked as a teacher, freelance writer, and book reviewer. He has published numerous articles about World War II and the Cold War and is the author of *The Soviet Union, the Communist Movement, and the World: Prelude to the Cold War, 1917–1941* (Praeger, 1990).